The Mau Mau Rebellion

A Mau Mau Oath

I speak the truth and before God
And before this movement,
the movement of Unity,
The unity, which is put to the test,
The Unity that is mocked with the name of Mau Mau,
That I shall go forward to fight for the land
The lands of Kioriyanga that we cultivated,
The lands which were taken by the Europeans.

And I fail to do this
May this oath kill me
May this seven kill me
May this meat kill me.

The Mau Mau Rebellion

The Emergency in Kenya
1952–1956

Nick van der Bijl

Pen & Sword
MILITARY

First published in Great Britain in 2017 by
PEN AND SWORD MILITARY
an imprint of
Pen and Sword Books Ltd
47 Church Street
Barnsley
South Yorkshire S70 2AS

ISBN 978 1 47386 457 3

A CIP record for this book is available from the British Library

Printed and bound in England
by CPI Group (UK) Ltd, Croydon, CR0 4YY

Typeset in Times New Roman by
CHIC GRAPHICS

Pen & Sword Books Ltd incorporates the imprints of Pen & Sword
Archaeology, Atlas, Aviation, Battleground, Discovery,
Family History, History, Maritime, Military, Naval, Politics, Railways,
Select, Social History, Transport, True Crime, Claymore Press,
Frontline Books, Leo Cooper, Praetorian Press, Remember When,
Seaforth Publishing and Wharncliffe.

For a complete list of Pen and Sword titles please contact
Pen and Sword Books Limited
47 Church Street, Barnsley, South Yorkshire, S70 2AS, England
E-mail: enquiries@pen-and-sword.co.uk
Website: www.pen-and-sword.co.uk

Contents

Preface and Acknowledgements

The Kenya Emergency was a peasants' revolt against dominant colonists who had occupied the land they used less than 50 years previously. It was fought by peasants who knew how to exploit the forest against young British and African soldiers who had to learn how to survive in a hostile environment. Militarily, the peasants were defeated. Politically, they won and are still in power. This book is designed to be a companion to others that I have written on British military campaigns between 1945 and 1990 and focuses on the British military presence in 1952–1959 Kenyan Emergency. The story of the British soldier and airman is hardly mentioned in other books on this subject, so focused are their authors on other matters, in particular the detention camps.

There is a mass of information on the history of Kenya, as there is on the Emergency and the impact it still has on the nation today. There is also a great deal of information on the Mau Mau and the settlers and colonists, much of it useful, although authors often have a political point to make. Not much has been written, however, about the Regulars and young National Servicemen who fought in the dark and dank forests, some of them already veterans of the Korean War and the deteriorating situation in Egypt. The book is not based on research in the academic sense; it is instead a collation of information from published works, regimental periodicals, the internet and some interviews with and recollections of 'those who were there'. I do not discuss the history of the detention camps because that has been adequately examined elsewhere. *Fighting the Mau Mau: The British Army and Counter-Insurgency in Kenya* by Huw Bennett (Cambridge Military Histories) provided the first detailed history of British military operations in Kenya and is a mine of information. Malcom Page in his

King's African Rifles; A History (2011) gives a brief overview of the regiments. Guy Campbell in his *Charging Buffalo: A History of the Kenya Regiment 1937–1963*, gives a subjective history of this colonial regiment. The charging buffalo was the unit cap badge.

I must thank Dr Anthony Clayton, who was a police officer in Nairobi and is a military historian, for peer reviewing the book. My thanks for their assistance also go to Colonel Cecil West of the Queen's Own Buffs for his experiences in Kenya; Christopher Yates for information on his father; Major (Retd) P.R. White MM of the Queen's Own Buffs Regimental Association; Richard McKenzie of the Black Watch Museum; Phil Mather of the Fusiliers Museum; Christine Benarth of the Shropshire Regimental Museum; the Hampshire Records Office for access to 1 Rifle Brigade archives; Rebecca Blackburn of the Royal Engineers Museum; the National Army Museum; and Alan Grace for information on Forces British Service (Nairobi).

In relation to photographs, I have sourced some images that have lacked a copyright trail, and therefore I am uncertain about their origins. As always, I would be pleased to hear from anyone who can help.

I am again indebted to George Chamier for his crucial insistence and patience during the editing process; to Brigadier Henry Wilson and Matt Jones at Pen & Sword Military Books, who, as always, were invaluable for their encouragement and administration; to Peter Wood, of GWR, who has again produced the maps; to his wife, Lyn, who supplied her recollections as the child of a soldier in Kenya; and to Richard Munro, who again has produced an exhaustive index.

As always, my wife, Penny, again proved a patient and understanding proof-reader.

MAP 1 - COLONY OF KENYA - 1959

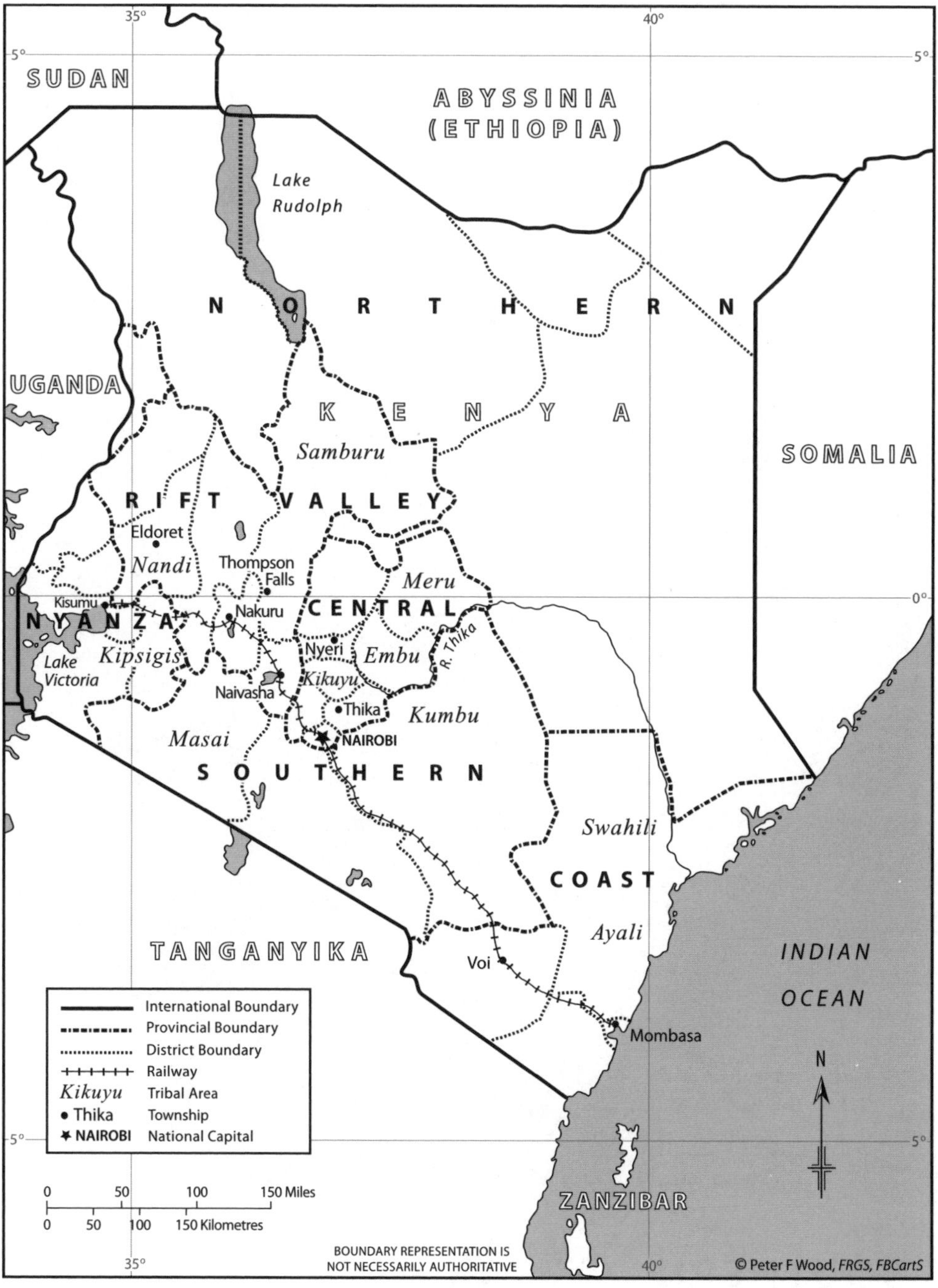
35°
40°
5°
5°
SUDAN
ABYSSINIA
(ETHIOPIA)
Lake
Rudolph
N O R T H E R N
UGANDA
K E N Y A
Samburu
SOMALIA
RIFT VALLEY
Eldoret
Nandi
Thompson
Falls
Meru
0°
Kisumu
Nakuru
NYANZA
CENTRAL
Nyeri
Embu
R. Thika
Lake
Victoria
Kipsigis
Kikuyu
Naivasha
Thika
Kumbu
NAIROBI
Masai
SOUTHERN
Swahili
COAST
Ayali
TANGANYIKA
Voi
INDIAN
OCEAN
Mombasa
International Boundary
Provincial Boundary
District Boundary
Railway
Kikuyu Tribal Area
Thika Township
NAIROBI National Capital
N
5°
5°
0 50 100 150 Miles
0 50 100 150 Kilometres
ZANZIBAR
35°
40°
BOUNDARY REPRESENTATION IS
NOT NECESSARILY AUTHORITATIVE
© Peter F Wood, FRGS, FBCartS

MAP 2 - MAIN AREA OF OPERATIONS - CENTRAL PROVINCE

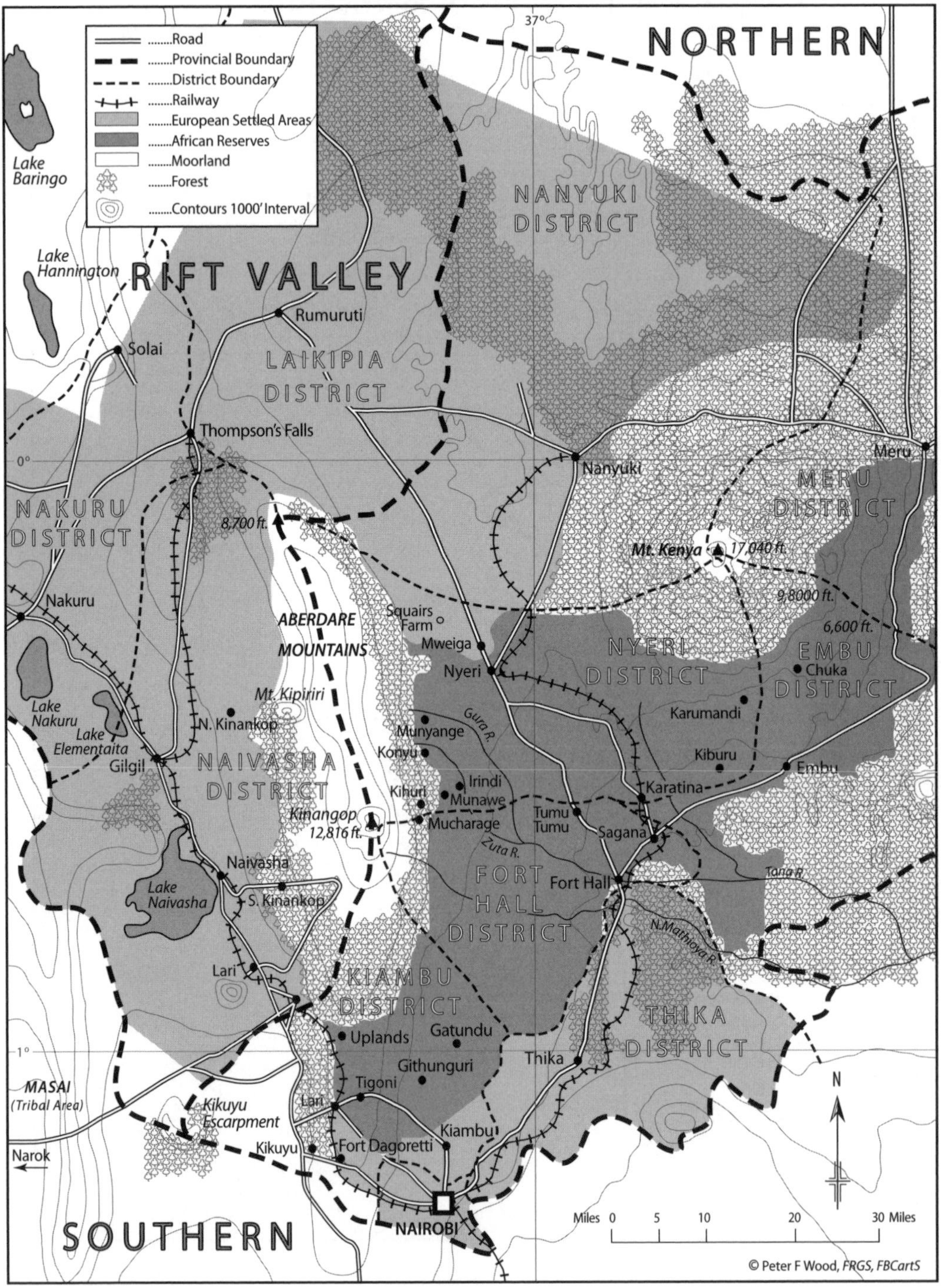

.......Road
.......Provincial Boundary
.......District Boundary
.......Railway
.......European Settled Areas
.......African Reserves
.......Moorland
.......Forest
.......Contours 1000' Interval
37°
NORTHERN
Lake Baringo
NANYUKI DISTRICT
Lake Hannington
RIFT VALLEY
Rumuruti
Solai
LAIKIPIA DISTRICT
Thompson's Falls
0°
Nanyuki
Meru
MERU DISTRICT
NAKURU DISTRICT
8,700 ft.
Mt. Kenya
17,040 ft.
9,8000 ft.
Nakuru
ABERDARE MOUNTAINS
Squairs Farm
6,600 ft.
Mweiga
NYERI DISTRICT
EMBU DISTRICT
Nyeri
Chuka
Mt. Kipiriri
Karumandi
Lake Nakuru
N. Kinankop
Munyange
Gura R.
Lake Elementaita
Konyu
Kiburu
Gilgil
NAIVASHA DISTRICT
Irindi
Embu
Kihuri
Munawe
Karatina
Kinangop
12,816 ft.
Mucharage
Tumu Tumu
Sagana
Zuta R.
Naivasha
FORT HALL DISTRICT
Fort Hall
Tana R.
Lake Naivasha
S. Kinankop
N.Mathioya R.
Lari
KIAMBU DISTRICT
THIKA DISTRICT
Uplands
Gatundu
1°
Githunguri
Thika
MASAI (Tribal Area)
Tigoni
Lari
Kikuyu Escarpment
N
Kiambu
Narok
Kikuyu
Fort Dagoretti
SOUTHERN
NAIROBI
Miles 0 5 10 20 30 Miles
© Peter F Wood, FRGS, FBCartS

Introduction

In 1846, two German missionaries, Johann Ludwig Krapf and Johannes Rebmann, exploring East Africa were staying with the Kamba people when they were told that a distant snow-capped mountain that looked like a Christmas pudding was known as *Kĩ-Nya*, seemingly because its volcanic rock and white snow resembled the feathers of the cock ostrich. Krapf recorded the African pronunciation as *'kenja'*. However, members of the Geographical Society of London did not believe that snow could fall so near the Equator and concluded that the sighting was the hallucination of malaria-stricken missionaries. Krapf had been sponsored by the Church Missionary Society of England; Rebmann later became the first European to see Mt Kilimanjaro.

Straddling the equator on Africa's eastern coast, the 224,960 square miles of modern Kenya share borders with Sudan and Ethiopia to the north, Uganda to the west and Tanzania to the south. Coral reefs, sandy beaches, rocky inlets and muddy mangrove swamps protect the 250-mile coastal belt from the long rollers of the Indian Ocean. Geographically, the country can be split into highlands in the south-west filling a third of the country, and the remaining two thirds which are lowland. The massive volcanic fault stretching from the Jordan Valley south to Mozambique through Kenya is known as the Great Rift Valley and is fertile. The highlands are dominated by the 17,100ft Mt Kenya, the 13,000ft Aberdares Range to its west and the 10,000ft Mau Escarpment to the south. Overlooked by the Aberdares and spreading west to the 10,987ft Mt Kipipri is lush savannah. Lieutenant Colonel John Windeatt OBE, who commanded 1st Battalion Devonshire Regiment (1 Devons) between 1954 and 1955, describes the ecology of the mountains in his *The Devonshire Regiment August 1945–May 1958*:

> Tree Belt – 6,000 to 8,000ft
> Semi-tropical forest with luxuriant undergrowth at the base of some very large trees, particularly camphor, some of which grow

> to the height of 120 feet, almost blotting out the sky. In places, the undergrowth was so thick that it was impassable except by hacking a way through it, with the resultant noise.
>
> Bamboo Belt – 8,000 to 10,000ft
> The trees give way to bamboo which grows from thirty to sixty feet, the stems being from two to five inches in diameter at the base. Owing to the density of the stems, in most places the bamboo is impassable, except along game tracks, which made taking avoiding action difficult if a rhinoceros decided to select the same track as a patrol. There were areas of dead bamboo where the stems had fallen, making a false surface to the ground through which a man could sink, making progress extremely slow and laborious.

The bamboo belt was approximately four miles wide. At 11,000ft are moors of tussock and tall elephant grass, swamps and lakes. In the middle there is a depression where the lakes are bigger and the cold water seeps slowly through the tussock. It is breezy and the sun shoots a fierce glare. At night it is cold, particularly in swirling mist.

The profusion of rivers cascading through steep-sided, heavily wooded gorges is great, especially on the lower slopes. The mountains experience similar weather patterns of rising morning temperatures from the sun, followed by moisture from Lake Victoria and anabatic winds inducing rainclouds at about midday, then a bright afternoon with the prospect of clear night skies. Elsewhere, twelve hours of daylight is common, with seasons generally governed by rainfall and predictable almost to the date. The 'long' rains pour between March and May and the 'short rains' from October to December, with the coast and highlands having an annual average precipitation of 40in. Ian Henderson, a colonial police officer, describes the rains:

> The long rains . . . usually go on without any real pause for the first week, then taper on into spasmodic afternoon thunderstorms. Within minutes of the first deafening clap of thunder, the rough forest tracks become quagmires and everything, everywhere, is drenched. Frightened by the lightning

> and thunder, the larger animals come out on to the tracks and wallow in the mud, tearing deep craters with their feet and making travel yet more difficult. These heavy storms are often preceded by hail which falls with great force, tearing leaves and even branches from trees, destroying the beautiful wild flowers, driving the animals frantic, and covering the ground with a white, pebbled crust . . . landslides are a constant danger . . . Vehicles are of little use . . . all the little streams swell and become formidable barriers . . . there are the animals. Terrified by the thunder, elephant, rhino, and buffalo would crash wildly through the bush as if trying to escape from their own shadows; warthog and bushbuck would race aimlessly backwards and forwards; and even the monkeys would leap down from their branches and huddle together in terrified little groups at the foot of the trees.

The summer is between mid-December and the 'long rains', the winter being June and July. The climate is of tropical humidity, giving an average 27°C (81°F). The average temperature in Nairobi, the capital south of the Central Highlands, is 19°C (66°F), whereas in the arid northern plains it is about 25° (76°F). Mountain temperatures decrease about 2°C (3°F) or every 1,000ft in altitude. Most British units found the even-tempered climate agreeable, and although enduring soaked clothing and equipment, few soldiers caught colds.

The peoples who inhabited Kenya were as diverse as those living in Eastern Europe, and for centuries they dwelt in harmony with their surroundings and adopted similar cultures. The Embuhad drifted from the north and settled to the south-east of Mount Kenya. Meru mythology has it that they escaped enslavement from the 'red people', that is Arabs, and settled on the northern and eastern slopes of Mt Kenya. The Maasai and Kipsigis drifted from southern Sudan with their herds and settled in the fertile savannah west of the Aberdares. Generally stocky, the Kikuyu, the largest group, had wandered from western Africa and settled between Mt Kenya and the Aberdares. As they expanded, they developed a system that regulated land use. Governance was broadly similar in the different tribes and conducted through brotherhood age-sets and marriage. In anthropology, an age-set can be defined as:

> A social category or corporate social group, consisting of people of similar age, who have a common identity, maintain close ties over a prolonged period, and together pass through a series of age-related statuses.

The system provided social continuity and stability, even when an age-set broke new ground. Land management was through a system of tenancies controlled by the age-set. In the absence of writing, binding oaths ensured integrity. During drought and epidemics, communities sheltered in the forest. Religious faith developed in three layers. On the snowy summit of Mt Kenya lived *Ngai*, a Supreme Being. The second layer was reverence to ancestors, and the third was the belief that the earth was alive through the presence of spirits in waterfalls, streams, isolated rocks and strangely shaped trees in the forest seen as protectors. Fig trees were favoured sacred places. There was strong belief in magic, and individuals with second sight were regarded as prophets.

Arab traders frequenting the East African coast during the first century AD were followed, 400 years later, by Greek merchants filtering from the Red Sea and South-East Asian traders focusing on gold imported from modern Zimbabwe, ivory, slaves, tortoise shells and rhinoceros horn. The first Europeans to penetrate the region were sailors commanded by the fifteenth century Portuguese navigator Vasco da Gama on his first voyage to India, briefly landing at Mombasa in 1498. As spice began to enliven dour European menus, Venice dominated overland and sea trade routes to the Indian Ocean, until Ottoman expansion blocked the overland routes. Portugal exploited the route pioneered by da Gama by settling in Mombasa in 1505. When Omani expansion captured Mombasa in 1698, within 30 years Portugal had left East Africa, except for Mozambique until 1975. The Omanis confined themselves to the coastal strip, where they developed clove plantations and intensified slave raids, which eventually attracted European scrutiny as part of the attempt to eradicate the trade.

Chapter 1

British East Africa

Zanzibar soon became such a thriving port and trading post that the British, French, Germans and Americans opened consulates. Elsewhere, Afrikaner farmers spreading north to escape British influence in South Africa came into conflict with the Zulus. Intrusion by imperialist explorers and earnest Christian missionaries clashed with African cultures and began to threaten the equilibrium of the vast emptiness of Africa, occupied by millions of animals, birds, reptiles and isolated indigenous tribes. The people living in the area around Mt Kenya were receptive to the 'red men', as they nicknamed Europeans, and their technological magic, but were far less impressed with the idea that their *Ngai* should be replaced by an invisible god. Nevertheless, those who recognised that reading, writing and arithmetic were worth practising professed to follow Christianity in order to learn and were persuaded to be baptised, attend church and take communion. But this came at a cost, as fathers often disinherited such sons.

Among the missionary-explorers was Dr David Livingstone, a Scottish Congregationalist who had offered his medical qualifications to the London Missionary Society. His exploration of eastern Africa and his crusade against the slave trade led to his becoming a Victorian hero, with his clarion call that Africa be redeemed by Commerce, Civilization and Christianity. When sixteen European countries agreed to carve up Africa at the 1884/85 Berlin Conference, they imposed their rule on millions of bewildered Africans in an unsavoury process that became known as the 'Scramble for Africa'. One of the four agreed General Principles of the Conference was: 'To watch over the preservation of the native tribes and to care for the improvements of the conditions of their moral well-being.' Moral well-being meant Christianity.

Another principle was that no signatory could retain a sphere of interest unless it had established 'effective occupation' by a settlement, a garrison or an administrative function. When Great Britain and Germany, the belligerent new boy on the imperial block, agreed to share East Africa in 1886, five German warships trained their guns on the palace of the Sultan in Zanzibar and invited him to surrender his territories. On advice from London, the British consul recommended that he did so. Within the year, Germany had occupied what became German East Africa (now Tanzania). The British Government delegated responsibility for its own 'effective occupation' to Sir William MacKinnon, a Scottish ship-builder and, as was customary, issued him with a Royal Charter to form the Imperial British East Africa Company (IBEAC) with its head office in Mombasa. The Sultan was left a 10-mile-wide coastal strip. A year later, MacKinnon leased the strip from the him.

When hostilities broke out between Muslims, Protestants and Catholics in Kampala in Buganda (now Uganda), the IBEAC intervened. Meanwhile, Mackinnon's dreams of constructing a railway inland foundered when differences within the company jeopardized investment, and he was relegated to developing a 600-mile ox track from Mombasa north-west to Busia on the Bugandan border. Although the Berlin Conference had agreed that Buganda was within the British sphere of influence, Dr Karl Peters, an ultra-imperialist in German East Africa, recognized that its occupation was key to German expansion and claimed that since Buganda lay beyond Lake Victoria, it was therefore outside the British boundary. In 1890, he persuaded its king to accept German protection, but Captain Frederick Lugard (East Norfolks), who had led an expedition of Somali and Sudanese soldiers against Arab slavers in Nyasaland, persuaded the king to a cede Buganda to Britain. London then offered Berlin the tiny island of Heligoland off the German coast, which had been a British possession since 1814, in return for recognizing the settlements of Zanzibar, Buganda and Equatoria (now South Sudan) as British. Germany accepted, and converted Heligoland into a useful naval base.

Meanwhile, two Royal Engineers, Captains James Macdonald and Wallace Pringle, had surveyed the Arab caravan track between 1891 and 1892 and concluded that a railway could be built 1,000 miles from Mombasa to Buganda, thereby opening up Central Africa to exploitation. When Lugard was instructed to build a string of forts along the route, one person he contacted was Chief Waiyaki wa Hinga, a respected Kikuyu chief whose first contact with Europeans had been with two Germans accompanied by a notorious Arab slaver. These forts were usually oblong and defended by a ditch, barbed wire, a palisade of stakes and two drawbridges. Inside were brick living quarters for the Europeans and African huts of grass, mud and wattle. Most were built near rivers and streams. In spite of misgivings from his fellow chiefs, Waiyaki saw benefit in establishing a relationship with Lugard and, entering into a blood-brotherhood treaty, gave him a plot of land on the forest edge near Gataguriti (later known as Dagoretti) in Kikuyuland. Lugard then departed, leaving a 30-strong garrison commanded by an officer named Wilson with instructions not to compromise Waiyaki's power by taking land or property.

As detailed surveys began, Lugard returned to Kikuyuland to find that Kikuyu hostility had forced Wilson to abandon Fort Dagoretti; his force had been unable to prevent the Kikuyu harassing the caravans. The fort itself had been looted and burnt and a steel boat destined for Uganda stolen. Helped by men from the fort at Machakos and some Maasai, in a first act of confiscation Wilson had fined the Kikuyu fifty goats daily and instructed them to find 300 men to rebuild a new fort. Wilson was replaced by Captain Eric Smith, who had lost an eye and an arm while serving in the Life Guards and was now organizing the convoys. Waiyaki returned some of the property looted from the fort, but Smith incensed the Kikuyu by arbitrarily pitching the new Fort Smith in Waiyaki's homestead in a place rejected by Lugard, completing it in mid-1892. Angry at this trespass, Waiyaki threatened to flatten the fort. Tension increased when several Kikuyu ambushed an ally of the Company. Since British retaliation was inevitable, Waiyaki retreated with his people and livestock to their ancestral refuges in the forest of the Aberdares.

Smith then undermined the relationship that Wilson had developed with the Maasai by attacking them, which led to retaliatory assaults on caravans in which about forty IBEAC employees were killed. Captain W.P. Purkiss, a former sailor with a talent for bricklaying, was appointed as Superintendent, Kikuyu Province, and while Smith dealt with the Maasai, he led an expedition against the Kikuyu that involved burning homesteads and shooting scores of spear-carrying men. During negotiations with Waiyaki at Fort Smith, both men became involved in a brawl which ended with Waiyaki being concussed and either being locked up in a room or handcuffed and chained by the neck to the fort flagstaff. Convicted in court the next day, he was exiled permanently 'from the country, where he had proved such a treacherous enemy, and the cause of so much bloodshed'. Waiyaki rejected rescue and was quoted as saying, 'You must never surrender one inch of our soil to the foreigners, for if you do so, future children will die of starvation'. Next day, 17 August 1892, as he was being marched to Nairobi, he died from the complications of his wounds. Some suggest that Purkiss had him eliminated and then buried upside down in Kibwezi, something which was considered sacrilegious by the Kikuyu.

Mutual understanding had been undermined by imperialist arrogance. The garrison left the fort only to raid homesteads for food and cattle to feed the IBEAC. In 1893 Captain Francis Hall (Bengal Native Infantry) arrived to command Fort Smith and further undermined the treaty with punitive raids against the Kikuyu that included confiscating 180,000 livestock. On occasion, he leaked warnings about the raids; nevertheless, he wrote to his father that the only way to deal with the Kikuyu was wipe them out – except that they provided food for his soldiers. His letters are among the earliest records of life in British East Africa. He died from blackwater fever aged forty in 1901.

In 1894 East Africa was swamped by epidemics such as smallpox, locust plagues stripping fields and rinderpest decimating thousands of wild and domestic animals. The Maasai lost 90 per cent of their cattle. The Kikuyu abandoned their homesteads for the Aberdares. Meanwhile, as financial and managerial incompetence led to the British Government disbanding the IBEAC, from it emerged, on 1 July 1895, the Protectorate of British East Africa, to be governed by a Commissioner appointed by the Colonial Office. Within the year, the building of the railway from Mombasa to Kampala was approved, as a strategic response to Italian and French threats from the east and north and Belgian incursions from the west. Mr George Whitehouse, the Chief Engineer and Manager of the Uganda Railway, his British managers and technicians and the first of 32,000 Indian labourers and clerks recruited under terms and conditions agreed by the British and Indian governments, arrived. The small port of Mombasa soon swelled in importance as ships sailing though the Suez Canal arrived with steel and other equipment.

In January 1901 Sir Charles Eliot arrived as the second Commissioner. The author of books on Finnish grammar and the history and philosophy of the Ottoman Empire, he opposed violence and big game hunting, which was becoming a popular pastime for wealthy Europeans. Between 1900 and 1906, John Ainsworth, an administrator, converted the one-street tented encampment centred around a waterhole known to the Maasai as *Enkare Nairobi* (place of cool waters) into a seven-district town divided by blue gum trees that became known as Nairobi. The Europeans lived on the high ground while the Indians assembled as traders and businessmen in the Bazaar. The African communities were to the east and in the village of Kileleshwa. Attributing the completion of the Uganda Railway to British pluck, while professing he had no idea why it was built, Eliot wrote in his 1905 *Report on the East Africa Protectorate* that it had opened up a civilized territory and a possible residence for Europeans. After leaving Mombasa, the line ran through luxuriant coastal vegetation, climbed to a plateau of thorny scrub before again climbing through rolling countryside to Nairobi and thence through cultivated fields to Kikuyuland. The line then descended rapidly to the Mau Escarpment, where it perched on ledges alongside the Rift Valley, crossing ravines on twenty-seven viaducts, and then dropped to Naivasha before heading north to Nakuru. Rain, late deliveries, bridge-building, man-eating lions near Tsavo, derailments, theft of copper telegraph wire, bolts and rivets by the Nandi people for ornamental purposes and inaccurate financial assessments led to the railway terminating in 1902 at Kisamu (Milestone 584), which was renamed Port Florence in honour of Whitehouse's wife. A branch line was later built through Kikuyuland to Nanyuki.

Eliot launched a campaign in South Africa to encourage emigration on the promise of abundant land, high yields and cheap labour to grow tea, coffee, maize and wheat. When London proposed in 1902 that Jews be given a homeland in the Central Highlands, a settler named Ewart Grogan escorted a Zionist Congress commission; however, he presented them with a poor case by camping on a track used by elephants, then entering an area frequented by lions and Maasai warriors. Between 1897 and 1900 Grogan was the first man to walk from Cape Town to Cairo in order to prove to his prospective father-in-law that he had the character to marry his daughter. Generally, the response from Great Britain was small, with only 2,800 people arriving between 1903 and 1905; but those who emigrated were mostly from upper class families, including about 200 acquaintances of Lord Delamere. Most retained the Edwardian clothes they had worn at home and were determined that British East Africa would become a white colony like South Africa, Canada, New Zealand and Australia. The Rt Hon. Hugh Cholmondeley, 3rd Baron Delamere, was a descendant of Prime Minister Sir Horace Walpole and owned a large estate in Cheshire. Born in 1870, he first visited Africa in 1891; while hunting lion in British Somaliland he had been mauled by one, leaving him with a limp. He is credited with coining the term 'white hunter'. In 1896 he arrived at the head of a large caravan after a long safari across desert and semi-arid country from Somaliland, then crossed the empty, rolling and lush slopes temporarily abandoned by the Kikuyu, not dissimilar to the Wiltshire Downs, bathed in an ideal climate and too high for malaria-carrying mosquitoes. His first land application in May 1903 was rejected by Eliot on the grounds the land was too far from any population centres. His second application, for land near Lake Naivasha, was rejected on the grounds that it might cause friction with the Maasai. His third application, in 1906, saw him given a long lease on 100,000 acres near Gilgil on the shores of the picturesque Lake Elementaita near Njoro; the estate later became known as Soysambu. Briefly returning to Great Britain, he married Lady Florence Anne Cole, from a privileged Anglo-Irish family; the rigours of a pioneering life in a mud and grass hut with no close neighbours, while her husband was colony building, would be a far cry from a mansion in Ulster.

Among the Christian missionaries in the territory were Harry and Mary Leakey, at the Katebe Mission near Nairobi. One of their children, Louis Seymour Bazett, was born in 1903 and grew up among the Kikuyu. Indeed, aged thirteen, he was initiated into the tribe. The parents of Arundell Gray Leakey arrived in 1906 to help build the church at Kabete and lived on a farm five miles from Nyeri on the slopes on Mount Kenya. Arundell was also accepted into the Kikuyu as a 'blood brother', spoke their language fluently and was known as *murungaru* ('tall, straight' in Swahili). The Leakeys became a well-known Kenyan family. As the epidemics faded, the Kikuyu emerged from the forests to find that their arable and grazing lands had been grabbed by several hundred white people waving 999-year Crown leases. Kikuyu culture prohibited the permanent alienation of land to non-tribe members, but the Kikuyu had been weakened by the epidemics and were unable to do anything except watch as their tribal lands were converted into farms split by barbed wire fences. This fertile region soon became known as the White Highlands. Waiyaki had been right. Kikuyu resentment simmered, and as their livelihoods and traditions were destroyed by the necessity to find work as labourers, farm hands and maids, they retaliated. Meanwhile, the Maasai occupying the fertile land around Naivasha and Nakuruwere arbitrarily moved into two reserves, one in the highlands of Laikipia, north-west of Mt Kenya, and the other on the arid plains near the border with German East Africa; a treaty specified that the land was theirs 'so long as the Maasai as a race shall exist'. The illiterate chiefs signed with their thumbprints, but settlers quickly began agitating for the lush land in Laikipia.

By 1 January 1902 the War Office had amalgamated the several regiments in East Africa into the King's African Rifles (KAR) of 1st and 2nd (Nyasaland), 4th (Uganda), 3rd and 5th (Kenya) and 6th (Somaliland) Battalions, with an initial establishment of 104 British officers seconded from the British Army and 4,579 other ranks. Between 1902 and 1920 4 KAR was engaged in a campaign fighting Sayyid Mohammed Abdullah Hassan, the 'Mad Mullah', whose revolt threatened to destabilize the Horn of Africa. During the year, Kikuyu resistance reached such a peak that troops were sent to restore order. Captain Richard Meinertzhagen (Royal Fusiliers) serving with 3 KAR in 1903 focused on the confiscation of livestock but he also retaliated for the murder of a settler with the slaughter of an entire homestead, apart from the children sheltering in the forest. In a punitive expedition against Kikuyu and Embu homesteads, about 1,500 Africans were killed and 11,000 animals confiscated, at the cost of three soldiers killed and thirty-three wounded. Pangas and bows and arrows were no match for rifles and Maxim machine guns. When Meinertzhagen was implicated in the killing of a spiritual leader that led to peace negotiations, he successfully orchestrated a cover-up. The death of an American Quaker, allegedly caused by Nandi ambushing caravans, raiding settlements and stealing wire and other metals from the railway, led to Meinertzhagen's troops killing all the adults involved. However, the War Office had become sufficiently concerned about him that he was recalled by his regiment.

In 1904 he wrote, 'I am convinced that in the end, the African will win.' Nevertheless, he had spilt as much human blood as he had in shooting animals for sport.

Eliot resigned in 1905 after refusing to give two South Africans of the East Africa Syndicate 500 square miles of land between Ol Kalou and Ol Bolossat, pledged to them by Foreign Secretary Lord Lansdowne on unduly advantageous terms. The Syndicate was a company associated with IBEAC. Among the most successful settlers were Afrikaners, who arrived in 1903 to escape the depression of the two Boer states after their surrender in 1902. Thirty-three families trekked north to German East Africa but when they found its brand of colonialism far more rigorous than what they had practised, they headed north to British East Africa and settled beyond Thomson's Falls, north of the Aberadares. Major Robert Foran, one of the first six European officers in the British East Africa Police, wrote of them:

> They were an exceptional stamp of colonist, accustomed to giving and taking hard knocks in life. Even better still, they had mostly farmed in southern Africa and fully understood the handling of native African peoples.

Ten months later, the Protectorate passed under the control of the Colonial Office, the Commissioner was retitled 'Governor' and the Executive Council, entirely composed of settlers, moved from Mombasa to Nairobi. Among its members was Delamere as President of the Colonists' Association. The settlers were also heavily represented in the Legislative Council. Delamere experimented with imported sheep, cattle and crops and battled against disease and crop failure until, in 1914, he succeeded with maize and saw his profits rise. In 1906, Eliot wrote an interesting report on British East Africa in which he compared its colonization with that of Uganda:

> [Uganda] is adapted to be a black man's country, like other African colonies. But in the East African Protectorate, the case is different. The native population is very small; only two districts (Kairondo and Kikuyu) can be said to be thickly populated; large areas are uninhabited, and those areas, with others, are climatically and

> otherwise suited to European colonisation. In other words, the interior of the Protectorate is a white man's country. This being so, I think it is mere hypocrisy not to admit that white interest should be paramount, and that the main object of our policy and legislation should be to found a white colony.

He insisted that while there should be no violence against the Africans, European settlers must help to develop the land 'for the benefit of mankind' and that the nomadic tribes be prevented from monopolizing land for which they had no real use. Kikuyuland had a climate and country suitable for European settlement, and there was a sufficient native population available for labour. However, he also predicted that the Kikuyu would resist. A believer in the Victorian ideology of a 'moral duty to civilize the resident population' by conversion to Christianity and sure that the working class should be docile and compliant, he dismissed concerns that the British had no legal or moral right to purloin land from the Africans:

> There seems to be something exaggerated in all this talk about 'their own country' and their 'immemorial rights'. No doubt on platforms and in platforms we declare we have no intention of depriving natives of their lands, but this has never prevented us from taking whatsoever land we want for Government purposes, or from settling Europeans on land not actually occupied by natives. We should face the undoubted issue, namely white mates black in very few moves . . . The sooner the native disappears and is unknown, except in anthrolopogy, the better.

While visiting several African colonies, Under Secretary of State for the Colonies Winston Churchill arrived in Mombasa in 1907 and found that the roughly 2,000 settlers were keen to persuade the government that British East Africa was a 'white man's country'. Their perceived superiority was typified by Grogan, now President of the powerful Colonists' Association, and four friends, who in front of a magistrate whipped two Kikuyu rickshaw boys at Government House for their 'impudence' in jolting a carriage and 'impertinence' when they answered back to some white women. When one died and the other spent three months in hospital, the Colonial Office insisted that Grogan be tried for murder; however, the charge was reduced to common assault and he was sentenced to eight weeks hard labour – as a clerk in a hotel. Churchill doubted that the Protectorate would ever be a 'white man's country', not so much because of settler attitudes but because of Africa and its tropical diseases.

In 1908, Governor Percy Girouard offered farmland in the Central Highlands to Afrikaners in the Transvaal, and 48 families totalling 247 people, led by Commandant Janse van Rensberg, loaded their 47 wagons and 90 horses on to a chartered German ship. Landing at Mombasa, they took the train to Nakuru, where they purchased oxen and joined the first Boer cohort. Elspeth Huxley wrote in her book *No Easy Way*:

> To get heavily-loaded wagons up this steep escarpment along the rough, narrow, treacherous track, with inexperienced oxen and in a wet year, was a truly remarkable feat, and only Afrikaners could have performed it.

Van Rensberg, who had collaborated with the British as an 'irreconcilable', had reconnoitred British East Africa the previous year and found the plateau to be fertile and isolated, something that Afrikaners were entirely comfortable with, having spent 200 years in isolation in southern Africa – until the British arrived. Eventually, 700 'irreconcilables' settled in the region and developed the town of Eldoret, which seems to have been something akin to the Wild West. In 1911 60 more families arrived, which led to Lord Cranworth, a very good friend of Grogan, complaining about the 'solid mass of utterly disloyal colonists'. Cranworth believed there were just two reasons to go to East Africa – big game shooting and shortage of cash. He had arrived in May 1906 and bought 15,000 acres of land to farm coffee and sisal, but the business failed as did his other projects. However, the Afrikaners had a skill which few if any of the British gentlemen farmers possessed, expertise with ox teams for ploughing and transport, and soon they were much in demand.

When the Committee of Imperial Defence decided in mid-1907, in the early stages of hostilities, that 'native levies' would not be used to defend the African colonies, the caveat was 'unless the circumstances demanded change'. This resulted, three years later, in the role of the KAR changing to internal security and the regiment being reduced to three battalions. Consequently, 3 KAR decreased in size and some discharged askaris (native soldiers) joined the *Schutztruppe* (Protection Force) in German East Africa. German colonies were defended by regular and locally-raised Protection Forces; their basic tactical unit was a Field Company of usually three German officers, two German NCOs, a medical officer, 160 askaris organized into three platoons, a machine gun section, logistic support that included a military hospital and 250 porters, and 200 irregulars known as *rugarugas*.

In 1911, the Kikuyu failed to reclaim land grabbed by settlers when Governor Girouard caved in to settler pressure. He also reneged on the 1904 treaty and ordered the Maasai in Laikipia District to assemble south of the railway. Although a leader, Parsaloi Ole Gilisho, suggested that the proposed land was of inferior quality and lacked water, white chicanery and promises of land north of the railway to the settlers saw the signing of the Second Maasai Agreement. The transfer of the people and their thousands of livestock in the cold and wet of the 'long rains' was a near disaster and was suspended. On the advice of Dr Norman Leys, a Colonial Office medical officer, who had reported on the breach of the treaty to Parliament in London and stated that it was 'a crime against peaceful people', Gilisho engaged British lawyers in Mombasa to challenge the signatories of the 1911 Agreement. Although Girouard admitted deceiving the Colonial Office about the selling of land in Laikipia and was forced to resign, this did not stop the Administration blocking every move that Gilisho took to meet his lawyers, refusing the Maasai permission to contribute to his legal fees and threatening him if he travelled to London. In 1913 the case was dismissed on the technicality that the Maasai had retained sufficient sovereignty to sign the 1911 treaty and therefore the Administration was not responsible for their welfare and interests. Gilisho led the move into the expanded Maasai Reserve south of the railway.

The 384,000 square miles of German East Africa (now Burundi, Rwanda and Tanzania) contained about 5,000 settlers, most living in the north-east, and about 8 million Africans. The Central Railway connected Dar-es-Salaam with Lake Victoria, while the Usambara Railway linked Tanga and Arusha, south-west of the forested slopes of Mt Kilimanjaro and the border with British East Africa. When in January 1914, Lieutenant-Colonel Paul von Lettow-Vorbeck took command of the *Schutztruppe*, he developed a strategy to defend German East Africa by using guerrilla tactics. As the likelihood of war increased, the KAR Inspector-General, Colonel Arthur Hoskins, recommended that the Regiment increase its establishment; but he met indifference, as he did when he suggested battalion-level training. Sir Henry Conway Belfield had arrived as Governor in October 1912, after twenty-eight years of colonial service in Malaya, and met with Governor Heinrich Schnee of German East Africa; they discussed the unrealistic idea that in the event of hostilities in Europe their colonies would adopt a stance of neutrality.

By August 1914 the few thousand white settlers in British East Africa were firmly in control. During the past thirty years the indigenous Africans had seen their cultures, fields and livelihoods destroyed by imperialist settlers, paternalistic and weak colonial officials and subversive missionaries. They were about to be pitched into a war way beyond their comprehension.

When war was declared in Europe late on 4 August, Belfield declared martial law; but when he formed the War Council, the settlers saw it to be Nairobi-centric and demanded representation. Among those who raised militias was Captain Arthur Wavell (Welch Regiment), the owner of a sisal farm near Mombasa, who had been refused permission to join his Regiment in England. He formed his 150 Yemeni and Adeni Arab employees into No. 2 Reserve Company, or unofficially 'Wavell's Arabs' or 'the Arab Corps'. The East Africa Transport Corps organized a motorcycle despatch service. On 13 August Lieutenant Colonel Oscar Watkins was instructed to form the Carrier Section of porters as part of the Transport Corps. He had fought in the Second Boer War as an infantry sergeant and then joined the British South African Police, before moving in 1907 to the Protectorate, where he was appointed a District Commissioner and magistrate in the Slave Courts, freeing slaves from Arab raiders. Within the month, he had raised five porter battalions each of 1,000 Africans divided into companies of 100 led by a headman. Most joined for adventure and the money. The railway workshops in Nairobi produced an armoured train to complement patrols and provide a quick-reaction force.

The settlers initially supported conscription, but as the social and economic impact bit, enthusiasm drained away, particularly among the

Afrikaners, who regarded the war as not their problem. When the question of the future security of the Protectorate after the war was examined, Belfield predicted that a large number of European soldiers would not wish to return to a sedentary life and that East Africa could offer them opportunities. He wrote to the Colonial Office:

> I am satisfied that the influx of a large additional number of white settlers would materially minimise any risk of native aggression, and should be encouraged.

The main German threat was from two cruisers, the *Emden* and *Königsberg,* sailing through the Suez Canal and threatening:

- Maritime lines of communications to and from India.
- Deployment of the Imperial strategic reserve, namely the Indian Army, to the Middle East, Africa and Europe.
- The Suez Canal.
- Coal bunkers and Admiralty signalling station at Aden Settlement.

The sinking of a merchantman by the *Königsberg* led to two British cruisers bombarding Dar-es-Salaam and knocking out its wireless station on 8 August. Meanwhile, von Lettow-Vorbeck established a German presence in the Protectorate and threatened the Uganda Railway by overrunning the weak garrison at Taveta, a dozen miles inside British East Africa, and by seizing the strategically important Salaita Hill. In mid-September the Indian Expeditionary Force C (IEF C) landed at Mombasa as reinforcements. Tension increased when the *Königsberg* sank the ageing cruiser HMS *Pegasus* in Zanzibar, and then the *Schutztruppe* threatened Mombasa by capturing the fort at Majoreni, 25 miles to the south. Belfield ordered the evacuation of people, rolling stock and supplies and left Wavell to provide a military presence in the port. During the second week of October, Wavell's men and a 3 (Kenya) KAR detachment reinforced by 1 (Nyasaland) KAR forced the Germans to withdraw to Vanga. Wavell and the KAR detachment commander were both severely wounded and command passed to an African sergeant-major. Wavell was later killed in action near the coast.

Meanwhile, German patrols raided the railway between Voi and Tsavo, and mounted detachments emerged from the Longido Hills. The landing of IEF B at Tangaon on 3/4 November in a plan to meet IEF C counter-attacking from the north was disastrous and is described in the *Official History of the War* as 'one of the most notable failures in British military history'. Captain Richard Meinertzhagen, the IEF B Intelligence Officer, had predicted:

> From reliable information received it appears improbable that the enemy will not actively oppose our landing.

Among those abandoned in this disaster were 2,000 African porters adrift in lighters without food, water and shelter.

IEF B returned to Mombasa in near-disgrace from a population fearful of German retaliation. The British formed the Nairobi and Mombasa military districts and defended the border. In early January 1915, von Lettow-Vorbeck attacked the fort at Jassin, about ten miles south of Vanga, but suffered such heavy casualties among his Europeans that he ordered, 'Harass, kill, fight, but don't get caught.' One feature that emerged was that while the two Indian brigades were welcome, the operational effectiveness of the KAR was often restricted by unrealistic tactical and logistic planning by Indian Army officers unfamiliar with conditions in Africa.

When the Allies had agreed an offensive in January 1916 and Lieutenant General Jan Smuts, a former Boer commando leader, was appointed to command the East African Expeditionary Force (EAEF), a sizeable portion came from the South African Overseas Expeditionary Force. He later commented, 'Swamps and jungles . . . what a dismal prospect there is in front me.' Edward Paice uses a cricketing analogy as the title of his history of the war in East Africa – *Tip and Run* – and summarises the situation thus:

> The expense of the campaign to the British Empire was immense, the Allied and Germans 'butchers' bills' even greater. But the most tragic consequence of the two sides' deadly game of 'tip and run' was the devastation of an area five times the size of Germany, and civilian suffering on a scale unimaginable in Europe.

Smuts ignored advice not to fight in the rainy season and, opening his offensive on 18 March, drove the Germans from the border positions; by September he was occupying the area north of the Central Railway. A measure welcomed by the settlers as making 'idle and irresponsible Africans work' was the June 1916 Native Followers' Recruitment Ordinance. When Lieutenant Colonel Watkins was asked to supply 160,000 porters for the advance, he told the General Staff that the request was unrealistic; nevertheless, by the end of the war he had recruited 63,000 British East Africans, 183,000 Ugandans and 9,000 from Sierra Leone into the East Africa Carrier Corps. It essentially had four components:

- Carriers of porters and providers of intelligence guides and scouts.
- Gun Carriers of guns, machine-guns, ammunition and spare parts.
- Medical Carriers of stretcher-bearers, medical orderlies and buriers of the dead.
- Military Police.

Conscription left families bewildered, homesteads supported only by boys and elderly men and farms without employees. The journey by train to Mombasa and embarkation into the stuffy holds of noisy and dirty ships was a terrifying prospect for those who had never seen the sea and did not know what a ship was, particularly when it pitched and rolled. Nevertheless, the Corps played a crucial role, carrying 50lb loads on 2lbs of food daily in long marches alongside mules, oxen and horses in harsh field conditions and supported by unreliable medical and welfare services. Pay was at the lowest band. By January 1917 Smuts was forced to halt and evacuate thousands of soldiers, mostly white South Africans, on medical grounds. Initially, he was replaced by Major General Hoskins, the former KAR Inspector-General, who used the rainy season to rebuild the EAEF with a greater number of African troops. Smuts claimed in London that the Germans were near defeat, but Hoskins was reluctant to advance until he was ready. This annoyed the government and he was replaced in May by Lieutenant General Jacob van Deventer, who had been Smuts' deputy during the Boer War. In March, as the lines of communication lengthened and the demands on the Carrier Corps grew, Colonel John Ainsworth, the founder of Nairobi, recruited able-bodied male Africans under the 'Grand Levy'; but as injured and wounded porters in poor health returned home with accounts of the campaign, young men reluctant to become beasts of burden in a war about which they understood little, fled into the forests. This forced Watkins and Ainsworth to suggest to district commissioners that they use press-gangs to fill their quotas. Although they did their best to ensure African welfare, they were faced by settlers demanding greater government control over the African population, thereby igniting post-war squabbles about labour. Deventer recommenced the advance in July and although he outflanked the Germans by landing in ports, von Lettow-Vorbeck remained at large until he surrendered in Northern Rhodesia on 25 November 1918.

Paice gives a total of 22,000 British casualties, of whom 11,189 died, from the total of 126,900 troops. Meanwhile, 60,000 Africans were battle casualties. About 450,000 Africans were conscripted into the East Africa Carrier Corps, of whom 95,000 died, most succumbing to disease, exhaustion and inadequate medical facilities. Fewer than 13,000 hospital beds were available for the Carrier Corps and most were too far from the front lines to be reachable by those injured or struck down by malaria, dysentery or pneumonia. While the Ugandan Administration expressed concern at its 3,870 dead and 4,650 missing, British East Africa ignored its 25,891 dead and 13,748 missing porters. When Surgeon-General Colonel William Pike investigated the EAEF casualty list and concluded in his 1918 *Report on Medical and Sanitary Matters in German East Africa* that 'there was much to regret in the medical history of the campaign', it was a damning indictment of a chaotic situation which resulted in several senior medical officers facing disciplinary action. Although particularly critical of the treatment of the Carrier Corps, he was told his report would not be published unless he concluded that responsibility for the death rate among the Corps should not solely rest with the medical authorities. One Colonial Office official concluded that Pike 'only stopped short because the people who suffered most were the carriers – and after all, who cares about native carriers?' The tragedy of the East Africa Carrier Corps left a lasting impression that resonates today in East African history.

Chapter 2

The Colonization of Kenya

Despite shipping shortages, closures of some markets during the war, the failure of the 1917 autumn rains and the absence of white manpower, British East African farmers had increased the exportation of plantation crops, chiefly sisal and coffee, as well as beef on the hoof and horses and mules for the campaign in German East Africa, and settler prosperity had rocketed. In contrast, the Africans had seen increased wartime taxes, demanding labour laws and conscription; many were scratching a precarious subsistence on their small plots, a far cry from the plenty they had enjoyed before the invasion of the settlers. Victory had seen German East Africa annexed as Tanganyika, but when the global Spanish influenza epidemic struck East Africa in September 1918, 160,000 people died in the Protectorate and famine took its toll, the worst affected regions being Kikuyuland and Nyanza, on the eastern shores of Lake Victoria. As the medical authorities struggled, Colonel Ainsworth set up a welfare organisation. Discharged soldiers unwilling to resume their former servitude found that employment was difficult, and this added to the feeling of oppression.

Sir Edward Northey had served in the Boer War and on the Western Front with the King's Royal Rifle Corps until wounded in 1915. He had then commanded the Nyasa-Rhodesia Field Force during the East African campaign. When he arrived as Governor on 31 January 1919, the Colonial Office instructed him to implement the recommendations of the Land Settlement Commission appointed by Governor Belfield in 1916 and to develop a strategy to allot a million acres in Central Province to 1,000 applicants in the Soldier Settlement Scheme. The Scheme was devised to encourage economic growth throughout the British Empire, restore social mobility after the long casualty lists and pay a debt of honour to veterans. In British East Africa, one aim was solidify the status of settlers faced by Africans no longer in awe of them. In April, three lotteries in London and Nairobi distributed over a thousand farms to existing residents and new settlers. The 250 Class A farms of over 300 acres were awarded as free grants. Applicants for the 800 Class B farms of 300 acres or less were required to invest £1,000. Awards were based on the ability to raise capital and to manage the investment. Farming experience was desirable but not required. But once again the selling of land squeezed African communities, particularly among the Kikuyu and the Nandi. While the Scheme was also designed to cater for 'poor whites', the new arrivals, in stark contrast to Australia, Canada and New Zealand, were largely drawn from the British and Anglo-Irish upper and middle class; they possessed similar educational, social, professional and military backgrounds to officers who had served in the British, colonial and Dominion armed forces, men attracted by adventure, an agreeable climate and a determination that the Protectorate would be a white colony. Poorer whites gained little from the Scheme except as officials and businessmen. The new colonists were thus an elite before they arrived and were determined to exploit their political clout to preserve their status and influence in the same way that the British influential classes had done from the hill stations of British India. Where there were differences, they were generally between the demands of wealthy farmers and the requirements of urban merchants. The impact of the Scheme can be seen in the remarkable fact that the 1926 census showed no single white resident aged twenty-six or over had been born in Kenya. The principal debt of honour paid by Northey was to offer 25,000 acres near Kericho in the south-west to the British East Africa Disabled Officers' Colony, men who had been severely wounded or were suffering the after-effects of battle and who could invest £600 in a joint venture; 4,000 acres were grabbed from the Kipsigis Native Reserve to grow flax. Public school stoicism and an ability to manage wounds were important.

The rigours of war had sunk the stuffiness of the pre-war Edwardians. In British East Africa, fear of the sun was now ignored by a relaxed society embracing the Charleston and jazz, and by young women known as 'flappers', who wore knee-length skirts and short bobbed hair and disregarded accepted norms of behaviour. Wanjohi Valley near Nyeri achieved a reputation for hedonistic settlers and adventurers indulging in riotous and decadent lifestyles that led to the area being known as 'Happy Valley'.

By the time that the East Africa Protectorate became the Colony of Kenya on 11 June 1920, about 5.5 million acres of land formerly occupied by Africans had been long-leased to about 10,000 expatriates. Administrative power remained with the Governor and his Executive of colonial departmental administrators. White representatives elected to the Legislative Council outnumbered Indian and Arab councillors. African representatives rejected the offer of two seats on the grounds that this failed to represent the size of their community. During the year, African males over the age of fifteen were required to carry their *kipande* identity document when they left a Reserve. The *kipande* listed the bearer's name, fingerprints, ethnic group, employment history and employer's signature and was aimed at auditing the labour pool. It was detested because it was discriminatory. Most kept the document in a small metal container, which they hung around the neck and called the 'goat's bell'. Failure to produce it on demand could mean a fine or imprisonment or both.

The new land distribution saw further marginalization of the Kikuyu, now squeezed into a Reserve that encompassed the districts of Kiambu, Fort Hall and Nyeri, surrounded by white farms, living on barely enough land for subsistence farming and paying Hut and Poll Taxes amounting to about two months worth of African wages. This meant that they had little choice but to seek work or squat on colonist farms where, under the 1918 Resident Native Ordinance, they had to pay rent in labour. By 1930, about 120,000 were squatting on 20 per cent of farms. They were not permitted to raise cattle in case disease affected colonists' animals and were forbidden to grow cash crops in order to prevent competition with the colonists. Coffee could be grown, but licences were difficult to obtain. Forced labour, which had been used before the war to build the transport infrastructure and administrative buildings and clear forest for farms, continued. Some colonists saw the practice as an act of benevolence towards an idle people. By 1918, a squatter was required to work for three months; however, although the size of their plots decreased, the liability was increased to six months in 1925. In 1939, the Colonial government purchased a large amount of land to relocate 30,000 landless evictees; however, it was poor quality land, and the

Kikuyu, who constituted the majority of the squatters, refused to move. On the south-western borders the Nandi exploited their 'good' African image to curtail white expansion. Elsewhere, Kikuyu militancy was growing.

In June 1921, a young government employee named Harry Thuku exploited restlessness among African veterans to form the Young Kikuyu Association (YKA) as a protest against the inequality of African political representation, the land grabs, the Hut Tax, legislation restricting the ability of Africans to move employment and the *kipande*. Thuku was born in 1895 into an influential Kikuyu family and after being educated at the Kiambu Gospel Mission had found employment in 1918 as a typesetter for the *Leader*, a European newspaper, and then as a clerk-telegraphist in the Treasury, where he gained administrative experience and became fluent in English. He also managed to acquire a criminal record for theft of a cheque and served two years hard labour. Politically aware and seeing opportunities for African prosperity disintegrating, in order to attract a wider presence he renamed the YKA the East African Association. For the first time, an educated and politically astute African was setting out to restore African dignity using a political organization outside colonial influence. The Association attracted significant tribal membership and to some extent set the benchmark for future African liberation struggles. The Legislative Council rejected its aims by claiming that Kenya was not ready for African representation, hardly a surprising decision given white power and the depths to which some indigenous populations had been driven. In early 1922, Thuku ratcheted up his demands by accusing the Administration of stealing Kikuyu land and suggested that the colonists should leave Kenya. He also encouraged people to throw their degrading *kipandes* on to the Government House front lawn. His suggestion caused such concern that he and two followers were arrested by the Head of the Criminal Investigation Department (CID) and remanded to Nairobi Central Police Station. A fractious demonstration of thousands of Africans followed, during which a woman displayed her disrespect to the police cordon by raising her dress above her head and showing her genitalia in a brazen act of defiance known as the *Guturama* (incidentally, the role of women in the struggle for independence has largely been undervalued). A constable then opened fire. The press reported 27 killed, while eyewitnesses claimed 200. The

1960 Corfield Report investigating the causes of the Mau Mau rebellion claimed that there were just three fatalities. Thuku and his colleagues were exiled to Somaliland, without trial, for eight years.

In the crowd was Kamauwa Ngengi, a Kikuyu born in the village of Gatundu in October 1891. When his father died the child and his mother, as was customary, were adopted by his eldest brother. When his mother died in childbirth, Kamau moved to Muthiga to live with his grandfather and board at the Church of Scotland Mission school at Thogoto, about twelve miles north-west of Nairobi; he raised the fees by working as a houseboy and cook. He then became an apprentice carpenter and was initiated into manhood in 1913. Two years later, he converted to Christianity and took the name of John Peter, which he later changed to Johnstone Kamau. During the First World War he worked for the Administration as a carpenter and as a clerk for an Asian contractor. In 1920 he married and fathered a son, Peter. Kamau then became a Nairobi High Court interpreter and ran a store at his home at Fort Dagoretti. Two years later, he was working as a store clerk and water-meter reader for the Nairobi Municipal Council Public Works Department which gave him the opportunity to create networks in the Kenyan and Asian community.

Before the First World War, Lord Delamere, his political allies in Great Britain and some officials made unrealistic demands for greater settler representation in the administrative decision-making process. By 1923 the Colonial Office had lost patience with their persistence and issued the Devonshire White Paper listing the following principles:

- Independent government in Nairobi was out of the question.
- The Indian population should have elected representation.
- The interests of the Africans were paramount. If they conflicted with those of the colonists, African interests should take precedence.

But the colonist mindset of Kenya as a white colony was strong and, rejecting the notion of African political representation, the Legislative Council banned the YKA two years later, only to see it morph into the Kikuyu Central Association (KCA). An applicant in 1924 was Kamau, and although his English lacked fluency it was better than most others', and four years later he became a translator for and then editor of the monthly Kikuyu-language newspaper *Mwigithania* ('He Who Brings Together'), a publication tolerated by the Administration. In 1927, the Indians were given five seats on the Legislative Council to join the eleven Europeans. Kamau, now calling himself Johnstone Kenyatta, was appointed the KCA's General Secretary in 1928. After the party gave evidence to the Hilton Young Commission investigating the amalgamation of the three East African colonies, a principle supported by leading colonists in the expectation that self-government might follow, the Commission's proposals were distinctly unfavourable to Kikuyu interests. When Governor Edward Grigg refused to meet the KCA, in February 1929 Kenyatta and Isher Dass, an Indian lawyer, sailed to London to testify against the proposals but, not surprisingly, their presence was hardly noticed; indeed, Secretary of State for the Colonies Leo Amery refused to see them. Nevertheless, Kenyatta met senior Colonial Office officials and reinforced KCA demands for political representation, improved education for African children, removal of restrictions on cash crop growing and the return of African land. He raised the plight of Kenyan Africans in several eloquent letters to British newspapers. On 26 March 1930, *The Times* published his letter demanding:

- Security of land tenure.
- Improved educational opportunities for Africans.
- Repeal of women's hut and poll taxes.
- Representation for Africans in the Legislative Council.
- Freedom to pursue traditional customs, in particular female genital mutilation. The Church of Scotland had been denouncing the practice since 1906 as unchristian and in 1919 demanded its abolition. However, the Kikuyu resented this further interference with their traditions which then led to tension between the Church and the KCA.

Meetings with the Church of Scotland were less than fruitful, largely because there was mutual distrust, which was hardly surprising given that the parties had had minimal contact in Kenya. Kenyatta met with other activists in revolutionary and liberation movements such as George

Padmore, a black Trinidadian communist promoting the idea that imperialism be replaced with equality, worker solidarity and hope. After visiting Moscow for several months, Kenyatta returned to London equipped with a militant approach and predicted in a letter to *The Times*:

> We hope to remove all lack of understanding between the various peoples who form the population of East Africa, so that we may all march together as loyal subjects of His Britannic Majesty along the road of Empire prosperity. I would like to ask if any fair-minded Briton considers the above outlined policy of the Kikuyu Central Association to savour in any way of sedition? The repression of native views of subjects of such vital interest to my people of legislative measures can only be described as short-sighted tightening of the safety valve of free speech, which must inevitably result in a dangerous explosion – the one thing all sane men wish to avoid.

Kenyatta returned to Kenya in late September 1930 with little gained except the right for Africans to develop independent educational institutions.

During his absence, Kikuyu politics had been dominated by the refusal to abandon female circumcision. Meanwhile, as the global economy began to collapse in 1929 at the start of the Great Depression and farmers bought modern machinery, pressures on the Africans mounted. A devastating drought and migrating swarms of locusts from the north assaulting farms between 1931 and 1935 sparked fears that East Africa would become a dustbowl and led to cash cropping of non-food items and consequent famine among Africans, in spite of the efforts of the Famine Relief and Food Control Board. Their predicament induced concern that Kenya's survival was at risk, particularly as export costs rose. By the mid-1930s, about a fifth of the agricultural land and supporting economic infrastructure and labour was under colonist control. Nevertheless, the Legislative Council ratcheted up pressure on the Africans with stricter controls on their way of life, educational supervision and changes in land use. The traditional channel of communications also veered from village chiefs and homestead headmen towards young men possessing communications skills learnt from missionaries and employment in the colonial administration. When the farmers in the White Highlands gained political representation as a reward for their contribution to the economy, they protected their interests by banning Africans from growing coffee and reduced the acreage given in exchange for their labour. These impositions saw further displacement of unemployed Kikuyu, who drifted to the squalor, anonymity and militancy of the townships, leaving the farmers without sufficient labour.

With his status on the rise, Kenyatta returned to England in early 1931, leaving Thuku, who had returned from exile, as leader of the KCA. Kenyatta associated with the India League and the League of Coloured Peoples and met the Indian nationalist Mahatma Gandhi in London. In 1932, he testified on behalf of Kikuyu land claims at the Carter Land Commission which, while it offered compensation for some, also supported restricting the Kikuyu to the overcrowded Reserves. During the year Kenyatta paid his second visit to the Soviet Union, whose Marxist-Leninist ideology regarded racism as a feature of capitalism and consequently criticized imperialism and took every opportunity to subvert it. To blacks living in the USA and some indigenous people living in European colonies, Moscow offered alternative political ambitions, and consequently during the 1920s several hundred African-American and Afro-Caribbean 'pilgrims' travelled to the 'Red Mecca'. Few were actually communists. From 1932 to 1933 Kenyatta studied economics at the Communist University of the Toilers of the East in Moscow but left disillusioned with the ideology. After learning about Western culture in other European countries, he studied anthropology under Professor Bronisław Malinowski at the London School of Economics. His mentor was so impressed with his pupil's thesis on Kikuyu life that he wrote the preface for his book *Facing Mount Kenya* (1938), written under the name Jomo ('Burning Spear') Kenyatta. As an active member of the International African Service Bureau, he joined black intellectuals such as Kwame Nkrumah from the Gold Coast and Paul Robeson, the singer, and protested against the 1935 Italian invasion of Abyssinia. In the summer of 1939, Makhan Singh, General Secretary of the Labour Trade Union of East Africa, asked Kenyatta to represent his organization at a conference planned for the end of September, but the outbreak of war intervened.

In Kenya, challenges to his progressive agenda and colonial subversion led to Thuku forming in 1935 the moderate Kikuyu Provincial Association (KPA). Jesse Kariuki, a leading militant, took over the KCA, but Government controls on political activity at the outbreak of war in 1939 prevented KCA from achieving the same recognition as the KPA; indeed, it was banned in 1940. In 1943, Thuku and Eliud Wambu Mathu formed the multi-tribal Kenya African Study Union (KASU), with the former elected as its first chairman. Born in 1910, Mathu had studied at Fort Hare College in the mid-1930s and at Balliol College, Oxford between 1939 and 1940.

The Second World War again saw significant changes in Kenya as 98,000 Kenyans joined in the armed forces, many enlisting to escape squatting and the townships and to provide livelihoods for their families. The 12th (East African) Division fought the Italians in Abyssinia. Sergeant Nigel Leakey, son of Arundell Leakey, was awarded the VC for gallantry at the Battle of Colito when he climbed on to enemy tanks armed only with a revolver. After the Division was disbanded in 1943, the 11th (East African) Division joined the 5th Indian Division in the XXXIII Indian Corps in Fourteenth Army in Burma. After the hard-fought victories around Kohima and Imphal, the British ignored the monsoon and the Division advanced through the malarial Kabaw Valley, which had an average monthly rainfall of 16in. In spite of malaria, dysentery, scrub typhus, skin complaints and rain, roads were built through the primary jungle and across *chuangs* (streams and small rivers). Air supply and, once again, long columns of porters, proved crucial. The askaris were noted for stalking the Japanese. For nearly five months, the troops slept in their uniforms, washed in buckets of rainwater and survived on tinned food. The Division then took part in the Battles of Meiktila and Mandalay.

RAF Nairobi, located on the north-eastern outskirts of the capital, had been opened in December 1935 as Air HQ for RAF and Rhodesian squadrons and the Kenyan Auxiliary Unit. In October 1940 Air HQ reformed as Air HQ (East Africa) and RAF Nairobi a week after the Japanese attack on Pearl Harbor on 7 December 1941. Its units included No. 207 (General Purpose) Group of RAF and South African Air Force squadrons flying maritime sorties against German and Japanese naval operations in the Indian Ocean. When the Group was promoted to

Command status in January 1943, it was subordinated to Middle East Air Force, itself under the control of Mediterranean Air Command. Among the units using the base was the Anti-Locust Flight (Persia) in 1944.

Meanwhile, Kenya hosted twelve prison camps. It is not often that escaping prisoners break back into their camp; however, that is exactly what happened when three Italians did so in early 1943. Felice Benuzzi of the Italian Colonial Service, Dr Giovanni Balletto and Vincenzo Barsotti, a sailor, were in Prison Camp 354 near Nanyuki, and such was their combination of boredom and fascination with Mt Kenya that Benuzzi decided to climb it. Ignoring advice from an experienced mountaineer, the three escaped in January and using a map from an Oxo tin label and with only meagre rations, they trekked to a base camp where they left Barsotti, who had become ill. Benuzzi and Balletto negotiated the forest and the bamboo and using climbing equipment manufactured in the camp, reached about 14,000ft above Petit Gendarme. The three then returned to Camp 354 in mid-February and were awarded twenty-eight days in solitary by the camp commandant, reduced to seven days for their 'sporting effort'. Benuzzi later wrote a book, *No Picnic on Mount Kenya*, about his exploit.

Early on 24 January 1941, the Earl of Erroll was discovered shot dead in his car several miles outside Nairobi. A leading figure in the colonial community who had recently been appointed Military Secretary, he had a reputation as a seducer of other men's wives. No one was ever brought to trial over the murder, but it did expose the lifestyles of the bored colonists of Happy Valley and resonates today in similar scandals. The murder was dramatized in the film *White Mischief* (1987).

In 1944 Sir Philip Mitchell was appointed Governor. He was born in 1890 and his father had been in the Royal Engineers team that was defeated 1-0 by the Wanderers in the first FA Cup Final of 1872. Mitchell dropped out of Oxford University and, joining the Colonial Administrative Service in 1913, was posted to Nyasaland as an Assistant Resident. He served in the KAR during the First World War and learnt Swahili in addition to Bantu. While Tanganyika Secretary for Native Affairs in 1929, Mitchell claimed that every Bantu village was a co-operative society. He had been Governor of Uganda between 1935 and 1940 and of Fiji between 1942 and 1944. Like many colonial officials, he had a paternalistic attitude towards Africans and believed colonists had a duty to civilize them. In *The Agrarian Problem in Kenya,* he wrote:

> They are a people who, however, have much natural ability and however admirable attributes they may possess, are without a history, culture or religion of their own and in that they are, as far as I know, unique in the modern world.

In the same year, Eliud Wambu Mathu became the first African to be appointed to the Legislative Council and served until 1957.

Chapter 3

The Emergence of the Mau Mau

The Japanese surrender on 14 August 1945 concluded the Second World War. East Africa had raised forty-three infantry battalions, nine independent garrison companies, engineer and signal squadrons, transport companies and field ambulances. The Kenya Regiment were Territorials and formed in 1937 from colonists, with a permanent Staff mostly supplied by the Guards. During the war they served in Madagascar and Burma. Men conscripted under the compulsory Military Training Ordinance did basic training at the King George VI Barracks in Salisbury, Southern Rhodesia, pending completion of its depot near Nakuru. In 1950 the instructors were supplied by the 60th Rifles and Rifle Brigade. RHQ in Nairobi was opened by HRH Princess Elizabeth in February 1952. In early April, Lieutenant Colonel Guy Campbell, who had been second-in-command for four months, assumed command. Commissioned in 1931, he had served in Sudan, Libya, Eritrea and Palestine with 60th Rifles and soon found kindred spirits among the independent young British and Afrikaner colonials in the rifle companies, where every officer was considered to be one among equals. A friend told him:

> [The] true Kenyan is an extrovert who had never fully grown up, with a very simple outlook on life, who was quick to take offence and who would fight for a principle . . . This means they could be uncompromising. (*The Charging Buffalo* p.36)

Although most British units had returned home, in September 1945 twenty Royal Army Service Corps (RASC) officers and 100 other ranks commanded by Major R.W. Armstrong disembarked from HMT *Caernarvon Castle* at Mombasa and were dispersed among KAR Motor Transport platoons. During the war, the ship had been refitted as an auxiliary cruiser and had been badly damaged in an engagement with a

German surface raider off the South American coast in December 1940. Armstrong joined 39 Company, East African Army Service Corps (EAASC), which was commanded by Major Ivor Thomas. It first went to Moshi on the delightful slopes of Mount Kilimanjaro in Tanganyika before being sent to the former Prison Camp 361 at Athi River, where it was disbanded as part of the drawdown of the Army in Kenya. Armstrong was posted to 42 Company and was involved in repatriating demobilized soldiers from the Far East and from labour battalions in North Africa, the latter travelling by barge south along the River Nile to Juba in Sudan and then passing through several staging camps before returning home. Essential to East Africa Command was the East Africa Water Transport Company, which was equipped with several 46-ton trawlers, 48-ton high performance towing launches and landing craft tasked with supplying offshore and river forts, providing launches for Field Security boarding parties and target-towing for coastal artillery. Four trawlers reinforced water transport operations in Egypt.

Jomo Kenyatta delayed his return to Kenya in order to help organize the Fifth Pan-African Congress in Manchester in October 1945, which was managed by people of African origin. Manchester was selected because the city was judged to be politically conscious. Pan-Africanism is a political ideology that emerged from the anti-slavery movement in the late eighteenth century and aims to promote African economic, intellectual and political co-operation, unify people of African descent and ensure that the wealth of their continent be shared amongst its people. The Congress was chaired by William Edward Burghardt Du Bois, an American civil rights activist, and was a milestone because it addressed the decolonization of Africa. Delegates included Afro-Caribbeans and Afro-Americans, as well as Africans such as Kwame Nkrumah, then attending the London School of Economics.

After war broke out, Dinah Stock, the Secretary of the Centre Against Imperialism and colleague of the pacifist Fenner Brockway (later a founder of the Campaign Against Nuclear Disarmament), persuaded Kenyatta to stay with her in the West Sussex village of Storrington, where he became popularly known as 'Jumbo'. When Great Britain came under siege during the Battle of the Atlantic and the Ministry of Agriculture promoted home-grown products, he cultivated a smallholding, where he grew sweetcorn, and found employment in an agricultural company in Thakeham, near Horsham. He taught British troops attending the Forces Educational Scheme and lectured to the Workers' Educational Association on colonial issues. He married a teacher, Edna Clarke, and they had a son two years later. Her parents were killed in an air raid in May 1941.

Globally, the communist philosophy promoted by the Stalinist Soviet Union and Mao in China was destabilizing parts of Asia and Europe; indeed, on 5 March 1946, describing Europe, Sir Winston Churchill declared, 'From Stettin in the Baltic to Trieste in the Adriatic, an iron curtain has descended across the continent.' Elsewhere, British, French and Dutch colonialism was being challenged in Malaya, French Indo-China and the Dutch East Indies (now Indonesia). The British Mandate in Palestine was also being contested, not that Britain wished to stay there.

Sporting his trademark Van Dyke beard, Kenyatta landed at Mombasa on 24 September 1946, sixteen years after he had left, but without his family. Accompanied by a Kikuyu delegation, he took the train to Nairobi, where he received a tumultuous welcome from Africans who believed that, at last, here was a well known leader who would represent them. He returned to Kiambiu District, where he purchased and farmed several acres, and was later appointed Principal of Kenya Teachers' College in Gathunguri, the country's first teacher training college. He married for a third time, his new wife being the daughter of a chief.

The British military presence in Kenya was largely confined to officers and other ranks seconded to East African units and those posted to HQ East Africa Command based in Buller Barracks and still subordinate to Middle East Command. Communications were provided by the East Africa Command Signal Squadron through its cryptographic office and Signals Centre. Squadron HQ consisted of ten British seconded officers, thirty other ranks and 250 Africans. The Command incorporated HQ Northern Area at Nanyuki, HQ Southern Area in Moshi, Tanganyika and detachments in Hargeisa and Mogadishu in Somaliland. As nationalism escalated in Egypt, the War Office anticipated that the loss of its Middle East Command base would mean that Strategic Reserve could be moved to Kenya. In 1947, the East African Pioneer Corps, which had played an important role in Middle East ports and harbours during and since the war, was disbanded in favour of using prisoners and labourers. When locally employed

Egyptians refused to work in the Suez Canal Zone, the Corps was reformed, including former KAR on two-year engagements. Of the 7,000 from Kenya, 416 were formed into 2201 Company in Machakos on 23 December and arrived in Suez a fortnight later. A further 10,000 were recruited to replace those completing their contracts. In preparation for the projected loss of Egypt, the War Office began converting the former Fleet Air Arm base and prison-of-war camp near the small railway station at Mackinnon Road near the road between Mombasa and Nairobi into a major HQ and Advanced Ordnance Depot capable of holding 200,000 tons of materiel. Royal Engineers improved roads and built a water pipeline from the River Tsavo, 70 miles to the west. Then 51 Company RASC arrived from Palestine and used tank transporters to move heavy plant vehicles, and 4 Armoured Brigade Company, consisting mainly of National Servicemen from Palestine, kept the project supplied with deliveries from Mombasa, using the AEC Militant six-wheel 10-ton truck nicknamed 'Milly'. Later, 242 Company, also from Palestine, replaced 51 Company. The Royals Signals formed the Mackinnon Road Signal Troop from 7 (Lines of Communication) Signals to support the project. In 1948, 1 Special Operations Team in Nairobi was re-titled 1 Special Communications Troop and in due course became 602 Signal Troop (Special Communications). Their power supply was, at best, variable. It was reported that soldiers made elements to heat water in their metal drinking/shaving mugs which led to a drop in voltage from 230 to 80 volts for about an hour after reveille; this led to FBS going temporarily off air. Although a fully functioning camp and the Depot were built within two years, the British withdrawal from Egypt seemed unlikely to be imminent, and Cyprus and Aden were seen as alternatives for HQ Middle East Command. There were also fears that the railway from Mombasa would not survive the projected build-up of 200 tons per day of vehicles, stores and ammunition.

Lieutenant Colonel Thomas had been instructed to form the EAASC Corps Depot and Training Centre at the former Italian Prison Camp 361 at Athi River, with the intention of forming nine companies. The failure of the Groundnut Scheme at Kongwa in Tanganyika meant the local recruiting pool of largely former KAR counterbalanced the slow arrival of British Army officers and instructors from the UK, mostly National Servicemen. Driver training was conducted on week-long 'safari' convoys into the bush. By the late 1940s the Austin Champ had replaced US Willys Jeeps, and trials of Series 1 Land Rovers were establishing that they were cheaper, more stable, consumed less fuel and were an ideal light transport. By 1950, six of the nine EAASC companies were supporting the six KAR battalions of 30 (East African) Brigade.

Kenya had again profited from the war, but little benefit had reached the squatters on the farms and in the reserves. Indeed, in 1945 most Africans were contracted to nine months indentured labour and were restricted to owning fifteen sheep and working about two acres of land. When the men had left to fight, the women took their place as agricultural labour, in addition to managing the home. The demobilized African servicemen and women who had helped humble the three belligerent nations of Germany, Italy and Japan had received education and, unlike the First World War veterans, had mixed with servicemen and women from across the world, had seen non-white troops being treated with respect and had met British people who sympathized with their plight; some, too, had seen the joy of liberation from occupation. Their experiences and the movement of international opinion against colonialism generated a steely determination for equality; indeed, those who had been commissioned or were senior NCOs challenged the colonial status quo by seeking middle-class employment and social privileges, and an African middle class began to develop. But with 60,000 colonists pressurizing Governor Mitchell to consolidate their power over 7 million Africans, the colonial machine seemed unlikely to budge and acknowledge their contribution.

The restrictions placed on Africans led in 1946 some dissatisfied veterans who had enlisted in 1940 to form the secretive *Anake a 40* ('Young Men of 40'), usually known as the Forty Group. Their primary aim was to conduct militant action to express their dissatisfaction. In contrast, Kenyatta openly espoused the belief that all Kenyans should direct their representation through a national movement. Within months, the Group locked on to a cause when they spread disinformation about an Administration decision that Kikuyu women tilling their fields in Fort Hall District should dig terraces on the Central Province slopes in order to improve agricultural output; this, the Group alleged, was actually to prepare land for another wave of emigrants. These would be people abandoning the austerity of post-war Britain, many of them ex-armed forces, coming under a secret plan devised by Major Ferdinand Cavendish-Bentinck to ensure the Colony maintained its white aspirations. Cavendish-Bentinck, heir to the dukedom of Portland, had been severely wounded in the First World War and had arrived in the colony in the 1920s under the British East Africa Disabled Officers Scheme. Also arriving were former Indian Army officers made redundant after Indian independence and intending to continue living the life they had been forced to abandon. Most were allocated units of about 700 acres in the Central Highlands, again at the expense of the Kikuyu, Embu and Meru. Other new arrivals included colonial officials, teachers, doctors, businessmen and artisans, most living in Nairobi, Mombasa and other towns, often in impressive ignorance of the plight of Africans living either as squatters or in the unhealthy squalor of townships, where unemployment and crime were rife and education almost non-existent, a state of affairs that resonates today. The 1.25 million Kikuyu were restricted to the 2,000 overcrowded square miles of the Kikuyu Reserve, while the 30,000 colonists occupied 12,000 square miles. An African joke was: when Europeans arrived in Kenya they had the Bibles and the Africans had the land, but now it is the reverse. This sort of subversion did not go unnoticed. The Central Province Commissioner and the Nairobi District Commissioner both wrote secret reports commenting on anti-European unrest among Africans, a pernicious African media and destabilizing political agitators.

With dissatisfaction seething among the squatters, 300 marched to Nairobi and entered Government House. In June, Kenyatta reformed the KASU into the Kenya African Union (KAU) and, declaring that blood would be spilt in the pursuit of freedom, quickly recruited 150,000 members who pledged their loyalty with an oath. The KAU usually met in the Indian National Congress offices in Nairobi, until police pressure forced them to meet in private houses. This led to the forming of a Study Circle of about ten intellectuals, including three expatriates, to determine direction and policies. Lieutenant Colonel Peter Wright (Intelligence Corps), formerly professor of history at Cawnpore University, was the headmaster of an Indian high school in Nairobi; Lieutenant Commander John Miller was also a teacher; Gama Pinto was a socialist Kenyan journalist. Former soldiers and young men and women provided security and acted as couriers.

While Kenyatta concentrated on the politics, Kikuyu radicals formed the Freedom Struggle Association, also known as *Muhima* ('The Movement'), the prime demand of which was independence. It preserved its security and solidarity with a simple oath:

If you ever argue when called,
If you ever disobey your leader,
If called upon in the night and you fail to come,
May this oath kill you.

While violations risked an automatic death sentence, the oath caught many between their Christian teachings, *Ngai* and their cause. Although the power of such oaths was of considerable concern to Europeans, they were, nevertheless, regarded as a bestial ritual that mocked Christianity, notwithstanding the many religions that use oaths to weld membership. The Administration acknowledged the practice to be psychologically powerful and declared participation to be an offence under the Penal Code, but nineteen early defendants were released after legal challenges. Suspects were later offered a 'cleansing oath' concocted by the anthropologist Louis Leakey and sworn on sacred stones. Louis and his wife Mary were internationally famous for their discoveries in the Olduvai Gorge of north-west Tanganyika that led to anthropologists accepting that *homo erectus* first evolved in East Africa. Since Louis had lived his life among the Kikuyu, Governor Mitchell used him as an advisor on African matters. According to John Nottingham, a Central Province district officer between 1952 and 1961, when some captured Mau Mau were forced into writing confessions, they were told they were now 'human beings', a phrase that meant nothing to them but implied that they had previously been animals.

The *Muhima* met weekly at the bungalow of Senior Chief Koinange Wa Mbiyu in Banana Hill, a suburb of Karuri in Kiambu District. Born in 1866, illiterate but politically astute, he had been the Senior Kiambu District Chief between 1942 and 1949 and was described by one District Officer as an 'evil genius'. Bildad Kaggia had served in the Middle East and while serving in Great Britain with the Repatriation of Allied Prisoners of War and Internees organization as a sergeant-major repatriating African prisoners-of-war, had met black US GIs. Many English people he met were astonished to hear about the aspirations of Kenyan colonists. Fred Kubia, a telegraphist, had first demanded independence in 1939. A senior member of the Forty Group, he had remained in Kenya during the war and became a senior trade union official.

Although Kenyatta was the only African leader in East Africa who had experienced international politics, and even though other British governors in the region had discussed nationalism as a threat, Governor Mitchell refused to meet him, denied him a place in government and, instead, placed him under surveillance. Civil disturbances and strikes escalated. After political meetings had been banned in parts of Kenya, in late August, at Kahuro in Fort Hall District, a chief and two policemen were chased when they opened fire as they tried to arrest two KAU from Nairobi who were addressing a large crowd on demands for 'more land, more money, more opportunity and self-determination'. Elsewhere, Kikuyu discontent increased, with arms and ammunition thefts from colonists' town houses and farms, the hamstringing of cattle and the disappearance of employees thought to be loyal. Militants also undermined loyalist elders and chiefs by accusing them of spurious but legally admissible criminal charges, thereby necessitating court hearings. Also active in Kiambu District were the *Dini Ya Jesu Kristo* ('Church of Jesus Christ'), who wore animal skins underneath their European clothes and believed that all Europeans should be driven from Kenya. After a clash on Mt Kenya with the police in December in which a European inspector and two constables were killed, four members were executed and the group was banned. This and continued reports of recruitment oaths led to the police recognizing that trouble was brewing.

In September, the Kenya Intelligence Summary reported that attacks on elders and chieftains in Fort Hall had been generated by the Forty Group. But when the Acting Provincial Commissioner raised the unrest with the Chief Secretary, such was his denial of the escalating trouble that the Commissioner's concerns were sent to the Member for Law and Order, John Whyatt. The Summary was compiled by the Director of Intelligence and Security and approved by the Member for Law and Order and the Commissioner of Police.

The military arm of the *Muhima,* the Kenya Land and Freedom Army (KLFA), first emerged in September 1948 as the youth wing of the KCA in Nyeri, providing couriers and sentries during oath-swearing ceremonies. As Kikuyu unrest escalated and the numbers of oath-takers grew, KLFA adopted a culture of commitment and discipline shifting towards militancy and the adoption of the young warrior spirit (*riika*) bound by the fighter's oath (*batuni*), with the single aim of driving the masters (*bwana*) from Kikuyuland and then establishing an independent Kenya. Although the KLFA rarely described themselves as 'Mau Mau', at least not until after independence, the term seems to have first emerged in March 1948 from witnesses giving evidence in the trial at Fort Hall of two women who had refused to terrace land. The District Commissioner believed they had been coerced by young urbanites connected to the KCA. On 21 September, the Director of Intelligence and Security used the term Mau Mau to describe a new dissident movement. Although 1948 was quieter than 1947, the Fort Hall District Commissioner predicted that 'gale warnings' of unrest should be sounded.

The origins of the term Mau Mau are shrouded in mystery. One version is that when the police broke up an oath-taking near Naivasha, the administrator shouted '*Uma! Uma!*' ('Out! Out!'). Another version is that during a police interview, a Maasai said that he taken part in an oath-swearing which he described as '*Mumau*', transcribed by the police as '*Maumau*'. In any event, the nomenclature stuck, and by 1950 'maumaued' was being used to describe intimidation by hostile confrontation or threats. One of the first said to have learnt about the movement was Lieutenant Colonel Meinertzhagen, now retired. On a trip to Kenya, he visited a chief he had known in the early 1900s who told him that a secret society known as the Mau Mau was planning direct action against the colonists. Meinertzhagen wrote to Governor Mitchell about it and about the unrest among the Kikuyu, but did not receive a response.

In February 1949 Michael O'Rourke was appointed as Commissioner of Police. A quiet and highly professional officer who had a good understanding of counter-insurgency operations from his service with the Royal Irish Constabulary and in Palestine, he arrived at a time when the Central Province and District Commissioners were warning Government House of Kikuyu unrest, midnight recruitment oath-taking and the Mau Mau, whose existence had been described in the world press since 1948. His first task was to re-organize and modernize the police. Under command of Police HQ in Nairobi were the regular Kenya Police, the Police Reserve and the Tribal Police, who operated in remote rural areas and were managed by the District Commissioners and District Officers, although a small cadre of Kenya Police controlled operations. The roles of the Rail and Water Police are self-explanatory. The main police departments included:

- Criminal Investigation. The Kenyan Police had been using fingerprints to identify suspects since 1907, and this was a valuable method of collecting forensic evidence.
- Special Branch. O'Rourke had authority to recruit four European, one Asian and a few African Special Branch constables, but costs meant that they were confined to Nairobi and Mombasa. They were inserted into the Criminal Investigation branch and became so heavily involved in investigating crime waves in Nairobi that reports of subversion, trade union and radical activity were left unassessed in O'Rourke's in-tray.
- General Service Unit. A 1,100-strong specialist paramilitary strike force organized into five Provincial companies of self-sufficient mobile platoons each consisting of a sergeant, two corporals and ten constables equipped with rifles and a Bren gun.
- Kenya Police Reserve Air Wing. Conceived in late 1948 by Wing Commander A.N. Francombe DSO, MBE, a former chief pilot of East African Airways. The Wing initially consisted of a single Auster, however he made arrangements to charter aircraft to form the Transport Squadron using East African Airways aircraft, the Communications Squadron of chartered aircraft and the Reconnaissance Squadron of Aero Club and privately-owned aircraft.
- Dog Section of trackers, patrol dogs and 'sniffers'.
- Signals Section.
- Inspection Branch for internal investigations.
- Training Department. Recruit courses ran for six months.

The police numbered about 6,000 officers in 1950 and, covering 224,560 square miles and a population of 5.5 million, was organized into 15 police divisions and 92 police stations, of which 12 divisions and 31 stations were located in the African Reserves and 45 stations were equipped as radio base stations. There were also 162 police posts. The Signal Branch managed 131 vehicles equipped with Marconi VHF radios.

In April, *Dini Ya Msambwa* ('Church of Ancestral Spirits'), another movement preaching Africa for the Africans and a return to traditional *Bakusu* faith, clashed with colonial forces; 29 were killed and 50 injured. Kenyatta tried to control the young firebrands, but his arrest meant that he and other moderates had little control over the murders of opponents, attacks on farms, the burning of crops and grasslands and intimidation, which manifested itself when the houses of several loyalist Kikuyu elders refusing to take oaths were burnt. In his 1949 Annual Police Report, O'Rourke concluded that the post-1945 African was no longer the politically naïve, uneducated, subservient and unsophisticated character of a few years earlier. As a consequence, crime had increased, in particular commercial crime, and therefore a modern police force was needed capable of meeting these new challenges. When the CID investigated the theft of thousands of rounds of ammunition from the KAR Ammunition Depot at Gilgil, it emerged that the depot was guarded by eighteen Africans armed with pick helves. A programme of protective security measures was implemented.

Although Governor Mitchell was an acknowledged authority on African affairs, and the Director of Intelligence and Security was regularly reporting increased subversion by Kikuyu, recruitment oath-taking and unrest, to some extent Mitchell allowed his paternalistic beliefs to mask the fact that a serious situation was developing. In a letter to the Secretary of State for the Colonies, Arthur Creech, in May, he wrote that Britain's task was 'to civilise a great mass of human beings who are at present in a very primitive moral, cultural and social state'. In short, Africans were primitive and could be expected to dabble in oaths and black magic ceremonies, therefore nothing unusual was taking place. To be fair, Mitchell had been ill with a heart condition for three years which had confined him to Nairobi and restricted his ability to meet Africans. He was out of touch.

At the same time, the Gold Coast (now Ghana) was also experiencing veterans returning to a colony beset by shortages, inflation, unemployment, black markets, discontented farmers ordered to fell cacao trees to control an epidemic and urban dwellers unhappy at the lack of improvements. A nationalist movement in 1947 called for African self-government 'in the shortest possible time', but when the colonial administration resorted to police action, riots ensued. Kwame Nkrumah moved into the void by forming a movement demanding immediate self-government. In January 1950 he instigated a campaign of strikes and passive resistance which inevitably dissolved into violent disorder and resulted in a short State of Emergency. Among those detained was Nkrumah, but unlike Kenyatta he was invited by Governor Lord Listowel to develop a constitution which, a year later, accepted greater African representation on the Executive Council.

As Kikuyu discontent spread, with recruitment oath-taking and clandestine committees proliferating throughout Central Province, the political focus moved to Nairobi, where on 1 May 1949 Kubia and six trade unionists formed the East African Trades Union Congress (EATUC). Kubia was elected president and the Punjabi-born Makhan Singh became general secretary. A year later they demanded:

- Independence under majority rule.
- Safeguarding of the welfare of Kenyan citizens and abolition of child labour.
- Free speech.
- Electoral representation in the Legislative Council.
- A 45-hour working week and a minimum wage.

Governor Mitchell had refused to acknowledge the EATUC as a representative organisation and consequently, in March 1950, it retaliated with general strikes in Nairobi, just as the white-controlled city council was about to celebrate the award of a Royal Charter. Mombasa port was paralyzed for two days by the African Workers Federation. But clashes and arrests in the provinces led to collapse of the EATUC. Kubia was charged with murder, Singh with sedition and others were arrested on various charges; although both leaders were acquitted, Singh spent eleven years in detention. Most of the remainder went underground. Political clashes and labour unrest unsettled Nairobi, and when several leading Kikuyu were arrested after allegations they had taken oaths at Banana Hill, on 4 August the Executive Council declared that the KCA, KAU and Mau Mau were indistinguishable and therefore there was no alternative but to proscribe the Mau Mau eight days later. It did not ban recruitment and organizational oathing.

Since the general strike had tested the Colony's emergency procedures, in August Mitchell formed the Internal Security Working Committee, instructing that it be chaired by the Secretary for Law and Order and giving it the prime remit of assessing internal security and reforming colonial defence. Other delegates included the East Africa Command, the police, the Chief Native Commissioner, the Director of Intelligence and Security, who was also Head of Special Branch, and the MI5 Security Liaison Officer. Scheduled to meet every six months, it lacked a sense of urgency, largely because, as Mitchell would claim in the 1960 Corfield Report examining the Emergency, Kenya had 'by far the most competent and effective intelligence service that I have met in the whole of my colonial service'. But one must ask what intelligence is in the military context. It is essentially the conversion of information about an enemy, or indeed a friend, disseminated in time for commanders to use it. It is then up to the commander to use or reject the product. Problems commonly associated with this most vital contributor to the battle are infighting with other organizations and preservation of the autonomy of intelligence organizations to conduct their operations under military and police conventions. The relative unsophistication of the Mau Mau meant that there were two prime sources of intelligence: human intelligence from captured enemy personnel, informants and gossip, and document intelligence from intercepted and captured letters, instructions and diaries.

As the internal security of Kenya began to creak in a period of active global communist subversion, Sir Percy Sillitoe, Director General of the Security Services, arrived to review the intelligence process. As Chief Constable of the Glasgow Police, he had pioneered the use of radios in vehicles and had defeated the notorious razor gangs. Learning from operational and intelligence failures in Palestine, the War Office had published the 1949 Internal Security Manual, which placed the highest value on accurate, timely and 'all-source' intelligence. This had been followed by Service intelligence staffs during the Second World War, but the principle was something of an anathema to police officers. The manual accepted that military intelligence staffs should not do the job of the Special Branch, which was still regarded as a major source of operational intelligence; instead, they should concentrate on developing close army/police cooperation and mutual confidence, with regular meetings and conferences to exchange information and ideas. Sillitoe believed those likely to be responsible for the unrest were radicals, dissatisfied ex-soldiers and trade unionists, and concluded that the potential causes of unrest were:

- Racial and inter-racial disputes.
- Economic difficulties.
- Religion.
- Political subversion.
- Inter-tribal disputes.

While he identified the risks of Africans attacking Europeans and/or European property, white retaliation was not listed as a factor. He recommended East African police forces should share information with the resident MI5 Security Liaison Officer for onward transmission to the relevant authorities.

At a time when integrated command was required, Mitchell adopted the weakest of leadership styles by forming the Colony Emergency Committee, with himself in the chair. He also chaired the Situation Report Committee overseeing operational matters. A major weakness was that there was no police or military representation and no Director of Intelligence.

In January 1951, Senior Superintendent Trevor Jenkins arrived as Head of Special Branch and Director of Intelligence and Security. Within five months, assessment of a legal KAU mass meeting at Nyeri induced a difference of opinion between the District Commissioner, who believed the 'extremists are becoming increasingly active violent', and his Provincial Commissioner, who was 'not seriously worried'. An attempt to counter the threat with anti-Mau Mau action in the Rift Valley soon foundered. Taking hints from the Gold Coast, Colonial Secretary James Griffiths arrived in Nairobi in May to investigate constitutional changes and was the first senior British politician to meet Kenyatta, who presented him a list of grievances and a petition demanding:

- Abolition of the colour bar.
- Government aid for African farmers.
- Free trade union activity.
- African political representation of twelve elected members on the Legislative Council.

Griffiths rejected the proposals and, instead, suggested a Legislative Council in which the 30,000 settlers would elect fourteen representatives, the 100,000 Asians six, the 24,000 Arabs one and the single African member currently representing 5 million people would be increased to five. It is perhaps not surprising that the suggestion was rejected by the KAU Central Committee. This led to Griffiths declaring, 'This is God's own country with the Devil's own problems.' On 10 August the Internal Security Working Committee finally acknowledged that the influence of militant colonists was a risk to the instability of Kenya by:

- Acting as an abrasive to other communities.
- Propagating well-meaning but impractical or misguided advice to Africans.
- Taking unlawful action against the Government or other communities

In November, the Internal Security Working Committee wrote to Governor Mitchell about the Mau Mau:

> It is a Kikuyu secret society which is probably another manifestation of the suppressed Kikuyu Central Association. Its objects are anti-European and its intention is to dispossess Europeans of the White Highlands . . . The potency of the organisation depends on the extent to which it possesses the power, latent in all secret societies, of being more feared than the forces of law and order . . . this society, like religious sects, remains a possible instrument for mischief in the hands of agitators.

Mitchell continued to reject the notion that Kenya was on the verge of a breakdown of law and order, highlighting his belief in a letter to Griffiths that the problem in Kenya was essentially social and land-based rather than one of nationalism.

In early February 1952, Princess Elizabeth and her husband, Philip, the Duke of Edinburgh, were on honeymoon at the Treetops game lodge when news arrived that her father, George VI, had died on 6 February. The news was given to her by Lieutenant Colonel William Beyts MBE, DSO, MC, the District Commissioner for Mweiga, in which Treetops was located. He had left India after Partition, thus severing a family link which had lasted for 340 years, and moved to Kenya, where he bought a dairy farm. But it had not paid sufficiently and he had applied to join the Administration.

The increasing instability led to Commissioner O'Rourke strengthening the police in Nyeri and opening Special Branch offices at the three provincial headquarters most at risk, namely Central, Rift Valley and Western, and Nairobi Area. Oath-taking was becoming bizarre, with greater demands for loyalty and willingness to murder Europeans. Louis Leakey suggested that Christian hymns being sung in Kikuyu had the word 'Jesus' substituted by 'Kenyatta' as a cover for Mau Mau meetings. The reality was that Kenyatta was having great difficulty in keeping the militants focused on a political solution. In a brief visit to London in February, Mitchell accepted that the political situation had deteriorated significantly and the prospects for peace were dim. On 21 June, Sir Henry Potter, who had recently arrived in Kenya as Chief Secretary, assumed the position of Acting Governor and Commander-in-Chief pending the departure of Mitchell a week later on retirement. Probably incapacitated by his worsening health, Mitchell had become increasingly distant and unwilling to accept African radicalism; he had advised the Colonial Office that there was no need to enhance internal security.

By mid-1952, the 'dangerous explosion' predicted by Kenyatta in 1930 began to get closer, a mere half century after European settlers started developing unspoilt country in pursuit of a white African dream at the expense of an indigenous culture who nurtured respect for community and nature. In 1950 Louis Leakey had begun chronicling the history of the Kikuyu, a project that he halted when the Emergency was declared in favour of a shorter volume explaining the emergence of the

Mau Mau. He linked several factors connected with Kikuyu grievances. The remaining 120,000 Kikuyu tenant farmers had no rights to the land on which they once lived, a state of affairs at odds with their culture of communal ownership and their belief that land is loaned from nature. Since Kikuyu decision-making was usually collective, the practice of appointing chiefs to promote colonial interests above the needs of the Kikuyu induced tension in an egalitarian society in which outcomes were enforced by oaths that no Kikuyu would dare to challenge. The white practice of focusing on private property rather than the good of the community was alien to Kikuyu culture and inevitably induced corruption and bribery. The seizure of grazing land prevented the Kikuyu from rearing livestock and thus bridegrooms were relegated to paying dowries in cash, which could not be repaid if the marriage failed. This led to abandoned wives turning to prostitution and to short-term liaisons, something previously unheard of in Kikuyu communities, as well as a crop of fatherless children. Leakey claimed the breakdown of marriage was a major factor in the unrest, because birth control had kept Kikuyu society stable. The drive to convert to Christianity, with promises of free medical treatment and education, led to youths being barred from ceremonies vital to Kikuyu culture and rejected by their families. This caused a fracture within Kikuyu society, with many disowned by one culture but not truly accepted by the other. Initiation into adulthood was crucial to Kikuyu culture, with circumcision the culmination of years learning the rules, manners and responsibilities of adulthood, and introduction to age-set bonding of loyalty, honesty and integrity bound by communal discipline. When mission schools began in 1929 to exclude girls whose parents would not renounce circumcision, as part of their initiative to eradicate the 'barbarous custom', opposition was considerable. Leakey claimed that 'book learning' mission education could not replace the moral instruction of the old system and that 'the failure to find a substitute for the age-old initiation rites is just one more cause of the present sad state of affairs in the Kikuyu tribe.'

On 14 July, O'Rourke wrote a highly classified report to Member for Law and Order Whyatt in which he compared the instability among the Kikuyu to the unrest that had occurred in Ireland, Palestine and the Gold Coast. He suggested that the police did not have the capacity or ability to deal with an internal security situation, and said he would be content to make suggestions if measures other than policing were required. Ten days later, in the face of colonist intimidation such as Michael Blundell demanding that the KAU be banned, Potter held a meeting at which various measures were agreed, mostly relating to further restrictions on the KAU and including collective fines. Although Potter was generally reluctant to deviate from Mitchell's policy, he was sufficiently concerned about internal security that on 17 August he advised the Colonial Office that Kenya was facing the possibility of revolution and drastic action would be required. His assessment confused London because Mitchell had previously been sending optimistic information. A week later, Potter imposed curfews in three Nairobi suburbs where several houses of Africans who refused to take oaths had been set on fire. He then sent Whyatt and Chief Native Commissioner Davies to London, intending that they should meet the Conservative Secretary of State Oliver Lyttelton to discuss the 'drastic action', but their arrival took officials by surprise and there was reluctance to authorize everything they wanted, including the closing of printing presses. Louis Leakey, who happened to be in London, attended the meeting. But arrangements were not made to visit the new Governor, Lord Baring, who was due in Nairobi within the fortnight.

Sir Evelyn Baring, 1st Baron Howick of Glendale KG, GCMG, KCVO was born in 1903 and was a member of the wealthy banking family. His father had been the first British ruler of Egypt as Consul General and he had been Governor of Southern Rhodesia between 1924 and 1944. He had no military experience. His departure for Kenya had been delayed for several weeks after he had injured his hand while felling a tree at home. The delay suited the Colonial Office because one method of determining the suitability of prospective governors was to place them in an acting role for several weeks. It also saved paying the outgoing and incoming governors.

Chapter 4

Declaration of the Emergency

During the night of 26 September, Nanyuki Police Station received reports from three farms of the killing and disembowelling of sheep and cattle, sabotage of farm equipment and burning of crops. Within the day, a hundred Kikuyu were arrested, most of whom had taken oaths the previous night to destroy European property. These incidents are generally regarded as the opening of the Mau Mau offensive.

Sir Evelyn Baring was sworn in as Governor on the 28th and, within the week, left Nairobi to conduct a five-day assessment of Central Province, where Provincial and District Commissioners told him that they believed Kenyatta was closely associated with the Mau Mau. Meanwhile, Colonel E.P. Roberts had formed the United Kenya Protection Association in the Rift Valley to promote criticism of the Administration's handling of internal security and demand summary justice. On his return to Government House, Baring wrote to Oliver Lyttelton:

> There is a clear determination by the Mau Mau to destroy all sources of authority other than that of the Mau Mau. It is now abundantly clear that we are facing a planned revolutionary movement. If the movement cannot be stopped, there will be an administrative breakdown followed by bloodshed amounting to civil war. We are faced with a formidable organisation of violence and if we wait, the trouble will become more serious.

After the loyalist Senior Chief Waruhiu Kungu, who was regularly accused of collaboration, and two policemen were murdered in Nairobi by three gunmen masquerading as police on 9 October, Baring, under considerable colonist pressure, recommended to the Colonial Office that a State of Emergency be declared throughout Kenya. This would give the government the ability to suspend and/or change some executive, legislative and judicial functions, as well as the power to restrict or suspend rights and freedoms usually guaranteed under the constitution. John Mbiu Koinange, a son of former Senior Chief Koinange, and the driver of the car used in the murder were later charged with the murder. Chief Koinange and several family members were charged as accessories.

Anticipating that an Emergency could be lifted by the third week of January 1953, an estimated period based on past events in the Gold Coast, Lyttelton made a statement to the House of Commons on 16 October:

> Mau Mau is a secret society confined almost entirely to the Kikuyu tribe. It is an off-shoot of the Kikuyu Central Association, which was proscribed for subversive activities in 1940. It encourages racial hatred and is violently anti-European and anti-Christian. It pursues its aims by forcing secret oaths upon men, women and children and by intimidating witnesses and law-abiding Africans. It resorts to murder and other brutal and inhuman methods.
>
> Early this year Mau Mau attacks began in the Nyeri District and then spread to the Kiambu and Fort Hall Districts in the Central Province. The situation became progressively worse. Accordingly reinforcements were brought from other areas; many arrests were made; curfews were imposed, magistrates given enhanced powers and public meetings banned in most areas.
>
> These measures proved insufficient because African witnesses were afraid to come forward and give evidence in face of the brutal methods and vicious reprisals of the Mau Mau against them. Africans who refused to take a Mau Mau oath have had ropes tied round their necks and have been strung up from rafters until they were unconscious. Those who have informed the police have later been found murdered. Charges against over 100 persons for administering or participating in the administration of Mau Mau oaths had to be withdrawn, because

> the witnesses had disappeared or been intimidated into changing their story.
>
> Up to 13th September there had been 23 murders, including two women and three children, 12 attempted murders, four suicides, 24 hut burnings, 12 serious assaults, a church desecrated and missions attacked.
>
> That was the situation when I received from the Acting Governor of Kenya draft legislation designed to enable the Kenya Government to deal with intimidation and to give them greater control over secret societies. On 16th September I discussed this legislation and the need for it with the Attorney-General of Kenya and the Chief Native Commissioner.
>
> From 13th to 30th September there were at least 13 further murders, three suicides and a large number of European owned cattle were slaughtered and mutilated. During October there have been further attacks, including the murder of two European women and Senior Chief Waruhiu, a Kikuyu who had served his community and the Government nobly and loyally for a great number of years. A European was seriously wounded while protecting his wife and on 10th October Lieutenant Colonel Tulloch, 74 years old, and his wife were savagely attacked.
>
> The Governor reports that since 1st October four Africans are known to have been murdered. These Africans had rendered assistance in anti-Mau Mau activities. I am pleased to say that Colonel Tulloch and his wife and Mr. Bindloss are all out of danger and making satisfactory progress.

The two women mentioned were Mrs Marie Chapman and Mrs Margaret Wright, murdered on 23 September and 3 October respectively. Mrs Wright, the wife of a civil servant, was stabbed at their farm near Thika.

The War Office agreed to send a battalion to reinforce East Africa Command. The General Officer Commanding (GOC) was Lieutenant General Sir Alexander Cameron MC, a Royal Engineer who had been wounded in the Third Battle of Ypres. From 1935 for the next ten years, he developed air defence and planned the protection of the D-Day landings, and after VE Day he used captured German rocket troops to test early missiles. Posted to Middle East Land Forces in 1951, he was sent to East Africa Command, then considered to be an undemanding posting, where he mainly prepared KAR battalions for deployment to Malaya.

Providing communications for Kenyan units was a mix of Royal Signals and East African Signal Corps (EA Signals), which had been formed in September 1939 for service in Abyssinia and Burma. When the war ended, the Corps was disbanded and communications transferred to KAR Signal Platoons and the East Africa Command Signal Squadron based at Killarney Camp, Nairobi. The squadron also controlled the Northern and Southern Area Troops. The Signals Training Centre was located at Nyeri, while the Chief Signals Officer East Africa Command was at Waterworks Camp, Nairobi. Brigades were supported by Signals Troops, typically ninety all ranks, mainly Africans, providing radio, cryptographic facilities, line laying and technical support. The Squadron also trained the KAR Signals Platoons. East Africa Command took as its insignia crossed pangas in a circle. The panga is a common blade in Africa, the equivalent of the South American machete. Weighing about 20oz with a 16in blade usually .08in thick, it is suitable for cutting through thick brush and chopping small trees and saplings.

Lieutenant General Cameron placed the three KAR battalions in Mauritius, Tanganyika and Uganda on notice to deploy to Kenya. Second Battalions were raised by 3 (Kenya) and 6 (Tanganyika) KAR, namely 2/3 and 2/6 KAR, and 7 (Kenya) KAR was also formed. Placing Lieutenant Colonel Gilbert Collins, commanding 7 (Kenya) KAR, in command of all troops in Kenya as a temporary brigadier, he then instructed Lieutenant Colonel Campbell that the Kenya Regiment would control internal security in Nairobi Area. The KAR deployed mainly in the Reserves, ready to support the Kenya Police. Medical support for each KAR battalion was provided by a Medical Centre consisting of a Royal Army Medical Corps doctor, five regimental medical orderlies, a dentist, a general ward for short admissions, the families wing of a general ward and a labour ward, all supported by Minor Operating Theatre and diagnostics and X-Ray laboratories. Serious admissions and consultancy were referred to Provincial Government Civil Hospitals. The Battalion medical officer was also required to join 'recruiting safaris' to weed out those unlikely to pass basic training. The East African Reconnaissance Regiment had fought in Abyssinia but by 1952 had been reduced to a squadron equipped with Daimler armoured cars and Dingo scout cars; it was particularly valuable for patrolling the bush. The several heavy, field and anti-aircraft batteries raised during the war were reduced to 156 (East Africa) Heavy Anti-Aircraft Battery equipped with Bofors 3.7in guns.

When Middle East Command placed 1 Lancashire Fusiliers on immediate notice to move, sixty-one soldiers nearing the end of their National Service were sent to support a major exercise in Aqaba, Jordan, while the remainder continued to prepare for the annual inter-divisional exercise in November. The Battalion was commanded by Lieutenant Colonel A.A. Agar OBE and was based at Arroyo Camp in Ismailia, Egypt, in an Expeditionary Force (Grade III) Camp that lacked electric lights in the Other Ranks tents and overhead cover in the ablutions. The Regiment was raised as the 20th Foot in 1688 and celebrated three Regimental Days commemorating, in turn, the Battle of Minden during the Seven Years War, the Battle of Inkerman during the Crimean War and, mostly famously, the landings at Gallipoli on 25 April 1915, when six men were awarded the Victoria Cross 'before breakfast'.

As Special Branch planned to decapitate the insurgent organization by compiling arrest lists of KAU and suspected Mau Mau, Governor Baring activated the Colony Emergency Committee and advised Lyttelton on 17 October:

> I have excluded any person against whom there is no evidence of participation in an organised campaign of violent intimidation and who are simply advocates of African self-government remedying of land grievances.

Shortly after midnight on 20 October, Operation Jock Scott launched the State of Emergency. Although the plan had been compromised by Kikuyu sympathizers within the police, the 150 prime suspects were picked up. Several thousand documents were seized, including a ton and a half from Kenyatta's house. Among those arrested were Jomo Kenyatta himself and most of the KAU leadership. After the house of Lieutenant Colonel Wright was searched, he was immediately expelled, protesting that he was not a communist and subversive even when incriminating documents were found. The property of Lieutenant Commander Miller was also searched; he was then appointed Coast Provincial Education Officer based in Mombasa. Despite international interest, Kenyatta and five other defendants, who became known as the Kapenguria Six, were convicted in April 1953 and sentenced to seven years hard labour in a jail at the remote town of Kapenguria. Many doubted that justice had been served. The failure to follow the Gold Coast's example of negotiating with nationalist leaders, and the belief that the KAU was associated with the Kikuyu militants, were serious misjudgements, because the possibility of a political solution had effectively been removed and the way paved for militancy.

Next morning, Governor Baring shocked Kenya by announcing the Emergency on the wireless. Measures included:

- Common Law remained in force.
- Those captured or arrested by the Army or who were behaving suspiciously were to be handed to the Police. Suspects could be arrested under detention orders and held in internment camps
- Buildings and huts could be searched.
- Magistrates were given powers to try offences connected with oath-taking, murder and assault.
- District officers and magistrates were given authority to order collective punishments by seizing property, including livestock, and to enforce evictions. This became known as Operation Cowboy. Confiscation constitutes the legal seizure of property by a government or public authority as a punishment or to enforce the law. It differs from a fine in that it is not intended to match the crime but rather redistributes to the law-abiding community the property of those committing or suspected of committing crime. The effect is to reduce the socio-economic status of the offender; however, it was unpopular and drew resentment because law-abiding citizens could be punished for the actions of the few about which they knew nothing. While the law allowed for owners to buy back confiscated items, property seized in Kenya was often transferred to loyalist communities as a reward, and this bred resentment.

The Emergency took the Mau Mau by surprise and most, fearing arrest, disappeared to their ancestral refuges, joining groups assembling in the forests of the Aberdares and Mt Kenya; thus current intelligence on their organization, weapons, dispositions, capabilities and intentions was weak. Provincial and District authorities gave advice to farms on physical security and personal protection and organized a watch system whereby in the event of an attack signal flares would be fired. Other tips included avoiding being alone at night and having firearms loaded and ready for immediate use.

A Company, 1 Lancashire Fusiliers was on tedious guard duties at the logistic and ammunition depot at Abu Sultan in Egypt when it was warned for deployment to Kenya as the Battalion Advance Guard. Within twenty-four hours it had transferred its duties to a Grenadier Guards company and then concentrated at the 10 Base Ordnance Depot at Geneifa. During the evening of Sunday, 19 October, the Fusiliers boarded RAF Transport Command 511 Squadron Handley-Page Hastings transport aircraft at RAF Fayed. The squadron had been formed in October 1942 as a transport unit flying Liberators, Albermarles, Dakotas and Yorks. The Hastings had an aircrew of five and could carry up to fifty soldiers, but its troop compartment could be so noisy in flight that normal conversation was almost impossible. Not all the Fusiliers were entirely clear why they were going to Kenya except to support the KAR. Since Lieutenant Colonel Agar did not know how long the Battalion would be deployed, he left most heavy equipment behind and split Support Company by attaching the Medium Machine Gun and Pioneer Platoons to A Company, Company HQ and Mortar Platoon to C Company and Anti-Tanks to D Company. Four Royal Signals from HQ 3rd Infantry Brigade joined Battalion HQ to provide rear link communications. The six-hour flight to the first stop at Khartoum was bumpy and most of the soldiers were airsick. The garrison of 1 South Lancashires provided accommodation and meals at their comfortable camp at the junction of the Blue and White Niles not far from central Khartoum. The next leg was to Juba, still in Sudan, and then the Hastings passed across Lake Victoria and landed at RAF Eastleigh at about 7.30 p.m. to be welcomed by officers from HQ East Africa Command, police officers, government officials and, more importantly, at least for the soldiers, a bottle of cold Tusker beer for each man. The beer was so named after the first chairman of Kenyan Breweries who had been killed in an elephant-hunting accident. The troops were accommodated in a large hangar.

Next morning, 21 October, Nairobi awoke to A Company, 1 Lancashire Fusiliers, sporting their distinctive yellow hackles behind their beret cap badges and dressed in desert uniform, conducting a flag drive around the streets in Army lorries driven by the Motor Transport Platoon, who were delighted with recently refurbished 3-tonners, a welcome relief after the battered rattletraps still in service in Egypt. Meanwhile, C Company in five Hastings was being entertained by the South Lancashires at Khartoum. One aircraft suffering engine problems approaching Lake Victoria at sunset diverted to Entebbe in Uganda, much to the surprise of airport staff because the soldiers were the first British troops to arrive by air in the country. They were entertained at the new Lake Victoria Hotel and impressed guests with their gentlemanly behaviour. The last to leave the bar were CQMS Sutherland and Sergeants Townley and Reid, the latter apparently excusing himself in a perfect English upper crust accent. The next day, a replacement Hastings flew the Fusiliers to RAF Eastleigh. D Company had followed C Company the previous day. The cruiser HMS *Kenya* with its Royal Marines Ship's Detachment arrived in Mombasa as first line reserves and provided the military presence in the port.

The murder of Senior Chief Nderi Wango, hacked to death on 22 October while trying to break up the oath-taking of about 500 recruits near the Gura River in Nyeri District, spread fear throughout the Kikuyu community. The river, spilling from the Aberdares, had the fastest flow of any in Africa. Five days later, Eric Bowker, a deaf, almost blind, elderly farmer and veteran of both wars living on a remote farm in the Kingapop district of the Rift Valley, was the first colonist to be murdered after the declaration of the Emergency, when he was stabbed to death while taking a bath. His two houseboys were also murdered. The killers then raided a small store he ran selling clothes and supplies to Africans working on neighbouring farms. Eleven Kikuyu were later hanged for the murders. Unlike most settlers, Bowker did not keep a weapon in the house. Oliver Lyttelton visited Kenya a few days later and, although harangued by colonists, later briefed the House of Commons that the murder was 'an irrational attack against the forces of law and order'. He denied that the affair had anything to do with the economic plight of the Kikuyu.

With internal security in Central Province a higher priority than Nairobi, Lieutenant Colonel Collins sent A Company, 1 Lancashire Fusiliers to Thomson's Falls, Naivasha and Nakuru. As became common for British battalions, the Kenya Regiment detached NCOs to British battalions to provide local knowledge and as interpreters. D Company moved to the Kenya Police Training School at Nyeri on 27 October to find that the recruits saluted those ranked as fusilier. The Nyeri Club proved a welcome watering hole for all ranks. Next night, in the middle of heavy rain, C Company were driven from Nairobi and, scheduled to be under command of 2/3 (Tanganyika) KAR, sneaked into Fort Hall at about 4.00 a.m. where they were welcomed by the KAR Quartermaster with hot sweet tea laced with rum. Their accommodation was the Indian School. No.8 Platoon, commanded by Second Lieutenant A.G. Stott, conducted a long flag drive through Fort Hall District and met a magistrate whose wife came from Oldham. The Company conducted its first raid when a composite platoon searched a small village six miles north of Nyeri, an operation that began with Drummer Myers signalling 'Fire Call' on his bugle. Thereafter, the Company developed two types of raid. The 'noisy' method entailed placing a man outside the door of each hut to be raided; then at a given signal, either a bugle call or a whistle, the soldiers hammered on the doors and entered. When fifty men from 12 Platoon and Anti-Tanks commanded by Second Lieutenant Filmer searched workers' accommodation at the Muiga Sisal factory on 14 November, the *Gallipoli Gazette* (the regimental journal) later recorded:

> The noise was sufficient to waken the dead – so loud, in fact, that it even roused the Kikuyu.

One Fusilier hammered so hard with his loaded Sten that it accidentally discharged.

The 'silent' method was first used by D Company to search several huts at Edmund Thorpe's coffee farm on the edge of the forest without alerting the entire homestead. D Company experienced a particularly difficult raid. On a cold, wet and moonless night, MT Platoon drove the Fusiliers about 30 miles to the upper slopes of the Aberdare Range, where they met their guide, Mr May, at his farm. He then led them along a game track through dark, thick forest and across a slippery log bridge over a river gushing through a ravine, without losing anyone. The column was then confronted by a series of steep climbs and deep ravines, and confusion reigned when the tail of the column caught up with the front. It subsequently became clear that Mr May was lost and Thorpe's farm was still several miles away, 10,000ft above sea level. Nevertheless, the Company raided the employees' huts at dawn and arrested three minor players. The total distance covered was about fifteen miles. For many Fusiliers, this was their first experience of jungle warfare, made more arduous by altitude and darkness. The first collective punishment dealt out by the Army followed arson to government property in Aguthi and Themgenge.

HQ Middle East Command did not agree with Baring's assessment that the unrest could be dealt with quickly, and on 5 November General Nicholson wrote to Lieutenant General Harold Redman (late Royal Artillery), Vice Chief of the Imperial General Staff at the War Office:

> It is evident that the Mau Mau is far more deep-seated than has been realised and it will take at least months to eradicate in the views of Government experts. What is at present envisaged is the Emergency Regulation will be retained, at any rate, until the end of January.

Sir Percy Sillitoe arrived in Kenya on his second visit with two experienced MI5 officers, Alec McDonald and Alexander Kellar. The latter had been in Palestine between 1946 and 1948 and then in Malaya. MI5 was then in the middle of the Cambridge University Soviet spy ring scandal, which had seen the defection of Guy Burgess and Donald Maclean in 1951. It later emerged that MI5 had been half asleep at the time. The delegation found that Special Branch was confined to Nairobi and Mombasa and was overworked, submerged in paper, housed in inadequate offices and lacked equipment and intelligence funds; also that Senior Superintendent Jenkins was so far down the police pecking order that he had no mandate to access the Governor and was thus unable to advise him and the Internal Security Working Committee on the worsening internal security situation in Central Province. The absence of a military intelligence structure meant that Special Branch information did not address the operational requirements of the Army. Within four days, Sillitoe recommended implementation of the 'three-legged' intelligence structure developed in Palestine and Malaya, in other words layers of Emergency Intelligence Committees. Before returning to the UK, he appointed MacDonald as Intelligence Adviser with a remit to develop an intelligence and security organization.

Between 9 and 10 November, 5 (Kenya) KAR launched Operation Cowboy as a punishment for suspected local support to Mau Mau activities in the Githathi area, north of Nairobi. Several days later, the Lancashire Fusiliers confiscated livestock in the Nyeri area because of hostility towards police investigations there. Over the next three weeks, C Company conducted several cordon-and-searches, ambushes and raids throughout Fort Hall District, resulting in the detention of 2,165 people, 118 of whom were known or suspected Mau Mau. Weapons, mainly bows, arrows and pangas, were seized. On the 21st, the Company minus Mortar Platoon and a small rear party moved to the East African All Arms Depot and Training Centre at Nakuru. Next day, Mortar Platoon found two missing African police constables stabbed and slashed in bushes near Gatheru. It was the Battalion's first exposure to the effects of panga wounds. Three days later, the remainder of the Company formed the Provincial Reserve, while 9 Platoon commanded by Second Lieutenant D.G. Hall was sent to the Afrikaner enclave at Ol-Kalou and Wanjohi Valley in Laikipia District and began operations in the northern Aberdares, until it was relieved a fortnight later by 8 Platoon.

Commander Ian Meiklejohn was a retired naval doctor who farmed about eight miles from Thompson's Falls in the Rift Valley. He had been torpedoed twice during the Second World War and was a former prisoner-of-war of the Japanese. He and his wife Dorothy were cousins and had arrived in Kenya in 1932. She was also a doctor. After supper on 22 November they were reading in their sitting room when five armed Mau Mau burst into the farmhouse, attacked the couple before they could reach for their pistols and slashed them savagely. Dorothy regained consciousness and although severely stabbed in the face, arms and chest, managed to drive the seven miles to Thompson Falls Police Station. When the police arrived at the farm, the barely recognizable Meiklejohn was found upstairs, where he had tried to load his spare shotgun. Both were rushed to Nukuru Hospital, but he died from his injuries the next day. At the trial in February of three men involved in the attack, it emerged that Meiklejohn had instructed several Kikuyu squatters on his comparatively small farm to move to the Kikuyu Reserve and the remainder to remove their sheep and reduce the numbers of their cattle. Two of three defendants were hanged and the third was acquitted. The day before the attack, five loyal Kikuyu were murdered. As a punishment for the attack, the Lancashire Fusiliers moved 750 Kikuyu and their belongings to the Reserve, burnt their huts and confiscated their livestock. Four days after the attack, D Company deployed to platoon bases throughout Laikipia District to support the police in an area that was rapidly becoming a centre of Mau Mau activity. D Company HQ and 12 Platoon were at Thomson's Falls, 11 Platoon was in a comfortable bungalow at Rumurati and Anti-Tanks were based on a farm on the slopes of the Aberdares. When the soldiers moved a large group of evacuated families, they earned a mention in *The Times*:

> The Lancashire Fusiliers who accompanied them arrived equally sodden. Their Yellow Hackles which they had placed in their pockets during the drive were quickly re-inserted in their hats on arrival and seemed a symbol of their resilience.

In early December, the Battalion re-organized. D Company took responsibility for internal security in Leshau and N'daragwa with its four platoons being given specific operational areas to police, a task that some experienced soldiers found difficult. During a raid on a suspected Mau Mau welfare centre and an Indian-managed sawmill that was difficult to approach, 12 Platoon used civilian lorries, then Major J.A. Grover, the Company Commander, and Sergeant Bennett conducted a reconnaissance posing as Canadian lumber men – so effectively that the manager asked Bennett how he would increase productivity. Lance Corporal Ruellan and Fusilier Whitford then drove their 3-tonners up treacherous, raid-sodden mountain tracks and delivered the Platoon to the factory. Operation Cowboy netted 3,000 cattle.

When Baring repeated his request in December for a military adviser, General Cameron sent his Deputy Chief-of-Staff, Colonel Geoffrey Rimbault, The Loyal Regiment (North Lancashire), to be the Deputy

Chief of Staff to the Governor; in essence, he became the Governor's Personal Staff Officer but he lacked a command remit. In his 1937 book on the Irish troubles, *British Rule and Rebellion*, Colonel H.J. Simson suggested that a fundamental factor in any insurgency was the fusion between direct action and propaganda, the insurgents' aim being to isolate the police and force the security forces on to the defensive, thus ensuring the survival of their organization. This would also disperse the security forces on defensive duties, denying them the initiative. Simson concluded that conventional military tactics were not designed to fight insurgencies and therefore a Director of Operations should be appointed to manage the destruction of such a campaign. Equally important was an effective intelligence organization.

When General Sir Gerald Templer was appointed High Commissioner in Malaya in January 1952, he was also Director of Operations and created the Director of Operations Committee consisting of the three Service Chiefs, the Commissioner of Police and the Director of Intelligence. Kenya avoided appointing a Chief of Intelligence and thus there was no co-ordinated approach to security force operations. This did not exist in Kenya. Compared to most people, the British had considerable experience of counter-insurgency, gained in the two Boer wars, the Irish War of Independence 1920–2 and the unrest in India between 1919 and 1947; by the mid-1950s they were, to a great extent, the world leaders in the field. Although General Cameron held weekly conferences on the Emergency, Baring actually managed it, but he lacked military experience. When he then suggested to General Nicholson that a Director of Operations co-ordinate Security Forces' operations in the centres of Mau Mau activity, General Redman declared on 28 November that 'Malaya and Kenya are not parallel problems and the appointment of a Director of Operations is not the best answer.' He was correct. Kenya's crisis was essentially a rebellion, whereas Malaya was at risk from communist subversion. Whereas Kenya had had a quiet war, Malaya and Singapore had been overrun by the Japanese, and Chinese communists supported by a few Allied officers provided the bulk of resistance. When the war ended, the Malaya Communist Party then conducted a campaign against the British. Before he was assassinated, High Commissioner Sir Henry Gurney had recognized that he could not manage the government and fight a war at the same time and that he needed a Director of Operations. He was fortunate that London appointed Lieutenant General Sir Harold Briggs, who formed a small committee consisting of a colonel, a police superintendent and a civilian, Robert Thompson, to develop an integrated counter-insurgency strategy of five principles that became known as the Briggs Plan:

- The government must have a political aim to establish and maintain an independent and united country that is politically and economically stable.
- Government must function in accordance with legislation.
- Government must focus on defeating political subversion, and not the insurgents.
- Government must secure its base areas before defeating the insurgents.

From these principles, the following strategies emerged:

- Win the political battle.
- Maintain continuous pressure on insurgency.
- Use minimum appropriate force to achieve the aim. This is usually governed by strategic objectives balanced against military circumstances.
- Form unified and integrated government, police and military command structures.
- Develop intelligence-based operations.
- Maintain continuous pressure on insurgency.
- Develop patrol-based tactics supported by all arms resources.
- Exploit 'turned' insurgents.
- Isolate populations from the insurgents.
- Establish and extend base areas in order to provide safe areas.
- Win hearts and minds in psychological operations to change mindsets.
- Balance 'hard' internal security measures such as curfews, moving populations and crowd control against 'soft' techniques such as education, medical and veterinary support and the manner in which security forces treat the population.

In comparison, Kenya lacked any formal police/military integration. Intelligence concentrated more on crime than on subversion. While the enemy was loosely organized, it used its supporters and intimidated others in order to collect information on Security Forces operations. There were no effective psychological operations, except to demonize the Mau Mau.

About 60 per cent of the officers, 80 per cent of JNCOs and over 90 per cent of the troops of ranks equivalent to private who served in Kenya were National Servicemen, who did not fully understand the situation and whose main objective was discharge after two years. The remainder were Regular officers, warrant officers and NCOs, the more senior having had battle experience during and after the Second World War. The remaining 10 per cent of junior ranks were Regulars, usually in specialist roles, such as Signal Platoons. The large percentage of National Servicemen meant that there was a high turnover of men arriving and departing; and since there was no centralized training school in Kenya, units were responsible for giving new cadres acclimatization induction, fitness training and schooling in the mysteries of fighting in the forest.

The Labour Government that ousted Winston Churchill in 1945 was not convinced of the need for post-war conscription; however, the combination of the need to discharge Hostilities Only servicemen called up during the war, address the loss of the Indian Army in 1947, provide forces to support British strategic and colonial commitments and sizeable garrisons in West Germany against the Soviet threat, in the Far East and the Mediterranean led to the 1947 National Service Act. Great Britain had sacrificed much during the war and thereafter continued rescuing Allied and civilian prisoners-of-war from nationalists in the Dutch East Indies, fighting Jewish terrorists (some liberated from concentration camps) in Palestine, and engaging in counter-insurgency operations in Malaya against Chinese communists, their former allies. Stricter rationing than that imposed during the war, austerity, the need to exploit growing export markets and higher taxation – this all led to political objections to conscription, and terms of service were reduced from eighteen months to a year. The outbreak of the Korean War in June 1950, however, led to the period of conscription being raised to two years. By 1952, some National Servicemen were languishing in brutal North Korean prison camps, exposed to communist indoctrination.

Others were involved in the unpleasant situation in Egypt, where servicemen were killed or wounded in action, kidnapped and murdered.

Men aged up to twenty-six and usually resident in UK were committed to two years National Service followed by three and a half years in the Reserve. All had experienced the rigours of war between 1939 and 1945, some having had family members killed in action, lost at sea or killed in air raids. Some had been evacuated to Canada, the USA and the British shires during the war. Those exempt included clergy, trawlermen and merchant seamen, some agricultural workers and those in government positions overseas. Deferments were granted to apprentices, university undergraduates and those undertaking professional articles. Northern Ireland was excluded, because of the fear of Catholic dissent, as were the Channel Islands, still recovering from German occupation. Twice a month, on Monday for the Royal Navy and Thursday for the Army and Royal Air Force, and once in December because of Christmas, about 6,000 men joined their training units after a selection process over the previous six weeks that included medicals based on a system introduced during the First World War and interviews to decide service preference. The Army absorbed about 72 per cent, the Royal Navy about 2 per cent and the remainder went into the RAF. Men with existing skills or trades were usually slotted into appropriate units. In general, about 40 per cent conscripted into the Army joined the Infantry. National Servicemen were backed up by a cohort of Regulars, some with medal arrays denoting active service experience.

Joining up was for many their first time away from home. The first six weeks were spent on basic training at depots or dilapidated camps consisting of either draughty Nissen huts or chilly stone barracks built in the eighteenth and nineteenth centuries during which disparate intakes from varied backgrounds were introduced to the Armed Forces culture of 'grin and bear it' and ticking 'chuff' to discharge day (chuff charts are typically used by Service personnel to count down the days until the end of a tour of duty). Royal Navy and RAF accommodation was usually better, and haircuts were less brutal than in the Army. Drill, physical fitness and weapon training, daily room inspections and making bed packs from sheets and blankets, the 'bulling' (spit-and-polishing) of leather hob-nailed boots and ironing of uniforms – all these were part of the indoctrination into Service life. Few regarded rantings by corporals, petty officers and flight sergeants, insistence on tradition and compliance with restrictions as bullying or an assault on their human rights; most recognized them as necessities of life in uniform. Food usually lacked the quality of Mother's cooking. It was a case of 'Take it or leave it, son'; indeed, rationing remained in force until 1954. Basic training was followed by about three months of trade training, in which the National Servicemen learned skills or languages with their chosen arm of service and unit.

Most officers had gained some military experience in public and grammar school Combined Cadet Forces. The Royal Navy and RAF sought experience in the Reserve Forces. Other Ranks talent-spotted as Army officers were assembled into potential officer training platoons at depots, where they prepared for the three-day commissioning War Office Selection Board known as 'WOSBee'. Those who failed completed their service in the ranks, and those selected for three-year Army Short Service Commissions (SSC) attended either Eaton Hall or Mons Officer Cadet Training Units (OCTU) near Chester and Aldershot respectively; they could then apply to convert their SSC into a Regular commission. Regular Army officers graduated from the Royal Military Academy, Sandhurst.

The standard rifle in use was the .303 bolt action Lee Enfield No. 4, which had been introduced into service in 1941. Equipped with a ten-round detachable magazine, its effective range was about 750yds. The standard sub machine gun was, initially, the cheap, short-range 9mm Sten Machine Carbine developed in mid-1941 out of desperation, at a time when the British realized that their infantry did not possess a short-range, quick-firing sub machine gun. Taking its name from its developers and place of manufacture, Major Reginald *S*hepherd and Harold *T*urpin, and its place of origin, *En*field Lock, the Sten was widely used in several guises during and after the war. Its 32-round detachable straight magazine slotted into the left hand side of the weapon and was usually rested on the left forearm to give a stable firing platform. In 1944, George William Patchett, chief designer at the Sterling Armaments Company in Dagenham, developed a replacement known as the Patchett; it was first used by some airborne troops at the Battle of Arnhem. In 1947, an Army competition that included the Sten, an experimental Australian design and the Patchett, saw the Army adopt the 9mm Sterling Sub-Machine Gun L2A1 in 1953. A reliable and accurate weapon, the British fitted it with a distinctive top-mounted curved box 30-round magazine. Most battalions converted their Support Company of machine gun, anti-tank and mortar platoons into a rifle company, often D Company, of three platoons. The standard platoon support weapons were the section .303 Bren Gun, which had been adopted from the Czechoslovak ZB 26 during the 1930s and which would remain in British service until the 1990s. The Ordnance portable smoothbore, muzzle-loading 2in mortar was found in infantry platoons. It could fire High Explosive, White Phosphorous Smoke, Smoke, Illumination and Signal Multi Star to an elevation of between 49° to 90° and a range of about 500yds. Each bomb weighed about 2½lbs.

Each man carried a First Field Dressing consisting of a bandage and a phial of morphine. Carried in each section was a first aid pack. Troops in Kenya were not only at risk of gunshot wounds and training injuries; there were also injuries from attacks by wild animals and snake bites. This led to the Medical Officer and his Medical Reception Station of about five beds being based at the Command Post as opposed to Battalion HQ. Soldiers were taught that first aid saves lives and that keeping calm was essential but not always easy with the seriously wounded. Schistosomiasis (bilharzia) was widespread in East Africa, picked up in rivers and streams from animal urine. All water had to be purified either by boiling, filtering through Millbank bags or using sterilizing tablets. Swimming in rivers below 6,500ft was not permitted because of the risk of leptospirosis from animal urine. Several soldiers were evacuated to the UK with poliomyelitis, a deadly infectious disease caused by a virus which can invade the brain and spinal cord, causing paralysis. A cause can be faeces entering water. The first recorded epidemic in Kenya occurred in 1921–2 and thereafter epidemics occurred on a three-year cycle, including in 1953, when the Buffs' medical officer and three others were given medical discharges. One was the military historian, Gregory Blaxland. Inoculations were not then available. Casualty evacuation from within the forest usually meant a long and exhausting carry of a stretcher manufactured from branches and ponchos by at least three soldiers to a rendezvous with a light ambulance, initially a Jeep and then a Land Rover capable of being fitted with stretchers. The casualty was then taken either to one of the British Military Hospitals at Nanyuki, Nyeri or Nairobi, or to the European-run

African Civil Hospitals at Embu, Fort Hall and Meru. The KPRAW provided air evacuation capability. Troops were warned against venereal disease and regular inspections were carried out by medical officers. They were encouraged to suntan gradually.

Commonly known as 'compo' (composite), the rations issued were designed to provide a soldier with enough familiar food to provide sustenance and energy. The rations came in 10-man boxed packs for bulk feeding and individual operational 24-hour packs. Three menus were used in Kenya:

Type A	Type B	Type C
Breakfast sausage and beans	bacon and beans	chopped bacon
Main meal • preserved meat, • vegetable salad in mayonnaise • mixed fruit pudding	• ham and beef, • spaghetti in tomatoes • treacle pudding	• liver and bacon • beans in tomatoes • rice pudding with raisins
Snack packet sweet biscuits, milk chocolate bar, clear gum sweets, boiled sweets, Mars bar, nuts and raisins, tea and sugar	sweet biscuits, milk chocolate bar, clear gum sweets, butter scotch, Spangles, nuts and raisins, tea and sugar	sweet biscuits, milk chocolate bar, clear gum sweets, boiled sweets, nuts, tea and sugar

When not on operations, British soldiers were fed locally-purchased or donated fresh rations prepared by Army Catering Corps and regimental cooks. For those arriving from the UK, in the grip of wartime rations until 1954, fresh meat and fruit were luxuries. Food was usually served into the soldier's mess tins and eaten with his KFS (knife, fork and spoon). Metal mugs were used for drinks. Officers' and Sergeants' Messes were much more civilized, with laid tables and waiters. On operations, African troops were issued with five-man No.9 Ration Pack. The scale for each man was:

African No. 9 Pack	
12oz rice (unpolished)	1oz dried fruit
6oz meat preserve	2¼ oz sugar
1¾oz Vil Ghee	½ oz coarse salt
4oz tinned vegetable	½ oz tea
4oz canned beans	1/16oz curry powder
6oz pitted dates	4½oz biscuits
4¼oz peeled groundnuts	2oz tinned milk

However, the Africans were not particularly taken with the quality of these rations and they often resorted to foraging for food from shops and villages.

Chapter 5

The Crisis Deepens

Intelligence emerging after Operation Jock Scott suggested that the Emergency had wrong-footed the Mau Mau before they were ready for organized revolution, although it was anticipated that attacks on farms would continue and intimidation would be directed towards Kikuyu, Embu and Meru disinclined to take the Mau Mau oath. The Emergency was largely confined to an area of about 14,000 square miles, about one sixteenth of the colony, with Nairobi, Central Province and three districts of the Rift Valley Province the centres of resistance. By its nature, guerilla war pits the weak against the strong, the outnumbered against organized security forces, the ill-equipped against the well-equipped. Critical for the Mau Mau were supporters in the Reserve to provide intelligence, supplies and support.

By January 1953, the Central Committee had been renamed the Council of Freedom. In contrast to other liberation movements of the period, it was dominated by the blue-collar class and generally lacked an ideological agenda. Command, control and conduct was exercised through the powerful Committee No. 4. The Mau Mau had split into two elements. The Passive Wing provided couriers and logistic support in the form of supplies and transport, and organized intelligence and recruitment. The Militant Wing consisted of the young, poor, semi-literate and landless. They entered with the rank of constable and progressed through corporal, sergeant, RSM, captain, major, major-general and general, each promotion being accompanied by an oath-taking ceremony. Meetings decided promotions. A few former servicemen joined, and it was they who instructed on weapon training and tactics. Discipline was enhanced by oaths and drill. When Kenyatta wrote *Facing Mount Kenya,* he claimed that oaths were so feared that no one swore them unless their belief was genuine beyond reasonable doubt. However, Christian dogma clashed with Kikuyu traditions, which led to an enduring division between the nationalist movement and the missionaries. There is no doubt that some oaths saw taboos violated, on the grounds that the more shocking an oath was, the greater its impact. In traditional Kikuyu society, oath-taking ceremonies took place in public, but those conducted by some Mau Mau were held in secret, which inevitably led to intimidation, beatings administered to those who refused to accede and death threats. Women and children were also required to take the oaths because they possessed knowledge about individual Mau Mau. Only about 14 per cent of militants were armed with conventional small arms, largely because no foreign government was arming the insurgents and colonial legislation made it difficult to acquire arms and ammunition except by theft. Police and colonists were expected to lock their weapons in gun safes when not in use. Blacksmiths therefore manufactured simple homemade guns, and weapon training included spears, pangas and bows and arrows. Indoctrination was also given on Kenyan politics and black aspirations and ambitions. At its height, the Militant Wing numbered an estimated 12,000 members.

The first wave of Mau Mau to seek refuge in the forests were militants avoiding arrest and dispossessed and disillusioned former squatters evicted from European farms in the Rift Valley. Mostly young, unmarried and illiterate agricultural workers, they had nothing to lose and every reason to fight. They were commanded by leaders who saw the KLFA as subordinate to the elder committees and the Kenya Parliament; indeed, some described themselves as *itungati* (soldiers of the rearguard). By June 1953, the leaders had adopted the rank structure ranging from corporal to field marshal, but in spite of the aspirations of Dedan Kimathi, there was no formal overall strategy. Leaders simply selected targets and the men they required. Generally, the *itungati* fought alongside their age-mates and neighbours. Some leaders also adopted *noms de guerre* that ranged from Kikuyu nicknames to place names of note. While it is easy to ridicule the number of field marshals, generals and colonels, the system provided a much-needed rank structure for impressionable illiterates.

Leader in the Mt Kenya area was Waruhiu Itote, alias General 'China'. Born in 1922 in the South Tetu parish of Nyeri District, he learnt writing and basic arithmetic at the Church of Scotland Mission School at Kiangure. Although his father encouraged him to farm, he left school aged seventeen and went to Nairobi, where he and two friends ran a vegetable business. He married in 1940. When the trio wound up the business, Itote enlisted in the Army in January 1942 and was posted to 36 KAR at Moshi in Tanganyika for six months, until the battalion was sent to Burma. Chatting with Itote in a trench near Kalewa, a British soldier was surprised to hear him say he was fighting for the British Empire and not for himself. An Indian soldier he met told him that independence should have been his price. He also learnt about the Haitian revolution and racial discrimination in the US Army from a black American soldier. On returning to East Africa in 1945 as a corporal, while part of a force sent to quell an uprising in Uganda, he met a man who suggested Kenyan soldiers should fight for independence and not rest until Kenyatta was their *kabaka* (king), then accused the Kikuyu of being a collection of women. It was these influences that led Itote to become a Kenyan nationalist, and although selected for promotion to sergeant as an instructor, he took discharge and with his savings started a business with five friends in Nanyuki supplying the East African Railways and Harbours Administration with firewood. When the railway converted to oil and the business collapsed, he found employment as a railway fireman. In 1946 he was active in politics in the KAU, the militant Transport and Allied Workers Union and the Forty Group. He was persuaded four years later by an Army friend to go to Naivasha, where he met members of the KLFA and took the oath to fight for freedom. Over the next two years he became a trusted member of the Nyeri Committee operating in Nairobi and was involved in oath-taking, intimidation and the elimination of those convicted by the Central Committee of being traitors. When the Committee formed the War Council in January 1952, Itote was nominated to powerful Committee No.4 and later adopted the nomenclature 'General China'. In mid-August 1952, he and several colleagues visited Kenyatta. When they learnt they were on police arrest lists, Itote led forty young men into the gloom of Mt Kenya forest, where he established a simple command structure, drilled his men and trained them in jungle warfare. He also set up a network of Passive Wing informers, co-ordinated his activities with the Militant Wing in Nairobi and established supply routes for weapons and ammunition.

In the Aberdares was Dedan Kimathi. An illegitimate child also born in Tetu, he grew up to be delinquent and dishonest, but was nevertheless selected to be the head of the household by his dying grandmother. He perfected his English at school and despite being adopted by an elderly foster parent was evicted after stealing from him. Although he loved Kikuyu traditions, he refused to be circumcised in a public ceremony. He made some money by selling tree seeds and was hired by the Forestry Department in Nyeri as a logger, but then stole the suitcase of a forestry officer. He was accepted into the Church of Scotland Mission School but refused to pay the school fees and was expelled. While holding down several jobs, he continued to steal. He spent three months in the Army, during which he hit a corporal and was involved in a drunken brawl. He was employed as a teacher at his old school in Tetu, but when he was accused of rape he fled to Ol Kalou, where he became something of a 'Robin Hood' figure to the uneducated Kikuyu in the Central and Rift Valley Provinces. He became a KAU oath administrator and Secretary of the Ol Kalou and Thomson's Falls branches until he was arrested after being implicated in the brutal murder of the senior chief in Nyeri District while he was investigating a large oath-taking ceremony on the banks of the River Gura. He escaped by bribing a warder and set off for the Aberdares with several followers. As militants made their way to his camp near Nyahuruns (now Nyandarua) he formed the 'Kenya Parliament', which he regarded to be the supreme Kikuyu body in the forests. In spite of a high-pitched voice, he was a skilful orator who frequently used quotations from the Old Testament. He was a strict disciplinarian but had little strategic vision.

Competing with Kimathi was the tough Stanley Mathenge a Mirugi. Born in 1919, he had fought in Burma and was handy with a .303 rifle. Uninterested in ideology, he focused on the Kikuyu winning back their status and dignity. A champion of the downtrodden and a firm believer in traditional Kikuyu religious practices, he had led the Forty Group and formed the Kenya *Riigi* of illiterate fighters as opposition to the Kenya Parliament. While Kimathi adopted the rank of field marshal, Mathenge did not seek status, to the extent that his camp did not possess an officers' mess. He developed strategy and planned and took part in attacks. Kimathi and Mathenge soon disagreed, not so much over policy and strategy, but over Kimathi's insistence on recording meetings. The conservative-minded Mathenge and other less educated militants considered literacy to be a damaging device that perpetuated white domination. The rivalry sometimes boiled over into conflict.

An *mbuci* (camp) was usually commanded by a senior officer, who maintained his authority with personal leadership, firm discipline and awareness of the needs of his men and women. Initially, camp life was well organized. General Matenjagwo inspired recruits to his Elephants' Camp by reminding that they were fighting a tough war:

> [We] . . . have neither aircraft nor tanks nor motor cars . . . We are the aircraft and armoured cars; we are also the food carriers and ambulances. But where unity exists and where nobody considers himself better than the others, victory must surely come.

The largest camp, at Kariaini about 25 miles north-east of Mt Kinangop secreted in the bamboo belt, reflected the military experience of Mathenge. Able to hold about 2,500 armed men and women, it had an armoury containing about 1,000 stolen and homemade firearms. There was an officers' mess, a workshop, a hospital, three kitchens, a stores area and accommodation neatly arranged according to rank, with all approaches protected by look-outs and sentries. Among the non-combatants were cooks, medical staff, foragers and women in a variety of roles. Clerks maintained nominal rolls and organized financial accounts. The wounded were treated by those with medical experience, usually using traditional healing plants and practices. Daily routine began with a breakfast of maize porridge, followed by prayers and then military training, weapon training and cleaning, drill, physical fitness, organizing the guard and foraging for game and wild vegetables. Supply columns, often of women, brought in food purchased from the Reserves. The second meal of the day was usually supper. Spells of leave allowed men and women to go home in relative safety from arrest. Discipline roughly equated to that applied in the British Army, with the accused tried in front of the camp's judge. Sentences included flogging, food deprivation and the death penalty. Most leaders wore parts of British Army uniforms, such as greatcoats and battledress jackets. A Mau Mau, Karari Njama, later wrote:

> Many of them were dressed in ordinary clothing while about 800 of them wore different Government uniforms, which must have been acquired mainly from dead security forces. Some had woven their hair like women while others had braided in with the hair to imitate the Masai . . . I could guess their ages; most of them were between 25 and 30 years old. There were a few old ones, well over 60 years (*Mau Mau from Within*)

Captain John Cornell, a Rifle Brigade Intelligence Officer who served in Kenya in 1954, describes a typical Mau Mau:

> He is an African youth of about 22, rather shorter than the average Englishman, his hair screwed into short rat tails, wearing a ragged beard. His clothes comprise a tattered khaki shirt and shorts over which he normally wears a torn black overcoat. He smells a good deal. He generally carries by a leather thong a woven reed bag which contains his few belongings – some matches, a tin of snuff, a strip of biltong, a few maize cobs, some battered cooking tins and some odd rags. He may also have a blanket and a home-made gun. This latter is carried more for morale than for lethal effect.
>
> Though he is not a particularly brave or aggressive opponent, the Mau Mau terrorist possesses an almost animal resilience and cunning which makes him a difficult man to finish off . . . Terrorists continually make good their escape with half a dozen bullets in them. We know of one Mau Mau, drilled clean through the body by a .303 bullet, who put gum from a tree over both the entry and exit wounds, lay up in a bush for several days without any food and then made his way 30 miles to join another gang.

A week before Christmas, information emerged that the Militant Wing were considering a co-ordinated attack on Christian Kikuyu attending Christmas Day services, but the fear of vigorous white retaliation led to the plan being cancelled in favour of small-scale raids on isolated farms and large-scale attacks against loyalists in the Reserve. Such was the anxiety among colonists in Nairobi that dinner parties and social events had almost ceased by late December, and a Home Guard of armed Europeans patrolled the streets. Nevertheless, colonial gossip focused on the arrival of Ava Gardner, Grace Kelly and Clark Gable to film *Mogambo* in Kenya. Another hot topic was the outspoken *Daily Mirror* journalist James Cameron, who in December criticised a heavy-handed internal security regime against 'decent Africans', accusing the colonists of being 'trigger-happy'. He had little to say about Mau Mau activity.

Since some sort of disruption was expected, the Lancashire Fusiliers celebrated Christmas Day on the 21st and then deployed on deterrent operations for the next month. The D Company patrol programme meant the seventy farms in its sector could be visited at least daily. Ambushes were laid on several tracks known or thought to be used by Mau Mau in the Odedaals Valley near the Van Landsberg settlement near Eldoret. In the event of an attack, a platoon would respond as quickly as possible, meet with the police and search the vicinity for spoor. To supplement the few lorries available, colonists lent several vehicles that ranged from powerful Chevrolets to battered rattletraps held together with wire, nails and luck. On 27 December D Company surrounded Thomson's Falls and detained 650 people, then conducted several raids in the vicinity of Marmanet Forest, about ten miles north-west of the northern tip of the Aberdare Mountains. When a patrol chased a gang ransacking Blain's Farm, Army Catering Corps Private Allenson, who was on a rest day from cookhouse duties, was left behind to guard the house. He challenged a houseboy smashing the door of his hut, but he was suspicious of the boy's claim that the Mau Mau had also burgled his house and reported the incident. The houseboy turned to be a Mau Mau informant. Operation Cowboy was activated on New Year's Eve, and D Company helped impound goats and donkeys. Meanwhile, nightly mobile patrols helped the police maintain relative tranquillity over the New Year.

Charles Hamilton Fergusson had been farming at Ol Kalou on the lower western slopes of the Aberdare Range for about thirty years. Since the declaration of the Emergency, he and his neighbour, Richard Bingley, had dined together for mutual security. Neighbours included the Afrikaner enclave around Eldoret. As was customary in a country in which the working day began soon after dawn, men and women usually had a bath at about 7.00 p.m. and then dressed for dinner in night clothes and a dressing gown. At about 8.00 p.m. on 1 January 1953, Ferguson's houseboy, Thuku, had just begun serving dinner when a dozen Mau Mau burst into the house and overwhelmed Bingley. Ferguson pulled his revolver from a pocket and had raised it to fire when a panga sliced his hand off. Both men were then stabbed to death and the house was looted. One of the first police to arrive was Inspector David Drummond, who had joined the Kenya Police on 19 December 1952. Bill Woodley was the son of a well-known safari guide and had recently been appointed assistant warden at the Tsavo National Park. He had recently completed his National Service training in Rhodesia and been seconded to 23 (Tanganyika) KAR in Fort Hall District as a Platoon Sergeant. He had formed a tracking section from Waate poachers who prowled the National Park. In the hunt for the killers, Woodley and his section were attached to 5 (Kenya) KAR and tracked the killers to a camp on the fringes of the Aberdare forest. The infantry then used the noise of a stream to mask their approach, killed four and captured several other Mau Mau, including four men alleged to have taken part in the murders. Among their possessions they found clothes belonging to the two farmers. Next day, a KPR inspector about thirty miles from the farms stopped a well-dressed African leading a bull and, noting inconsistencies on his *kipande*, escorted him to Thomson's Falls Police Station. The overcoat the suspect was wearing had the name tag 'Fergusson'. The African was Thuku. He was arrested, convicted of the murders and hanged, as were four others. As a collective punishment, the Government confiscated 4,000 head of livestock.

The next evening, 2 January, in a farmhouse 60 miles north of Nyeri, Mrs Kitty Hesselberger and her companion, Mrs Dorothy Raynes Simpson, both middle-aged, had planned what to do in case of an attack. After dinner, they were listening to the 9.00 p.m. news on their wireless, as they customarily did. Mrs Simpson was in a chair facing the door. In *Eyewitness 1950–59, Kenya*, she describes how Mrs Hesselberger had just cracked a nut taken from a bowl of sweets and nuts on the table when:

> The houseboy came through rather hurriedly – and made us a little suspicious – and we looked up and I said, 'They're here'. There were a number of figures in the room, all strangers. I leapt out my chair and luckily I had my revolver next to me, and I shot at the first boy that was coming to me and then I heard Mrs Hesselberger

> saying, 'Be careful'. I turned to her and I saw one of the boys on top of her.

Simpson shot the attacker, as well as her faithful boxer dog, who had become involved in the melee. As soon as Mrs Hesselberger had disentangled herself from her attacker, she picked up a shotgun and fired it along the unlit corridor that led to the kitchen. Hearing noises in the bathroom adjoining the sitting room, both women fired through the wall and later found a blood trail leading through the window. The women had survived the attack because they had ensured their weapons were immediately to hand. Mrs Simpson's bland account of a terrifying incident was described by Joanna Bourke, the historian, as typically English, especially the insignificant details like the bowl of nuts and sweets. Two days later, Chief Hinga Hinga was murdered by three Mau Mau while recuperating in bed in Kiambu Native Civil Hospital from wounds received when his car was caught in a Mau Mau ambush. He was one of thirty-four Africans murdered in the first fortnight of 1953.

Following the murders, Governor Baring declared restricted zones under the Emergency Regulations on 3 January:

- Special Areas (SA). Security Forces could open fire here only after two challenges. Geographically, they were confined to the Embu, Kikuyu and Meru Reserves and a small enclave west of Nairobi. .
- Prohibited Areas (PA). These were areas that were generally uninhabited and in which Security Forces could open fire without giving a warning. They were confined to the Aberdares, Mt Kenya and Mt Eburru to the north of Lake Navaisha. Anyone found in these areas was considered to be hostile.

Each area was separated from the remainder of Kenya by a one-mile wide zone kept free of vegetation to observe comings and goings and marked by white-painted boulders.

The seven-day Operation Blitz was launched three days later to probe the lower northern foothills of the Aberdares, but the Mau Mau simply melted into the forest. On the third night, a four-man 8 Platoon, C

Company, 1 Lancashires ambush commanded by Lance Corporal Morris was compromised by a charging buffalo that sent the soldiers scampering out of the forest until they met another patrol. The four-day Operation Yellow Hackle, which was completed on 19 January, was launched from the Wonjohi Valley and designed to drive insurgents in the Aberdares towards Operation Long Stop being manned by the KAR near Nyeri. Two Mau Mau were reported killed and 43 arrested by the KAR. Of 500 people screened, half were detained. Shortages of troops saw loyalist Maasai, Samburu and Kipsingi warriors armed with bows and arrows joining cordon-and-search operations in which 70 suspect Kikuyu were transferred to the police. Two others were killed by Maasai spears. During these operations, the Lancashire Fusiliers Signals Platoon was stretched to the limit providing signallers and ensuring that wireless sets were functioning twenty-four hours a day. Also on the command net was 1 Company, 5 (Kenya) KAR, whose African wireless operators tended to spell every word phonetically, which slowed down their delivery of messages. Donkeys usually carried the radios, and when one being used by two Fusiliers decided to go for a canter it deposited its load; fortunately, nothing was damaged. Such was the shortage of riflemen that when signallers were not on watch they were employed as riflemen and cooks.

A feature of these early operations was the use of KPRAW. Until the Emergency they had done very little police work, but they were soon found to be an indispensable asset supporting operations seven days a week with reconnaissance, supply drops, casualty collection and the delivery of stores to isolated outposts and patrols. With Air HQ in Nairobi, a Tactical HQ was formed at Marrian's Farm in Mweiga consisting of an Air Wing and an Intelligence Staff. The 1,100-acre farm on the extreme northern side of the Kikuyu country bordering the western fringes of the Aberdares had been bought under the Soldier Settler Scheme by two former Indian Army officers, William Sheldrick and Thomas Atkins, who intended to grow coffee and play polo. They then sold the farm to Peter Marrian, who had arrived in Kenya in the 1930s. Forward operating bases were located at Eastleigh and Nankuki. Most of the planes were PA-20 Pacer high-wing light aircraft, which proved to be rugged and fast. Aircraft were always on immediate stand-by and rarely took off without a box of thirty-six anti-personnel grenades. Among the pilots was Eric Garland, a former soldier who had won the MC during the retreat from Dunkirk and then joined the Army Commandos. He subsequently joined the RAF and was shot down flying a photo-reconnaissance mission during the Battle of Monte Cassino in Italy. He was captured but escaped and reached Allied lines. He later bought a ranch in Kenya and resumed flying with the KPRAW.

Also based at Marrian's Farm was the Tactical HQ for the seven Kenya Regiment companies dispersed in small forts on spurs high in the Aberdares. The common fort design adopted was a stockade surrounded by a ditch, wire entanglements and sharpened bamboo driven into the ground at an angle; they were manned by about two sections to a platoon. By January 1953, the Regiment was developing specialist forces at Squair's Farm. Captain Neville Cooper GM, MC (former Parachute Regiment), a B Company platoon commander, formed the Intelligence Force (I Force) and experimented with several innovations until it became known as I Company in February 1953. Tasked to find Mau Mau camps, the Company formed about 25-strong long range patrols, who spent a fortnight in the bush and developed techniques that later became common in British jungle warfare training and operations. Everyone and everything leaves a footprint of some sort. Today, it is a question of closed circuit cameras and social media. In the jungle, it is sounds, footprints, disturbed vegetation, discarded food, urine and faeces, light and smoke from fires, human odour, tobacco and soap. In Kenya, spilt maize was a sign of food collection, and flattened grass often indicated where someone had avoided walking on a track. Local knowledge of terrain, climate and ecology is essential. Trackers can determine whether footprints are male or female and the health and age of the target. After Bill Woodley and his team of poachers had proved so valuable in the hunt for the killers of Fergusson and Bingley, in February, a Game Department employee named Kibwezi Kilonzo, from the Kamba tribe, was the first African tracker to be enlisted into the Kenya Regiment. Woodley returned to the Regiment and was sent to recruit trackers from poachers in Tsavo. Others brought their own trackers, some of whom had been in the KAR and Kenya Police, and saw them enlisted. None could be promoted beyond sergeant major.

In late January 1953, A and C Companies, 1 Lancashire Fusiliers moved to Naivasha in the preliminary phase of Operation Red Rose to clear Mau Mau camps in the Aberdares bamboo belt. The town was a District administrative centre, road and rail junction serving farms to the west of the Aberdares. Early on 26 January, two Africans rushed to the Rear HQ reporting that they had found their *bwana* and a friend dead on the lawn of Ruck's Farm. The Company second-in-command, Captain M.F.V. Drake, immediately informed the police and took a small patrol to the farm where they met Police Reserve Inspector Tony Pape and found the bodies of Roger Ruck, his wife and their son.

Ruck ran a remote farm north of Kingapop. Aged thirty-eight and a man of strong views, he was a member of the Kenya Police Reserve. His wife, Esmée, who was several months pregnant with their second child, was a qualified doctor who treated Africans at local clinics and dispensaries. With no other white children on the farm, their six-year-old son Michael had African playmates. Although the family got on well with Africans, Roger had become less trusting of Kikuyu after the murder of his neighbour, Eric Bowyer; they therefore carried personal weapons and checked the security of the house before going to bed. Domestic staff were no longer permitted to remain in the farm after dinner and were accommodated in the labour lines. The implementation of the Emergency had meant that labour turnover had been higher than usual, and A Company had used the Rucks' farm as a base.

Unknown to the Rucks, about thirty squatters on the farm had taken Mau Mau oaths. Having seen strangers on the farm, Ruck had posted guards to protect his livestock. Mau Mau presence had become evident when Inspector Pape came under fire the previous evening. Shortly before retiring, the Rucks' groom shouted that Mau Mau were on the farm and one had been captured. Roger immediately grabbed his Beretta pistol and, as he left the house, told Esmée to arm herself with the shotgun. As he followed the groom to the workshops, he was ambushed and held while being slashed with pangas. His cries of pain alarmed his wife and set the dogs barking and cattle lowing. Armed with the shotgun, Esmée went outside but she was stabbed to death and her unborn baby was ripped from her stomach. A farm worker who ran to help was also murdered, and all three bodies were left on the lawn. In their customary fashion, the Mau Mau mutilated the bodies, then ransacked the house for weapons, ammunition, money and clothing, breaking into Michael's locked bedroom and murdering him too.

Images of bloodied teddy bears and broken toy trains strewn across the child's bedroom floor subsequently inflamed British and colonial opinion. The gang then returned to the neighbouring property of Colonel John Nimmo where they hid in a gorge before returning to the forests. It later emerged that several of Ruck's employees had been involved in the slaughter.

The murders of the Rucks, in particular, led 1,000 angry colonists to march on Government House, where they demanded that Governor Baring give them a greater say in running the colony and that tougher action be taken against the Mau Mau in Central Province. They blamed Governor Mitchell and the Executive Council for failing to address Kikuyu grievances, accused Baring of procrastination and criticized the slowness of the judicial system in bringing Mau Mau to trial. When Baring refused to meet a delegation, the crowd broke into Government House, where they were confronted by Michael Blundell. He had arrived in Kenya in 1925 aged eighteen and farmed in the Rift Valley. Before the Second World War he had supported the notion of Kenya as a white colony, but his wartime service with Kenyan troops had led him to sympathize with their ambitions and aspirations. Critical of the complacency of Mitchell, he was the only elected member of Baring's government. Press reports of a meeting at Nakuru reported that one colonist had demanded the shooting of 50,000 Kikuyu.

In response to colonist concerns, Baring announced that Major General William Hinde had been appointed as Personal Staff Advisor to the Governor. Commissioned into the 15/19th Hussars and with a reputation as a fearless rider that resulted in his being nicknamed 'Looney', he had represented Great Britain at polo in the 1936 Olympics. He had been wounded in France in 1940 and then commanded his Regiment until August 1942, when he was promoted to brigadier and to command, first, 20th Armoured Brigade and, two months later, 22nd Armoured Brigade in North Africa and Italy. Both were part of the 7th Armoured Division, which had found fighting in the countryside of Normandy markedly different from the desert. It had also been fighting without significant rest since 1940, and during the Battle of Villers-Bocage, senior commanders felt that it had lost its edge; Hinde was one of several officers who were consequently sacked. He was a keen ornithologist and while Deputy Director of Military Government in

Berlin from 1945 to 1948, showed considerable diplomatic skills when arrested in May 1947 by a Soviet patrol while bird-watching near the boundary of the Soviet sector in Berlin. He was escorted to the Soviet Kommandatura Headquarters but quickly released with an apology. Between 1949 and 1951 he was Deputy Commanding Officer, Lower Saxony in West Germany and then commanded Cyrenaica District in Libya, reporting to General Sir Brian Robertson, who had been his senior in Berlin and who had been Commander-in-Chief, Middle East Land Forces when the British moved from Cairo to the Canal Zone Base. While Hinde was being briefed at HQ Middle East Land Forces, Robertson told him, 'You are Chief Staff Officer to the Governor and your job is to jolly them along.' Hinde, who had some sympathy for the colonists because his brother was a farmer at Nanyuki, arrived on 1 February and replaced Colonel Rimbault. During the four months since the Emergency was declared, 177 Africans, nine Europeans and three Indians had died in Mau Mau attacks.

In the Aberdares, 9 Platoon, 1 Lancashire Fusiliers accompanied by two KPR inspectors and several Kipsigi trackers, with their rations of live goats, climbed to the top of the hills, patrolled during the day and laid ambushes at night. It seems that the combination of the altitude and Coca and Pepsi Cola led to some fusiliers hallucinating. Mortar Platoon was patrolling the Aberdares with HQ C Company and 8 Platoon after a group of Mau Mau were seen in the vicinity of Harold White's farm near Ol Kalou on 1 February. The next night, a patrol led by Second Lieutenant Stott shot one of three Mau Mau and captured another group.

In a strategy to remove increasingly successful businesses competing with colonists becoming alarmed at their success, in February Baring ordered under the Emergency Regulations the eviction of about 100,000 Kikuyu squatters on farms in areas of suspected or actual Mau Mau activity to Kikuyu Reserves. Although many were loyal, families were rounded up, often with little warning and occasionally at gunpoint, and sometimes forced to abandon huts, livestock, clothing and personal possessions before being moved on. It was not unknown in the chaos for parents to become separated from their children. The Lancashire Fusiliers evacuated families from Ol Kalou in their lorries. Even militant colonists considered the evictions to be inhumane, quite apart from the loss of their workforces. Major General Hinde was appalled, because the strategy undermined the counter-insurgency principle of keeping the people on side. Intelligence soon emerged of increasing sympathy for the Mau Mau and rising recruitment.

Reports now began to emerge that some police and soldiers were taking the law into their own hands in the belief that coercion and violence against the Kikuyu would convince them not to support the Mau Mau. Baring condemned the rough handling of prisoners, suspects and members of the public on 11 February, declaring that offences against humanity would be dealt with by disciplinary action. Naval and military commanders, at all levels, have always been fiercely protective of the reputation and culture of their units, even more so when given a hint of independence; investigations by civil police, let alone military police, were something to be avoided. There are four internationally recognized principles in armed conflict:

- Distinction. There shall be respect for and protection of civilian populations and objects. The military shall direct their operations only against military objectives and not civil property.
- Proportionality. Loss of life and damage to property *incidental* to attacks must not be excessive in relation to direct military advantage expected to be gained.
- Military Necessity. The conduct of military operations should only go so far as absolutely necessary. Everything beyond that is criminal. The killing and wounding of an enemy in battle is permitted, but torture is prohibited as is applying measures that have no military necessity.
- Unnecessary Suffering. The deployment of weapons and methods of warfare that would cause unnecessary suffering is prohibited.

The escalation in tension saw HQ East Africa Command allocating Central Province to its Northern Brigade and forming the operational HQ Kenya Garrison. Substantial recruitment to the Kenya Police saw police officers arriving from British constabularies and the British South Africa Police and constables from tribes in remote areas. Unfortunately, the force was gaining a reputation for brutality and dishonesty, and its biggest weakness remained the lack of decent intelligence, in spite of the enlargement of Special Branch.

In fulfilment of the 'three-legged' concept, in early March, Chief Secretary Potter wrote to the Provincial Commissioners, Commissioner of Police and the Legislature that the Kenya Intelligence Committee would be formed and that it would report to the Governor and the Operations Committee. Meeting fortnightly, it was to be chaired by the Intelligence Advisor. Members would include the Assistant Chief Secretary, Head of Special Branch and the Kenya Security Liaison Officer; representatives from the Chief Native Commissioner and HQ East Africa Command would also be in attendance. The other two 'legs' of Provincial and District Intelligence Committees were expected to:

- Collect and co-ordinate intelligence.
- Forward intelligence summaries and reports up the chain to the Kenya Intelligence Committee.

But Special Branch, because it had been starved of funds, had very little political intelligence on African matters outside Nairobi and Mombasa. Indeed, Commissioner O'Rourke had highlighted in his 1952/3 annual report that there was no point his seeking funding because the request would probably be rejected. The consequence was that Special Branch had been forced on to the defensive and become reliant on information passed on by provincial and district police headquarters. This had already led to the mistaken belief that the Mau Mau was directly linked to Kenyatta and the Kikuyu Central Association, and the consequent removal of the most influential African in Kenya. The presence of Special Branch at the top table was recognized by its most senior officer being promoted to Assistant Commissioner of the Police. When John Prendergast arrived as Head of Special Branch and Director of Intelligence, he bridged the police/military gap by having several Kenya Regiment sergeants transferred into the new Joint Army Police Operational Intelligence Teams (JAPOIT); however, since they were under the control of Special Branch, the focus remained on political intelligence. Although the military intelligence concept initially called for a General Staff Officer, Grade 1 (Intelligence) at HQ East African

Command to manage military intelligence collected by Army units, an overall Chief of Intelligence was not appointed because the Colonial Office and the War Office insisted there was no comparison between Kenya and Malaya. In Malaya, the Communist terrorists were experienced, well-organized and politically committed. In Kenya, there was no subversive threat, simply the desire for the return of land. Battalions brought their intelligence sections, and soldiers were posted to Brigade and Command HQ intelligence sections as collators. Specialist intelligence resources provided by the Intelligence Corps had been dismantled in 1945, predictably, because the War Office maintained its stance that there was no need in peacetime for permanent specialist skills such as interrogation, air photographic analysis and field security. As after the Boer War and the First World War, these military organizations had been disbanded.

Field Marshal Sir John Harding, the Chief of the Imperial General Staff, visited Kenya between 19 and 24 February. Unimpressed with the colonists, he wrote to the Colonial Office suggesting that they resented the Mau Mau disturbing their lives and predicted some hotheads 'will take the law into their hands, and indeed there have been cases, fortunately hushed up, of their so doing'. He noted the Afrikaners were particularly vocal in demanding action. Governor Baring was equally concerned about this internal threat to security. Harding did not share the optimistic official view promoted by Major General Hinde that the Governor had sufficient resources. Indeed, he wrote after his visit:

> One Brigadier with an attenuated staff and no signals cannot exercise effective command over five equivalent battalions deployed on a Company or Platoon basis over an area about 130 miles and 120 miles wide.

On his return to England, Harding instructed 39 Infantry Brigade, then commanded by Brigadier John Tweedie (Argyll & Sutherland Highlanders), then at Old Park Camp in Dover as part of 3rd (Strategic Reserve) Division, to deploy to Kenya. The Brigade had been formed during the First World War and was disbanded after seeing action at Gallipoli and in Mesopotamia. It was re-formed in April 1951 as part of the 3rd Infantry Division and had been in the Canal Zone until October

1952, its main components being 1st Battalion, Royal East Kent Regiment and 1st Battalion, Devonshire Regiment.

The bulk of the Lancashire Fusiliers were around Naivasha in the Rift Valley. D Company was at Thomson's Falls. Early March had been quiet, but then tension increased with 3,500 arrests in Thika, which was thought to be a Mau Mau centre and known to be a haven for criminals targeting Nairobi. A week earlier, 2,500 Embu had been arrested at Pumwani, about two miles east of Eastleigh. On 26 March, 8 Platoon, C Company, commanded by Second Lieutenant A.G. Stott, was warned that early next morning there was to be a raid on the Kikuyu Transit Camp at Naivasha which held detainees. The camp was located in the outskirts of the town and surrounded by a low wall of mud and stone with an embrasure at each corner. The wall had been recently widened and raised, and it was augmented by barbed wire entanglements; however, it had been badly laid and an inspecting officer ordered that the outer defences be reconstructed. The platoon was unaware that the Mau Mau were about to launch two of their most skilful actions of the Emergency.

At about 9.30 p.m., Major General Mbaria Kaniu, who was operating from the Kinganpop area, led about eighty Mau Mau armed with a total of three .303 rifles, a Sten, a shotgun and a pistol. Most were dressed in greatcoats to resemble police officers. They crept to two places previously noted to be weak in the barbed wire and the perimeter wall. The shooting of a sentry in the watchtower was the signal for a stolen truck to ram the compound gates. One group then stormed the front desk and killed the duty officer. Four others in an adjacent office escaped through the window. Resistance was weak because most of those on duty were new constables with little training and no combat experience. A second group made for the KPR Armoury and loaded weapons into the truck. Meanwhile, a third group released 173 prisoners from the detention camp. The raid awakened the off-duty police but they were trapped in barracks. As the Mau Mau began to withdraw, they tried to take a lorry parked in the compound but were unable to start it. The raid was well executed, and during the twenty minutes the raiders spent in the compound, they netted 29 rifles, 18 Lanchester sub machine guns and undetermined amounts of ammunition. Two policeman were killed and there were no Mau Mau casualties.

Lari, a town about 10 miles south of Naivasha, straggles along the steep decline from the escarpment on the road between Nairobi and Nakuru. The Police Post was manned by two former Kenya Regiment soldiers and 20 constables. The town was developed by Kikuyu evicted in 1939 from a tea plantation at Tigoni in Kiambu District to make way for colonists. They had been assured that the Land Commission would give them land, but loyalist chiefs, one of whom was Chief Luka Mbugua Wakahangara, sold plots to the highest bidders and, in so doing, ignored the Kikuyu cultural obligation to provide land for those who did not enjoy customary land rights. Lari had also attracted hundreds of squatters from Rift Valley farms. Discontent seethed there. When Chief Luka addressed a rally near the Kiambu District Officer's office in Kimende warning that anyone who had taken the Mau Mau oath risked retribution from the Administration, an oath administrator sent his ten-year son to transmit the content of the speech to Mau Mau in the Githunguri area. Even after intelligence surfaced on 18 March that Lari was a Mau Mau target, the 2/3 (Kenya) KAR company providing internal security in the area was sent to the Athi River prison camp at Lukenia on the outskirts of Nairobi in response to reports of anticipated trouble, leaving the 150-strong Lari Home Guard to provide security and patrols.

At about 8.30 p.m. on 26 March, as the Home Guard responded to the report of an African nailed to a tree about three miles from the town, about 400 Mau Mau wearing overalls and divided into about seven groups, each of about 100 insurgents, assembled on the fringes of Lari. Each group was divided into three sections: one wrapped cable around targeted huts to trap the occupants; the second splashed the huts with fuel and set them on fire with burning torches; the third protected the attackers and formed a cordon to prevent anyone escaping. The fifteen homesteads selected for attack included those occupied by headmen, councillors and prominent Home Guard members. At about 9.00 p.m. the Mau Mau stormed in unopposed. The slaughter that followed ranks among the worst massacres since 1945, but is rarely mentioned in the history books. A wife of Chief Luka recalled:

> We were woken up by gunshots. It immediately came to my mind that we had been attacked as we had always been warned by the

> Mau Mau because of our husband's collaboration with the colonialists. When I went out to investigate, there were many people outside and although the moon was shining brightly, I could not recognise any of them. Terrified, I quickly retreated to my house. Gacheri, my co-wife, was fast asleep and as I tried to wake her up to alert her that we were under attack, the attackers who were on my heels were at the door of our grass-thatched house where we were sleeping with our four children. As they broke down the door, I tried to escape, clutching Gacheri's one-year-old daughter, but the attackers mercilessly set on me with sharp machetes, vowing to kill me. By sheer good luck, I managed to escape and took cover near a tree a short distance from the compound, with blood oozing from the machete cuts. From my hideout, I saw my co-wife come out of the house carrying the three children, one on her back and the others in front. One of the attackers hit her and she fell to the ground. One of the children she was carrying, Mbura, rushed in my direction. The attackers brutally slashed Gacheri on the neck and head as I watched helplessly from my hideout. She did not die on the spot but the children, Wanjiku and Wairimu, were killed but we never found their corpses. After they were done, I took the two children I had with me and we ran for our lives towards the river. By that time, the colonial police officers had arrived and gunshots rent the air as the attackers ran away. We left our hideout at dawn and on getting home, were shocked at the sight that greeted our eyes. Hundreds of our cattle had been slashed to death and our entire homesteads burnt to ashes.

In all, 74 men, women, children and babies, all Christians, were killed, including Chief Luka and several of his wives and grandchildren. Although the Home Guard hurried back to Lari, they were too late; but angered by the slaughter, they and the regular and reserve police gave little quarter and singled out anyone suspected of being Mau Mau sympathizers. Major T.P. Shaw, the Battalion Second-in-Command, instructed A and C Companies to assemble at the Police Station. C Company, which was based at Njabini and was commanded by Major K.A. Hill MC, then deployed to Naivasha and helped collect weapons and ammunition dropped by the raiders. It also experienced several friendly fire incidents from jittery police and Home Guard while searching the bush for weapons and wounded terrorists.

The next night, after the Sten gun of one of the two European inspectors had misfired when he met a column of 60 Mau Mau on a track, HQ C Company took over a KPR ambush of a track junction covering the pipeline road in the bamboo belt about five miles from Njabini. Second Lieutenant Shaw led 8 Platoon on a clearing patrol and had a couple of contacts, during which Fusilier Hawkins shot an armed Mau Mau at a range of 400 yards; he was carrying a Lanchester and over 100 rounds. Heavy rain obliterating the road to Naivasha led to Battalion HQ, then in Nairobi, managing the ambush. The arrival of 30 reinforcements allowed Major Hill to re-form 7 Platoon under command of Sergeant Reid. On 1 April, Company HQ and 8 Platoon reacted to an attack on the Chaplin Farm on the edge of the forest; the only casualty was a houseboy, badly stabbed. Two days later, a group of Mau Mau let it be known that several houses about six miles from Njabini were going to be attacked – and then attacked the Company base, setting fire to several tents. The expected trouble after the sentencing of Jomo Kenyatta did not materialize; nevertheless, Hill was reinforced with three platoons. On the 14th, 8 Platoon provided stops for a sweep originating from Fort Hall after four Kenya Regiment had been killed in an ambush.

Another audacious attack occurred on the border of Nyeri and Embu Districts when a Mau Mau commander named Kibarawa Maran ('Chui'), dressed in a police uniform and masquerading as the new inspector, assembled the Home Guard and then signalled his gang to open fire. 'Chui' was born in 1927 and had gained some military knowledge by observing tactics, discipline and military protocols while employed as a cleaner with the KAR. When in 1952 he discovered that he was paid less than his Indian colleagues, he became disillusioned and managed to convince his father that the Mau Mau road was the only option. When the Emergency was declared, 'Chiu' joined General 'China' on Mt Kenya, led raids on police stations for weapons, rustled livestock and intimidated loyalists into donating food. But as he achieved notoriety, 'Chui' moved his operation in between Mt Kenya and the Aberdares.

Chapter 6

The Military Response

So far, strategies to lance the Mau Mau boil had largely failed, although 619 insurgents had been killed and 343 wounded. The sweeps had netted 103,379 individuals, of whom 89,820 had been screened. However, it was clear that the Administration was losing control, because it had no clear strategy.

The attacks at Navaisha and Lari shocked the Administration and colonists because they had not believed the Mau Mau could mount such daring raids, perhaps forgetting that some were Burma Campaign veterans. The raid on the Police Station supported the belief that attacks were generally based on good intelligence and had elements of vendetta about them. An inquiry into the attack at Naivasha blamed Commissioner O'Rourke, but it was not published because the post's deficient defence was evident at all levels. The brutality of the slaughter at Lari provided an opportunity to develop a Psychological Operations response.

Realizing that his counter-insurgency strategy was failing and that over-enthusiasm was causing friction between the Police, the Army, the Administration and civilians, Governor Baring decided that a supremo was required and agreed on 1 April that Major General Hinde be appointed Director of Operations in order to:

- Chair the Operations Committee, which advised on the conduct of operations.
- Direct the conduct of operations by the police and Armed Forces.
- Suggest changes to the Governor's Committee.
- Issue orders for the implementation of the Governor's Committee's instructions.

- Frame and issue operational plans for the guidance of Provincial Operational Committees.

Wing Commander Francombe quickly mobilized the Communications Flight of two Ansons, a Proctor and a Valetta. He had also strengthened the Reconnaissance Squadron by purchasing ten Piper Tri-Pacer 135s flown by full-time RAF pilots and ex-RAF and Aero Club pilots.

Nanyuki was a pleasant garrison town overlooked by Mt Kenya and a terminal for the railway line from Nairobi 130 miles to the south; the climate was warm during the day and cold enough at night to sit around a log fire. Among its facilities were clothes shops, garages, a pharmacy, a barber, a hairdresser, several doctors and a cottage hospital, lawyers and hotels catering for fishing holidays in the rivers teeming with trout, although the Mau Mau threat had reduced their bookings. Recreation focused on house parties, bridge, recitals, squash, golf, tennis and polo. Surrounding farms produced grain, dairy products, chickens and sheep, and on the lower, drier, slopes cattle munched lush grass.

The garrison housed HQ 70 Brigade, which was commanded by Brigadier Donald Cornah, the Kenyan KAR battalions, the KAR Depot and Training School, the East Africa Armoured Car Squadron, East African Signals and the cottage British Military Hospital. The askaris were permitted to leave camp in uniform on Saturday and Sunday afternoons and usually visited the native quarter, even though the Royal Military Policemen from 156 Provost Company had erected 'Out of Bounds' signs around it. One Saturday afternoon, the military police raided the quarter and arrested several askaris in brothels, locking them up in the guardroom. When 3 KAR heard about the arrests, a crowd of askaris stormed the cells and released the prisoners. Brigadier Cornah was furious and ordered Lieutenant Colonel Jack Crewe-Read's battalion to march toward Nyeri on Monday, a distance of about 25 miles, until ordered to stop. At 7.00 a.m. the battalion paraded as instructed and were given a diplomatic ticking-off by Crewe-Read; they then set off, with the askaris thoroughly enjoying the march. While lunch was being taken about 1.00 p.m., a mash for the askaris and a Fortnum & Mason-style meal including port and Stilton for the officers, Brigadier Cornah turned up in a Daimler armoured car and, rejecting a cold beer, told Crewe-Read that the battalion should return to barracks.

Bob Smith, who had been seconded to the battalion, describes their return:

> The African RSM asked the Adjutant if the askaris could take off their boots. That was the way they liked to march, with laces tied together and their wide-soled footwear, specially made for those who spent most of their lives barefooted, hanging around their necks. Permission was given, and when they were ready, the order 'Quick March' was given. If the singing on the outward leg of the march had stirred the blood, it was nothing compared with the enthusiasm the askaris felt when they had their noses pointing towards home. 'Tufunge Safari' and 'Mama na Dada' were two of the great marching songs of the KAR, but there were many more – all sung in that chanting, rhythmical style peculiar to Africans. It did not stop there. Soon, shoulders were bobbing, arms were waving, boots were flying and some of the Wakamba were gyrating and leaping as if they were at a Saturday night *ngoma* (dance) back in camp. Long before the Mexican Wave was thought of, askaris had a way of starting a similar snake-like movement through the ranks by taking three or four steps forward and one backwards. Not only did this increase the mileage, but it further increased the discomfort of the *wazungu* (British officers, warrant officers and senior NCOs), who had not yet mastered the African style of route marching. When they reached the tarmac, half a mile from Nanyuki, the African RSM gave the order to halt and replace footwear. Then the British RSM took over and the whole column marched to attention with rifles at the slope, through the main street and back to camp. 'Tufunge Safari', the regimental march, rang out again but, this time, played by the Bugle Band of the Battalion.

The next Saturday, the askaris visited the native quarter, no longer out of bounds. Those who had been arrested served seven days detention with enough free beer to make the week worthwhile.

Rejecting more reinforcements, Hinde re-formed 70 Brigade as 70 (East African) in order to:

- Assist the Police and Civil Administration in the main towns.
- Assist the Police and Civil Administration in the prevention of stock theft and terrorism of European farms.
- Eliminate Mau Mau gangs after incidents.
- Eliminate gangs in the Native Reserves.
- Assist the Police and Civil Administration in the restoration of law and order.
- Destroy the Mau Mau in the two Prohibited Areas.

The Rules of Engagement remained as follows:

- Prohibited Areas: shoot on sight any person seen in or entering the Prohibited Area.
- Special Area (virtually all of Kenya): open fire on anyone failing to stop when challenged.

Giving 70 Brigade responsibility for the security of the Reserves, Hinde allocated the Aberdares to 39 Brigade, although it would not be until early May that they were ready for operations. By the end of April, it was deploying to Kenya in a series of the longest air deployments thus far known. The Buffs had been raised in 1665 in a period when regiments were known by the name of their colonel. In 1744, two regiments known as the Howards were fighting in Holland and, in order to distinguish them, one became known as the Green Howards and the other as the Buffs, from the facing on their jackets. In 1685 1 Devons had been formed, and at the Battle of Salamanca in 1812 they won the sobriquet 'the Bloody Eleventh' for their stubbornness. The 1st Battalion had fought in Burma, and then in Malaya between 1948 and 1950, thus its Regular core had experience of jungle warfare. The Commanding Officer, Lieutenant Colonel Paul Gleadell, had been Second-in-Command of the 12th (Airborne) Battalion during the fighting in Normandy, during which he was awarded the Croix de Guerre for gallantry; he later won the DSO when commanding the Battalion during the airborne assault to cross the River Rhine in March 1945. From July to December 1950 he was G1 (Intelligence), GHQ Far East, where he was awarded the CBE.

As became normal practice, battalions earmarked for Kenya despatched an Advance Party, followed about three weeks later by the Main Body. In a journey that lasted about five days between leaving their barracks and arriving at RAF Eastleigh, they spent the night before departure at the London Reception Centre transit camp in Goodge Street Underground Station, which had been fitted with racks of beds. The worst aspect was struggling up and down the stairs dressed in the full Service marching order of webbing, kit bag and rifle. Next morning, the drafts took off from Blackbushe Airport in British Aviation Services Handley Page Hermes aircraft. British Aviation Services was formed in 1946 and was one of the first companies to move into Blackbushe in 1947, primarily in the business of aviation consultancy and ferrying contracts. It operated four Hermes. The soldiers were each given a flight map showing the route. For many soldiers, it was the first time they had flown. In an oral testimony recorded in *Remembering Scotland at War*, Private Bob Mitchell of the Black Watch, who arrived in Kenya in 1953, recalled:

> We took off and we flew over the Alps, Marseilles; it was beautiful. We got a lovely view. Touched down in Malta; by this time it was kind of dark and spent some time in Malta; a couple of hours. Moved on, touched down at El Adam; same thing there; refuelled. Then touched down in Khartoum and got off the plane there to have breakfast and change into our olive green dress, which was designed, you know, for the warmer climate. I remember getting to the door of the aircraft and the heat hit you like a brick wall. It was something. You weren't prepared for it. You can imagine; Khartoum about 11 o'clock in the morning, the hottest time, it was really stifling. You know that was . . . And remember, we'd never been out of Scotland before we went this trip. There was no package holidays in these days and going away to the likes of Africa was, now, like going to another planet.

Mitchell was an apprentice joiner, whose call up was deferred until he had completed his training. Stansted was also used by charter aircraft. The Hermes' payload was between forty-two and eighty-two passengers while the Avro York, derivative of the Lancaster bomber, had a passenger capacity of fifty-six. Those flying with the RAF joined their aircraft at a Transport Command base. Several overseas RAF stations were available in case aircraft needed to divert. When 1 Buffs deployed, there were several dramas. The departure of half of A Company was delayed for 48 hours by engine trouble. The aircraft carrying half of B Company ran short of fuel and, after diverting to Wadi Haifa on the Egyptian border, flew to Khartoum, where it mistakenly landed on an unused runway pitted with potholes. When the missing stick of A Company had arrived at RAF Eastleigh on Easter Saturday, Major S.G.P. Johnston and his Quartermaster staff experienced an immediate nightmare when a fire that started near the Quartermaster's Stores consumed rations, rifle company stores and vehicles. The MT Platoon managed to divert the flames from 500 gallons of petrol in jerry cans, but at the expense of their personal kit and tools and the platoon office. This meant that for several nights the drivers had to sleep wherever they could. The MT sergeant requisitioned the ambulance as his office and bunk.

On arrival, battalions generally established a field Command Post supported by a static Main Headquarters manned by the Adjutant, Quartermaster, Post Sergeant delivering official and personal mail and by the Paymaster. The delivery of classified and personal packages and letters was the responsibility of Royal Engineers Postal and Courier Units, with Nairobi designated as British Forces Post Office 10, usually 'BFPO 10'. Another means of contact with home was the Forces Broadcasting Service, which first set up in Mombasa in 1947 to support the Mackinnon Road project. It later moved to Nairobi. On a regular basis, the BBC Light Programme broadcast messages and a record to and from families, timed for Sunday lunch. Pay parade was formal; the recipient marched to a desk behind which sat the Paymaster, checked the cash and after announcing 'Pay correct, sir!' saluted and returned to the ranks. Command Post assets included the Intelligence Section, consisting of the Intelligence Officer, Intelligence Sergeant and four or five clerks. Companies were allocated tactical areas of responsibility. The classic tactical layout was to place Company HQ in the middle surrounded by its platoons. Platoons arranged their three sections in a similar format, as did sections. In bases, most of the troops lived in camps of marquees and 180lb tents, each surrounded by a maintained rainwater drain and connected by stone footpaths. Tents were more comfortable if the canvas was erected on a wall of horizontal logs, thereby giving greater headroom. Keeping all camps clean to prevent dysentery and insect-borne diseases was essential. Urinals were manufactured from biscuit tins placed over a soakaway pit. Lines of wooden latrines were dug over trenches 2ft deep and each was provided with a scoop or shovel. Such trenches were meant to be replaced every 24 hours and marked. All waste water, for instance from the kitchen, was passed through grease traps into soakaways provided by the Public Works Department. All other waste was, wherever possible, burnt or rammed into deep pits. Camps were surrounded by defensive positions of machine gun posts and slit trenches. On arriving in Kenya, the troops on operations wore, a 'Floppy Joe' jungle hat, Jungle Green shirt and trousers and (19)44 pattern webbing, designed specifically for jungle warfare. Lightweight windproofs were useful. Ankle-length green plimsoll jungle boots were issued, but soldiers preferred their leather boots and, if dry, issue plimsolls. An important aspect was that the capacity of the webbing could be increased by the addition of straps and fixing points. A man on a typical four-day patrol might carry rations, ammunition and grenades, first aid necessities, a panga and two blankets inserted into a ground sheet rolled around the pack.

Post-1945, British tactical thinking relied on a series of pragmatic doctrines that reflected the changing circumstances of British commitments and were expressed in a series of tactical manuals. Theatre-specific doctrine focused on decentralized command and control in which the decisions and initiative of junior officers and all ranks were crucial, particularly while operating from platoon bases. Rapid turnover of men leaving and joining units, in particular National Servicemen, saw most battalions form a training company. When on leave, some troops went to the Silversands Mombasa Leave Centre, not far from Nyali Beach, while others accepted invitations to 'safe' farms. One Royal Signaller who had been based at Nanyuki recalled:

> The leave camp was a marvellous place, right by the beach, with a thatched bar on the sand. Mombasa was hot, so most of us got up at 6am before the temperature rose, had an early breakfast then spent most of the day in the sea. One day I walked along the beach for half a mile and came to the Nyali Beach Hotel. I could see that swimming trunks were acceptable wear in the hotel bar so I

> popped in for a drink . . . Most nights in the cool of the evening Housey-Housey was played on a fairy-lit terrace.
>
> Beer flowed liberally and Bill Haley's Comets played over the PA. One morning I went into Mombasa, walked around in a temperature of 104F in the shade and had a boat trip round the harbour, where I saw Arab dhows in full sail. My tropical holiday ended all to soon but left memories for a lifetime. (*Royal Signals Contact Site – My National Service 1955–57*)

Maintaining physical fitness was essential, with formal exercises conducted by Physical Fitness Instructors and sports competitions. Units retained their inter-company competitions and organised inter-unit matches in soccer, cricket, rugby and hockey. Ranges outside the perimeter allowed for weapon training. It was usually about a month before the radios and other heavy equipment arrived by sea at Mombasa.

The main issue for signals was the high terrain and distances between Command Posts, sometimes tens of miles from their companies on the other side of high ground, and platoons ten miles from Company HQs. An example was when the Devons regrouped astride the Aberdares. Conditions were sometimes so bad that when the 1 Buffs Intelligence Sergeant asked to use a radio, he was advised to send a pigeon. One Immediate message took seven hours to be transmitted. A facet of High Frequency (HF) transmissions is that carrier waves are directed up to the ionosphere and then refracted back to Earth which can achieve intercontinental transmission distances; however, the lowering of the ionosphere layer at night, the changing seasons and solar activity can all induce heavy atmospheric interference. Very High Frequency (VHF), however, sees transmission hugging the terrain to a distance of about 100 miles. While less affected by interference, the carrier wave can be blocked by high ground, but is less affected in buildings. A well-placed aerial, or antenna, is key, and therefore commanders and radio operators were reminded to be 'aerial conscious'. Lieutenant Colonel John Shirley, a New Zealander seconded to the Royal Signals, was serving with the Army Operational Research Group (Malaya) when he invented the Shirley Aerial for static locations. It consists of two horizontal dipoles that use the ground as the carrier wave. 'Sky wave' aerials 100ft high suspended between two trees are also effective.

British HQs were equipped with semi-mobile ground and vehicle station No.19 and No.52 HF wirelesses operated by Royal Signals. British signal squadrons were typically six Regular other ranks, the remainder being National Servicemen. Originally designed for armoured units, many No.19 sets had instructions in Cyrillic because they had been earmarked for the Soviet Union during the war. They had a 'Flick' switch for rapid frequency change. A few No.76 wirelesses were also used, primarily for Morse. Four light vehicles each fitted with a semi-tropicalized No.62 provided Brigade HQs with mobile command posts. Battalion Signals Platoons managed communications with Nos.19, 22, 31, 46 and 62 HF radios. When the No.62 HF suffered from interference after dusk it was mostly used for Morse, at which most KAR signallers were proficient. Companies were usually equipped with manpack Nos.31 and 88 VHF. The No.31 was the British version of the American BC-1000 and had a range of up to five miles; however, it had limitations which led to its being placed on prominent features as a relay station. The No.88 had a range of about two miles and was the first British tactical VHF radio, replacing the No.38 in the late 1940s. In Kenya, No.46 HF, which had been designed in 1942 specifically for amphibious landings and was carried in a waterproof pouch, replaced the former to bridge the distances between companies and platoons. In relation to VHF aerials, in static positions, the usual 4ft rod whip was replaced by the locally-developed 'Nanyuki Mark 1' consisting of a 12ft rod fixed to a 40ft pole supported by guys; this increased communication distance to about 40 miles. The problem of the 4ft whip of the No.88 proving ineffective in forest and bamboo was solved by 30ft of copper wire being thrown into a tree and fed vertically to the radio. No.88s were fitted in KPRAW aircraft as an airborne communications and control platform. The Army also laid a network of field telephones connected by Don 10 landline that linked to command posts at all levels. The vehicles of the Signals Despatch Service Centre delivering documents were eventually replaced by an Air Delivery Service. But the predominantly military HF radios and the Police VHF network meant communications between the two were incompatible, until the Army purchased some VHF radios. The Mau Mau had no radio intercept capability, except with radios captured from the police, and relied on letters and couriers.

The Emergency was already arousing controversy about the conduct of the Security Forces – but not that of the Mau Mau. As the conflict was generally perceived to be a straight fight between colonists wanting to retain a 'white colony' and the Mau Mau agitating for independence, the British Government was sensitive to criticism, not only from the Houses of Parliament but also from within the Commonwealth, particularly as in South Africa the National Party was using 'apartheid' to strengthen segregation. Generally discipline held, but there were lapses. The Kikuyu were not that popular as a tribe and were thought to be disinclined towards militarism. While knowledge of the Laws of Armed Conflict was minimal, Queen's Regulations made all soldiers responsible for acquainting themselves with the 1944 Manual of Military Law and its amendments, such as:

> The fact that a rule of warfare has been violated in pursuance of an order of the belligerent Government or an individual belligerent commander does not deprive the act in question of its character as a war crime; neither does it, in principle, confer upon the perpetrator immunity from punishment.

Baring remained sufficiently concerned about reports of retaliation that on 17 April he again condemned indiscipline within the Security Forces. Three days later, Major General Hinde reinforced community defence by forming the Embu, Kikuyu and Meru Home Guards, placing them under the command of Colonel Philip Morcombe as Inspector-General with responsibility for training, provision of equipment and development of defence techniques. Morcombe had commanded 5 (Kenya) KAR in Madagascar and Burma and, most recently, 1 Suffolks in Malaya.

The Home Guard had its origins in early December, when several militias were raised in Central Province. Research by Bethwell Allan Ogot, the Kenyan historian, suggests that those who enlisted generally fell into one of the following groups:

- Christians, largely recruited by their church. Many chose to face both ways by also taking oaths. This group was the most numerous. General Gatunga particularly terrorized those in Embu and used a bugle to begin attacks on homesteads and people.

- Constitutionalists, who saw the Mau Mau as politically subversive and a threat to internal stability.
- Opportunists exploiting the Emergency for personal gain at the expense of the Mau Mau.
- Traditionalists opposing Mau Mau culture and misuse of oaths.
- Kikuyu sympathetic to the Mau Mau but enlisting to avoid being detained.

The Home Guard's principal roles were to:

- Protect homesteads.
- Deny and disrupt Mau Mau freedom of movement in the Reserves.
- Allow the military forces to concentrate on offensive operations.
- Collect intelligence.

Sergeant majors and above were paid and vetted. Arms were usually bows and arrows and spears. Neville 'Spike' Powell had been born in Kenya and after National Service training in Southern Rhodesia joined the Kenya Regiment. Commissioned in early 1954, he was seconded to the Home Guard as a District Officer and also commanded a Tribal Police Combat Unit. Three Kenya Regiment platoons in the Nyeri, Fort Hall and Kiambu Reserves commanded by Captain Ray Mayers and manning section-sized posts in Central Province supplied two soldiers to help command several Kikuyu Home Guards. This group became known as Ray Force.

As incentives to keep them on side, the Home Guard was exempt from the special Emergency taxes, had access to credit loans and school fees for up to three children and were excused forced labour repairing roads and bridges. Some district administrations giving them priority in commercial dealings led to accusations by the Mau Mau of collusion with the whites; they were nicknamed 'Black Europeans', 'running dogs' (a phrase used by communists to describe loyalists) or 'tie-ties' (from the European style of wearing ties despite the heat, adopted by some Africans). Since the forest Mau Mau had easy access to the

Reserves, it was not long before the Home Guard and Mau Mau became involved in a vicious turf war, particularly in Nyeri and Fort Hall Districts, that saw killings, posts overrun, weapons and equipment stolen, subversion, ambushes and intimidation, all of which affected morale and recruitment on both sides. Kiambu District was largely unmolested because it was on the main Mau Mau supply route between the Passive Wing in Nairobi and the Militant Wing. In April, the Kamba Central Committee of militant railwaymen decided not to sabotage the railway and thus attract attention; indeed, only three incidents were recorded. At the same time, Maasai unrest in Narok District was crushed. Realizing that some blue-collar unions were a hotbed of subversive activity, the Administration created the Kenya Federation of Registered Trade Unions (KFRTU) for white-collar unions as a moderating influence. By the end of 1953 it had a nationalist Arab general-secretary opposed to the revolt. Early in 1954 the KFRTU undermined a general strike called by the Central Committee.

On 10 May the Governor's Emergency Committee replaced the Colony Emergency Committee, with responsibility for:

- Policies for the conduct of the Emergency to the Chief Staff Officer to the Governor.
- Instructions to Government Departments on matters designed to further the restoration of law and order.
- Co-ordinating the decisions of the Committee for social and economic improvements with measures necessary to re-establish law and order.

Membership included:

- Chief Secretary. Responsibility for internal security was transferred from the Attorney-General to the Chief Secretary, thereby releasing the Attorney General to focus on his role as a member of the Executive Council.
- Member for Finance.
- Member for Agriculture.
- HQ East Africa Command.
- Michael Blundell.

While Africans were not represented on any committee, in addition to Blundell there was sometimes additional unofficial colonist representation, in the hope that the colonists would not become too demanding and to curb excesses. The Chief Secretary and Director of Operations worked together to ensure operational and administrative co-ordination. Sitrep Committees, renamed Emergency Committees and better staffed, could concentrate on controlling operations at all levels. Provinces and Districts were instructed to form subsidiary Emergency Committees to:

- Direct operations in their areas. An Executive Officer was appointed to manage operations from the joint District Operations Room.
- Carry out the instructions of the Director of Operations.
- Issue orders to security forces in their areas.

The Intelligence Corps provided protective security and counter-intelligence defence for the Army and its associated civilian elements against sabotage, subversion and espionage through its Field Security role. During the Second World War 277 Field Security Section (FSS) was formed in Winchester and was one of several sections sent to East Africa to undermine Italian subversion. During the Palestine emergency, several former KAR, mainly Burma veterans, were enlisted in order to monitor disruption engineered by militant Jews sent to the detention camps at Gilgil and to keep an eye on activity within the Jewish community. The Section was disbanded in 1950 and re-formed in July 1953 as FSS (East Africa), with the role of investigating Mau Mau cells that had subverted East African soldiers and civilian employees in military installations in order to acquire information, weapons and medical supplies. The FSS also vetted those applying for employment with the Army and RAF, investigated forged permits and bus passes, conducted inquiries at detention centres to collect information useful for Army operations and recorded the fingerprints of employees.

Chapter 7

Brigade Operations June/July 1953

General Nicholson visited Kenya in mid-May and announced at the end of the month that Britain would be leaving the Canal Zone in Egypt and that HQ Middle East Land Forces would be transferring conduct of East African operations to East Africa Command. He also announced that General Sir George Erskine would be taking over as Director of Operations and that General Cameron would remain responsible for operations elsewhere in the region. Major General Hinde, who had revealed his pro-colonist bias by remarking at a private function that '100,000 Kikuyu should be [put] out to work in a vast swill tub', had become something of an embarrassment and was demoted to Deputy Director of Operations.

Commissioned into the King's Royal Rifle Corps, Erskine had served on the Western Front during the First World War and had then commanded the 7th Armoured Division in North Africa, Italy and Normandy. One of his brigade commanders was Hinde. He had also fallen foul of Dempsey's purge of the Division, but nevertheless became Head of the Supreme Allied Headquarters Mission and was commanding 43rd Wessex Division during the advance to Germany. He had also commanded British Forces in Hong Kong, was Director-General of the Territorial Army and had commanded Middle East Land Forces, in which position he had gained experience in counter-insurgency. He was commanding Eastern Command when posted to Kenya.

With Special Branch suggesting that there were 2,500 fighters in the forest, of whom 600 were hard core, with General 'China' organizing operations, Fort Hall had become a ferocious battleground of farms raided, Home Guard attacked, weapons stolen and loyalists murdered. In spite of deploying additional posts, the Police struggled to maintain law and order; nevertheless, with every incident they were gaining counter-insurgency experience in small unit operations, ambushes and tracking. One of the most inspirational Mau Mau was Kago Mboko, a Church of Scotland-educated Kikuyu and member of the KAU who in 1953 had moved from Nairobi to the Rift Valley, where he took the Mau Mau oath. He had been among those squatters forcibly moved to the Kikuyu Reserve and, fleeing into the forest, proved himself a competent guerrilla leader. With a loyal bodyguard of about six and a gang of about sixty, he raided Fort Hall District from his camp in the southern Aberdares and, using support from the squatters, was known for attacking where he was least expected and announcing his arrival with a call from a military bugle.

Counter-insurgency is defensive in nature, and taking a lesson from Malaya, to begin with General Erskine adopted a four-phase strategy, first consolidating the position by localizing the threat and allowing 39 Brigade to become familiar with the situation. The strategy sent a clear psychological message to the Mau Mau that the Administration would prevail.

Initially, 39 Brigade spent a week acclimatizing by conducting 'Showing the Flag' parades and patrols to farms; it was then assisted by 70 (East African) Brigade, the Kenya Regiment and 1 Lancashire Fusiliers, which had joined the Brigade, and learnt forest warfare tactics and techniques by despatching progressively longer company, platoon and section patrols to dominate sectors, disrupt Mau Mau lines of communication, harass and ambush and collect intelligence on tactical areas of operations. The Lee Enfield No.5, or 'Jungle Carbine' as it became known, was introduced for use by British units. Shorter and lighter than the No. 4, it was originally designed for wartime airborne forces in Europe, but was ideal for jungle operations. It could be fitted with a No.5 bayonet, which also doubled as a sheath knife. But it took the same ammunition as the No.4 and therefore had a considerable kick to its recoil, which affected accuracy. Troops were taught to look *through* foliage for shapes and shadows, not at it. Patrolling was sometimes known as 'flogging the forest'. The gloom and density of the forest often confined troops to moving in single file along tracks. One mile an hour was the average speed. The moorland tussock also restricted movement to single file as opposed to the standard advance-to-contact V-formation. The normal organization was a reconnaissance group of scouts and trackers, followed by the headquarters, then the assault group and finally the support group, also providing the rearguard. Attacks by animals, such as rhino and elephants, were an additional hazard. Navigation was a major problem. Initially, maps were constructed from the air photographic coverage made of all Kenya during the late 1940s, but the density of the forest meant that features such as streams were not shown. Not infrequently, KPRAW pilots came to the rescue by supplying a grid reference, usually accurate to within about 100yds. In 1954, Royal Engineers of 89 Field Survey Squadron arrived at High Ridge Camp in Nairobi and began to produce quality maps. A culture of sign language was taught to patrols, for instance:

Enemy seen or suspected	*Thumbs down*
No enemy	*Thumbs up*
Support Group	*Clenched fist*
Assault Group	*V-sign*
Recce	*Thumb and forefinger formed as 'monocle'*
Obstacle, e.g. track junction	*Crossed forearms*
Dwelling	*Hands formed into inverted V to denote a roof*

Mau Mau fieldcraft was recognized to be of high quality, and although their ambushes were quite rare, counter-ambush drills were essential. The role of those caught in the 'killing zone' was to put down fire while the assault group rolled up the ambush; however, the forest's density meant that classic flank attacks often proved impractical, so charging the enemy was a risk worth taking.

Concerned at the lack of offensives against the Mau Mau in the Prohibited Areas, on 7 June General Erskine took the first step of releasing the Army from internal security on the Reserves by ordering several operations against known and suspected camps:

- 39 Brigade, supported by No.1340 Flight RAF and the East African Armoured Car Squadron, to patrol Mount Kenya and attack known and suspected Mau Mau camps in the Aberdares along a 40-mile stretch between South Nyeri and Fort Hall Districts.

- 70 (East African) Brigade to dominate the Reserve and areas where there was little or no subversive activity.

An emerging asset was that the KPRAW was becoming ever-present and indispensable in supporting operations with reconnaissance, supply drops and the delivery of stores to isolated outposts and patrols. Most of the Pacer aircraft had been fitted with military No. 88 radios in their aircraft and were thus able to provide target indication for the Harvards. The six former RAF pilots were on immediate stand-by.

General Harding also reversed Hinde's decision to refuse more aircraft by asking that four North American Harvard-111s be transferred from Thornhill in Southern Rhodesia when the Rhodesian Air Training Group closed. They were grouped in Kenya as No.1340 Flight and placed under command of Squadron Leader C.G.StD. Jefferies, a Hurricane pilot in the Battle of Britain and then in Burma. Designed as a trainer for fighters, the Harvard was used by the US Army Air Corps, the US Navy and the RAF. In Kenya, the aircraft were fitted with a fixed .303 Browning machine gun on the starboard wing for ground attack and racks on both wings capable of carrying 200lb bombs. While the aircraft possessed a psychological weapon in the form of a high-pitched propeller scream while diving, their engines proved temperamental and unable to maintain power in high African temperatures and at the height of the mountains; indeed, of the nineteen aircraft sent to Kenya, six crashed. While their crews survived, weapons and equipment were not always recovered, and the wrecks proved a rich source for scavengers. To provide close support, No.1340 Flight and the KPRAW established a rudimentary Operations Centre at Mweiga in Nyeri District, that included an Intelligence Staff. Between July and October 1952 a No.82 Squadron Lancaster had conducted an air photographic survey of Kenya, but there was no interpretation of it until Mrs Peterson, formerly Flight Lieutenant Vyvyan-Cooper, a wartime photographic analyst at RAF Medmenham, offered her skills and was enrolled into the Police Reserve. Ground defence was supplied by the RAF groundcrew until a small RAF Regiment detachment arrived. Since Erskine lacked an Air Desk at his HQ, the Brigade HQs managed close air support.

By the middle of May, Brigadier Tweedie judged his Brigade fit for operations and he sent the Buffs to a tented camp at Ol Joro Orok, six miles south of the District town of Thomson's Falls, on the Equator, not far from spectacular waterfalls and consisting of the railway station, police station, garage, Barry's Hotel, a golf course and a race course. When B and C Companies were given the northern and southern Aberdares respectively, both established their HQs on farms not far from the forest edge and used Austin Champs to patrol the countryside and visit farms, where the soldiers were welcomed by the Europeans. Nevertheless, life was frustrating as Captain C.M. Hamilton wrote to the *Kent Messenger*:

> The Mau Mau gangs operating in the Aberdares are very elusive and move very quickly – quicker than our men. It has become a game of a hide-and-seek war very different in some ways to that being waged in Malaya.

Although the Lancashire Fusiliers were reporting that the Mau Mau were 'suspiciously restrained', two Devons companies remained in Nairobi on internal security while the Battalion moved to Molo, north-west of Nakuru, and then regrouped as follows:

East of the Aberdares
Command Post at Othaya
A Company at Munyange
C Company on the edge of the Prohibited Area at Mucharage
West of the Aberdares
Battalion HQ and B Company at Gilgil in the Rift Valley
D Company at North Kinankop

In order to generate an offensive spirit in the Devons, Lieutenant Colonel Gleadell offered £5 to the first patrol to kill a Mau Mau, a bounty claimed simultaneously by two units: a D Company patrol led by Second Lieutenant Gray following tracks to a Mau Mau camp at dusk on 11 May and killing one insurgent and wounding two others; and an A Company patrol commanded by Lieutenant Frederick Legg also killing an insurgent in a clash. The Battalion suffered its first battle casualty when a patrol led by Lieutenant Edward Tremblett was ambushed and Private Cole was wounded.

When Erskine ordered operations against known and suspected camps in the Aberdares facing the 40-mile stretch between Muranga and Nyeri, Brigadier Tweedie launched the three-phase Operation Epsom that included bombing in Phase Two and food denial in Phase Three by ambushing paths connecting the Kikuyu Reserve and the forest. Although he believed hand amputations of dead Mau Mau for forensic identification were an intelligence necessity in counter-insurgency, when revelations of a serious case of ill-discipline began to unfold in 70 Brigade, Tweedie instructed that hand amputation was prohibited and ordered that the dead be buried.

The Buffs regrouped at Nyeri, described in the Regimental periodical *The Dragon* as a town 5,500ft above sea level with scenery not unlike England, except for large coffee and banana farms, and an abundance of wild animals. There were several Indian *dukas* (shops), the Outspan and White Rhino Hotels and a fine sports club with 'constant entertainment'. The Command Post moved to Kabage, north of the Aberdares. A Company was at Wallace's Farm, except for 1 Platoon, which was sent to Squair's Farm to replace D Company, which was scheduled to move to a forest hut at Madojoro. The rifle platoons were spread among farms. A Company was reinforced by two KAR platoons and an East African Armoured Corps troop. The Buffs recorded fourteen Mau Mau killed, and C Company were credited with five. Two others were captured.

At the end of the month, C Company, 1 Lancashire Fusiliers was tasked to eliminate an enemy hide, with the Harvards, for the first time, giving close air support. For four days the soldiers inched through a heavily forested gorge, through which snaked a fast-flowing river; CSM Barlow lost count after thirty-five of the number of times the column crossed it. On the first night, the Fusiliers wedged themselves into bamboo thickets to avoid falling into the river, and rum replaced a hot meal. The Company was in position as the Harvards began their runs, but no bombs fell because of system failures; in one instance, the troops could see bombs swinging in their harnesses. Although machine gunning proved more intimidating, the attack was fruitless. As the Company regrouped in a clearing, a KPRAW aircraft free-dropped boxes of 'compo rations', some bouncing off trees, some splitting open. Unit signallers soon became adept at dodging packages while directing the aircraft.

During Operation Epsom, the Devons Command Post and D Company crossed the Aberdares, intending to drive Mau Mau towards 'stops' provided by A and C Companies and Police Posts on the eastern slopes. These stops covered likely enemy withdrawal routes and usually evolved into ambushes. Typically, in a company attack on a hide, two platoons would deploy as stops. The two companies then joined A Company at Munyange. Major R.A.C. Ravenhill, commanding C Company, the Buffs, had established a base in several forestry buildings in a clearing at Kabage. When shouting and the blowing of bugles was heard, a patrol reported the noise was coming from the thunderous gorge of the River Chania. The undergrowth precluded the use of the 2-inch mortars, so C Company clambered down the steep sides until they saw a Mau Mau hide of several dens cut into the river bank As the soldiers opened heavy automatic fire, Second Lieutenant G.J.B. Edgecombe led the charge. Six Mau Mau were killed and the remainder were captured. Two days later, an Anti-Tanks Platoon of D Company, commanded by Lieutenant Tennent, stumbled on a hide and killed four. After he withdrew, the Harvards of No.1340 Flight and the Reserve Air Wing bombed the area. When police reported to Battalion HQ at Ol Jorok Orok that a gang was in the vicinity, Regimental Sergeant Major White assembled a patrol from the Orderly Room and cornered two. A Reserve Air Wing pilot then dropped a message in a canister to a B Company platoon that seven more Mau Mau had taken refuge in a hippo swamp. During its first week, the Battalion Intelligence Section recorded eighteen killed Mau Mau and nine captured. In Operation Royal Flush, the Battalion spent three weeks patrolling the Gura, Mumwe and Zuti river valleys. In Operation Rhino, launched on 18 June, A Company plus its Kenya Regiment attachments climbed 12,000ft to the Moorlands in four days of persistent rain and found several empty hideouts, from which they salvaged a teapot, a saw and a torch; they then returned to celebrate Coronation Day on the 23rd, an event that was widely marked across Kenya with parades and parties. The overall result of all three operations was minimal.

Tweedie then launched the fortnight-long Operation Buttercup next day with the intention of intercepting food parties coming from the Rwathia Ridge, in the Fort Hall District, to the forest camps, and to invest in loyalist support. Four Buffs from A Company were wounded when a No.3 Platoon section attacked a No.1 Platoon section in error. The lesson re-learnt was that 'talking or making any noise after dark is looking for trouble'. The success rate improved when Second Lieutenant Buxton and four soldiers killed three Mau Mau in an ambush, one of whom was carrying despatches between Mount Kenya and the Aberdares. Then 11 Platoon, usually the Medium Machine Gun Platoon, got lost in thick bamboo and undergrowth, stumbled into a hide and killed three Mau Mau. After four weeks systematically searching caves and river banks, checking treetops and forcing insurgents into ambushes and stop lines manned by the Home Guard and Kenya Regiment, the Rwathia Ridge was secured. The Kenya Regiment had formed a Support Company of Land Rovers mounting 3-inch mortars and Bren guns. During the month, the Devons accounted for fourteen enemy killed, five by C Company, and two captured. Meanwhile, as Lieutenant Colonel Gleadell was handing command of the Devons to Lieutenant Colonel John Windeatt, who had arrived from Iraq, he launched Operation Carnation 1 in response to good intelligence and located five camps eight miles south of the River Gura. Of particular interest was the 'Zuti Roundabout' of converging paths in the forest and bamboo belt overlooking the River Zuti.

Early on 12 July, C Company, commanded by Major Pat Nepean MC, left its base at Konya and, guided by eight trackers and with each man holding the face veil attached to the pack of the man in front, entered the pitch darkness of the forest with the intention of establishing a company base 6,000yds from the forest edge. On patrol, Nepean insisted on silence, and at the end of each day he allocated 30 minutes for the soldiers to erect *bashas* (shelters), using only windfall bamboo. The remaining companies protected the rear of C Company by setting up a platoon base between 3,000 and 5,000yds from the forest edge through which the platoons rotated about every three days. By about 6.00 a.m., C Company reached its first objective of Burnt Village, once a forest workers' camp at a track junction in a clearing. Leaving Lieutenant Peter Graystone and his 8 Platoon as a rearguard, the Company climbed towards a small clearing about 3,000yds to the north-west known as Green Knoll; within 400yds the leading section engaged two Mau Mau skinning a cow on the path but lost them in pursuit. At about the same time, firing was heard from Burnt Village, and Nepean sent a fighting patrol commanded by a sergeant back to investigate. Shots were fired at a man walking along the path toward C Company, but he also disappeared. The sergeant returned, reporting that 8 Platoon had dispersed four Mau Mau driving rustled cattle up the slope from the River Zuti. He also brought a prisoner, one of the rustlers, who had been captured by 8 Platoon hiding in undergrowth. Interrogated by Sergeant John Williams (Kenya Regiment), he divulged that:

- The previous night, he had been in a party of forty Mau Mau who had rustled about 110 cattle.
- Their camp was about three hours walk south-east across the River Zuti and it was occupied by about 300 Mau Mau led by Stanley Mathenge.
- At first light, Mathenge held a muster parade and issued his orders for the day which included occupying several observation posts overlooking the 'Zuti Roundabout'.
- The Roundabout was about 1,000yds north of his camp.
- Mathenge withdrew into the camp perimeter at night – a standard jungle warfare tactic.
- The prisoner was prepared to lead C Company to the camp.

With one of the three top Mau Mau within his grasp, and recognizing that conducting a fire and movement assault in the dense bamboo was out of the question, Nepean split C Company into an Assault Group of five two-man Bren gun teams and five riflemen and two section 'stops', one among the enemy observations posts and the other covering the ford on the track heading south toward the Mau Mau camp. Green Knoll would be the base for the remainder of his Company. The march continued into the night, until Green Knoll was gained at 3.30 a.m., although it was too late to reach the enemy camp by muster parade. C Company moved off 80yds from the track and lay up in the bamboo for the day. Two Brens covered the entry point from the track with orders to fire only at Mau Mau. Intending to attack the next morning, at 7.00 p.m. Nepean instructed the Assault Group and the observation post stop to get into position. At 3.30 a.m. next morning, 14 June, the river stop left with just a mile to cover. As C Company set off at 4.45 a.m. full of confidence, the niggling drizzle of the night had developed into rain, and the troops slipped and slithered down a steep and muddy path toward the ford, catching up with the river stop, who had covered just 500yds. Approaching the southerly track junction of the Roundabout about forty minutes later, smoke seen 30yds from the path turned to be coming from the soaked and freezing Assault Group and observation post stop huddled around a small fire. Soon after leaving Green Knoll, a navigational error in the darkness had left them still two miles short of the Mau Mau camp. With little time left to assault the camp, Lieutenant Colonel Windeatt gave Major Nepean permission to continue with the operation and consolidate at Green Knoll.

At 10.00 p.m. the Assault Group and its observation post stop left camp, crossed the river, struggled up the rain-sodden path and found a sheltered spot to huddle together and generate some warmth. By 4.00 a.m. the Assault Group were inching along the path from the ford toward the camp and froze when three Mau Mau reported by the observation post to have used the ford padded by along the track. When movement was heard to the right and behind them, the soldiers again lay still in the mud. Soon afterwards, when more movement was heard behind them, the Assault Group commander, believing that he was in danger of being compromised, gave the order to fire. While the Bren gunners raked the camp, firing four magazines, and the riflemen, each with 25 rounds, selected their targets, pandemonium erupted, and the Mau Mau, most shaken from their sleep, abandoned the camp in all directions. Nepean regrouped C Company by calling 8 Platoon, and over the next few hours they saturated the forest with patrols, killing three insurgents to add to the eight Mau Mau killed in the attack. Prisoner interrogations over the next months suggested that several others had died from wounds. It seemed the first noise heard came from Mau Mau heading south after meeting Mathenge, and the three leaders had been in the Reserve.

Operation Grouse in Embu and Meru Districts between 10 and 15 July and Operations Carnation 1 and 2 between 12 July and 7 August continued to disrupt Mau Mau activities. In an rare display of Mau Mau aggression in the forest, a Buffs patrol commanded by Sergeant W. Histed were attacked from behind just as they were about to fire on a party ahead. Fortunately, enemy musketry was poor. During Operation

Plover in the Rift Valley between 18 July and 7 August, the Devons forced Dedan Kimathi to move deeper into the forest.

The Buffs continued their success, with A and D Company moving to Charity Farms at night at the end of July and quickly surprising the Mau Mau by their presence. An A Company patrol led by Lieutenant Minto ambushed a gang on the forest edge and then another gang at its hide. Two months earlier, Lieutenant P.O.R. Gatehouse had carried the Queen's Colour at the Coronation Parade and with three soldiers was now following a path used by food carriers. On 3 August he placed two soldiers as 'stops' and the third as a rearguard, while he searched the undergrowth. But as he emerged from the gloom, bending low, he was unfortunately shot in the head by one of the 'stops'. This was about 10.30 am, and not until a Reserve Air Wing saw a soldier frantically waving from a clearing was it realized that was something was wrong. Guided by a tracker, Sergeant Kay and three men from another patrol found Gatehouse being nursed by his men. The density of the undergrowth meant that Kay was unable to organize evacuation, so he sent Private Griggs and a tracker for help. By the time that Lieutenant Tucker RAMC arrived with a stretcher party, it was dark and twelve hours since the officer had been wounded. It took all night to carry him out of the forest to Nyeri Hospital and eventual discharge. After Operation Carnation 2 and several months which tested communications with Battalion HQ, the Buffs concentrated west of the Aberdares near Major General Hickman's Farm not far from Mweiga, in an area similar to the Weald of Kent orchards. Sergeant Dave Currie RAVC joined the MT Section with a train of six mules. The Bedford one-ton lorries were replaced by Morris Commercials, also one-ton but lacking rough ground tyres. An Army Kinema Corporation projectionist showed films. There was the usual turnover of National Servicemen and men going on postings. During the month, C Company lost Colour Sergeant Horswell killed on 18 August in a friendly fire incident, and two privates wounded.

Private R.E. Dixon, a National Serviceman from Oxford, a lad about nineteen, serving with the Buffs, described a 72-hour patrol of Aberdares to his parents. Armed with a Lee Enfield Jungle Carbine, fifty rounds of ammunition in a bandolier and grenades, he thrust his Mark V 7.85-inch bayonet into his jungle boots. After a 20-mile drive from Ol Joro Orok, the section of nine men commanded by their corporal entered the forest:

> We did several patrols in the gorges, horribly thick, tangled undergrowth, very steep and packed with tall, unbelievably, tall trees. On Thursday morning, our section found a Mau Mau hideout, luckily deserted because we should have been wiped out if any natives had been hidden there . . . You can guess how proud we were to have stumbled across this hideout but our pride was short-lived for as soon as we had returned to base camp and had a wash and a meal and were unrolling blankets, we were told to go out again, for as we had found the hideout, so we must return and lay an ambush.

At 9.00 pm, Dixon was on guard:

> 'Solo' – all alone behind a tree; patience – waiting for something, anything, to happen, midst all the noises of the jungle. I could hear an elephant eating and scratching itself; the screeching of a school of baboons; the occasional snorting of a rhino – the sort of noise like the winding of a clockwork monkey. Homework – well, homework that I couldn't leave to do another night or in a 'break' – I had to stay awake and alert, for the lives of myself but of my section depended of my efficiency and good hearing. I couldn't see a single thing except directly in front of me and the crazy-work pattern of the sky away down the mountain and directly above me. Nothing happened during my period of duty, but believe me, I've never been so scared in all my life, and, strangely not of the Mau Mau but of the animals.

Dixon describes how, for him, the night was tense, and when he was relieved, he lay with his rifle in the crook of his arm and hardly slept:

> We waited until it was quite light and found our way back. I knew I had heard queer noises during my period of guard, but seeing the fresh spoor of elephant, rhino and buffalo right outside the ambush only made me realise how very near the danger had been.

Extensive search operations took place in Nairobi, the largest being Operation Ratcatcher, during which 17,000 people were screened by Special Branch between 18 and 31 July.

The insurgency in Meru District had been as severe as anywhere in the Central Province, with 233 loyalists being killed in Mau Mau raids. The village of Chuka in Eastern Province on the eastern slopes of Mt Kenya and about 40 miles north of Meru had remained reasonably peaceful, despite the number of people there in exile from Nairobi. Its headman, Chief Petro Njero, was generally well regarded, although there was still simmering resentment of his support of the 1945 terracing proposal. He had raised a Home Guard and had effectively supported operations in early June, although the district commissioner was concerned that this commitment was diverting labour from the fields. But the KAR had a long history of conflict with local authorities. Generally, KAR morale was satisfactory, although there were lingering grievances over the quality and quantity of rations – in particular, their preference for fresh food over Army compo (composite) rations – and therefore an expectation that local people would supplement their food supply.

In early June, 4 (Uganda) KAR and the Home Guard trapped about 50 insurgents and food carriers on a track alongside the River Thika and killed 34 of them. In mid-June, 5 (Kenya) KAR was conducting operations to disrupt Mau Mau activity south and east of Mt Kenya. Controlling a cordon-and-search sweep in a Special Area near Nyeri was then Acting Major Gerald Griffiths commanding B Company. Aged forty-three, he had been commissioned into the Royal Tank Regiment in 1931, but on being jailed for a serious crime, had had no option but resign. Granted an Emergency Commission in the Durham Light Infantry in October 1940, his offence apparently overlooked when the British Army was re-forming after Dunkirk, he saw active service in the Middle East until evacuated to the UK with battle fatigue. He then moved to Kenya, established a stud farm near Nanyuki and joined the KAR. Under command he had an East African Armoured Car Squadron troop, as well as two 7 (Kenya) KAR platoons: 4 Platoon commanded by Second Lieutenant J.M. Howard and 5 Platoon commanded by Second Lieutenant D. Innes-Walker (Royal Warwicks). The shortage of platoon commanders in the KAR was alleviated by British regiments detaching young officers, many recently commissioned and impressionable. CSM W.P. Llewellyn, who had recently arrived in Kenya, was attached to B Company to gain experience.

At about 7.30 a.m. on 11 June, three Kikuyu forestry workers approached a stop manned by two 7 KAR askaris, who had orders not to open fire unless in an emergency or if ordered to do by CSM Llewellyn. Shortly afterwards, Griffiths arrived in a jeep driven by Captain Joy of the REME, with an escort of two askaris in the back. He asked the two 7 KAR why they had not shot the three men and, after inspecting the workers' *kipendes*, told one to leave because he was too old to kill, then returned their passes to his workmates and told them they could leave too. They had walked about ten yards away when Griffiths emptied a full 30-round Bren magazine into them, then left in his jeep with Joy and Llewellyn. Llewellyn later returned to the scene to find the two workers were both alive and lying in the road gravely wounded. As he diverted traffic, one crawled into the middle of the road, apparently trying to be run over. About half an hour after the incident, Griffiths returned, accused one of the wounded men of shooting his horse in Nanyuki, then shot him in the head with his revolver and again left. Llewellyn was still at the scene when a British officer arrived and instructed him to kill the surviving African, which he initially denied doing but later admitted he had done.

Two days later, Griffiths established a Tactical HQ near Chuka, midway between Embu and Meru. The 7 KAR Commanding Officer, Lieutenant Colonel L.W.B. Evans, had instructed the two subalterns to establish platoon bases and every day for the next week to send two patrols into the Protected Area, where it was thought that the Mau Mau had a training camp. Either an Embu District Officer, Mr Lakin, or Mr Gardner, a Forestry officer, would accompany each patrol. The Chuka Home Guard, which had a good reputation, would patrol the forest fringes and capture any insurgents flushed out by the two platoons. Evans reminded the two officers to assume anyone found in the Prohibited Area was hostile and that, in accordance with standing orders, patrols were not to enter the nearby Kikuyu Reserve Area. On the 14th, Evans, Griffiths, Major Day, who was the 5 KAR second-in-command, and the two subalterns collected two prisoners from Embu Police Station. Both had agreed to act as guides. That evening, Griffiths interrogated them at his Tactical HQ and, grading their answers as unsatisfactory, gave Private Ali Segat his Somali hunting knife to threaten one of them with emasculation. Although Innes-Walker removed the trousers of the terrified man, Segat refused; instead, he amputated his right ear. Innes-Walker, who had accepted Griffiths' instructions without question, left the scene and about fifteen minutes later heard shots. Returning to camp, he learnt that the mutilated prisoner had been shot while 'attempting to escape', which was impossible because he was handcuffed to a tree. Next day, Griffiths instructed Ali to pierce the ear of the second prisoner with his bayonet and feed wire through the wound so that he could be tethered. At some stage over the next two days, this prisoner was also shot while allegedly attempting to escape.

The malaise that had infected B Company became even worse over the next two days. When Chief Petro heard that military operations were planned near the Meru Reserve, he met Griffiths, District Officer Lakin and Forest Officer Gardner and confirmed that his Home Guard would confine its activities to inside the Reserve. Undertaking to supply food to the askaris on the 17th, he delivered one goat, not the three requested, several chickens, sugar cane, maize and bananas to the B Company base. At about 2.00 p.m., a ten-man patrol led by the 5 Platoon Warrant Officer Platoon Commander Kipsigi detained ten armed men about 100yds from the forest edge and ordered them to lay down their weapons, take off their shirts and lie prone on the ground, so that their backs could be checked for Mau Mau tattoos and markings; during the course of this operation they were beaten with rifle butts. When one prisoner sent into the village to fetch beer failed to return, the askaris instructed another to go for maize and sugar cane, with the threat that if he did not return, his colleagues would be shot. In the meantime, three women were raped. At about 4.00 p.m. Innes-Walker interrogated the prisoners, and they were then led into the forest and shot. Griffiths learnt about the killings from one of the subalterns. During the evening, District Officer Collins sent a Tribal Policeman with a message to B Company asking if the missing ten Home Guard had been seen. Chief Petro was in his HQ at about 6.30 p.m. when he heard a short burst of firing from more than one weapon. When one of his headmen then appeared and reported that rumours were spreading in Chuka that the men from the Karigine Home

Tanga, 1914. Captured British officers guarded by African *Schutztruppe* being marched to a prison camp.

First World War. Members of the East African Carrier Corps haul a lorry through a fast-flowing river.

Burma 1944. KAR and their porters.

A Mau Mau gang in the forest.

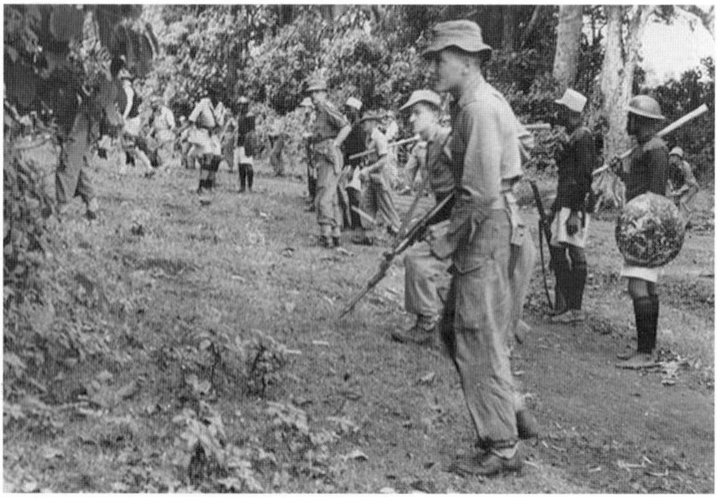

Lancashire Fusiliers and police about to conduct a sweep into thick forest.

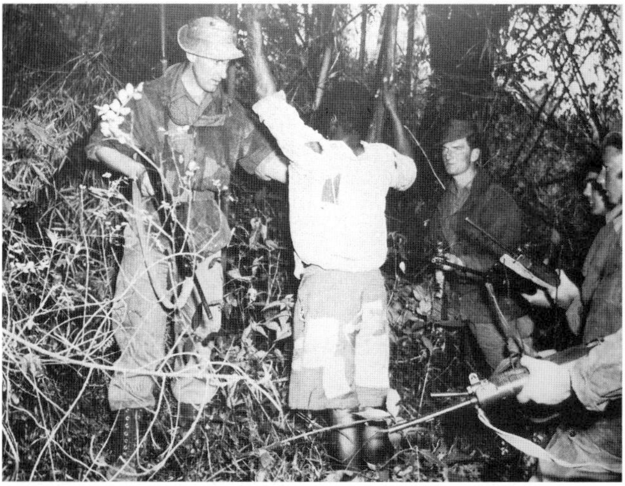

A soldier searches a Mau Mau suspect.

KAR *askaris* guard Mau Mau prisoners.

A Kenya Police Reserve Air Wing Pacer dropping supplies to a patrol.

'Dodd's Field' airstrip at Kikuru. Named in honour of the former Hurricane pilot and Kenya Reserve Police Air Wing pilot, Jimmy Dodds DFM.

A Lincoln bomber flying over the summit of Mt Kenya shrouded by cloud.

A Harvard-2B Trainers 'pancaked' on the runway at RAF Eastleigh. The aircraft sent from Southern Rhodesia struggled in adverse flying conditions, nevertheless they provided useful close support.

1954. A Handley Page Hermes operated by British Aviation Services (Britavia) at Blackbushe Airport, England. The company had been providing passenger and freight services, including trooping to and from Kenya, since 1945.

A Royal Irish Fusiliers sergeant weights a section prior to departure by air. The fusilier on the scales carries a 2-inch mortar.

HMT *Georgic* was one of several troopships that supported British operations and garrisons, including Kenya. Built in 1941, diesel-powered, she had been refloated after being sunk in a German air raid on Port Tewfik, Egypt in 1941.

A Kenya Police officer uses a fingerprinting kit. The kit proved unsuitable in wet conditions. Fingerprinting was a reliable forensic method for suggesting identity.

A Rifle Brigade 'pseudo' patrol flanked by two former Mau Mau, 'Chatterbox' and 'Curly Locks'. The tall figure is Sgt Oulton (Kenya Regiment) (*Hampshire Records Office*).

A combined British troops and Home Guard patrol. The Home Guard are equipped with bows and arrows. Judging by the revolver in a leather holster, the soldier nearest the camera may be Kenya Regiment.

4 (Uganda) KAR on the ranges with Bren light machine guns. While the *askaris* were happy with small arms, they were less confident with mortars (*National Army Museum*).

A King's Own Yorkshire Light Infantryman escorts a butler suspected of being Mau Mau from a farm. The soldier carries a Patchett SMG and wears a windproof smock.

A posed Rifle Brigade patrol. The first two soldiers are armed with 7.62mm SLRs, the third with a Sten gun, the fourth with No 4 Lee Enfield and the fifth with a No. 5 'Jungle Carbine'. The SLRs were introduced during the course of the Emergency.

Members of the Kenya Regiment after a patrol.

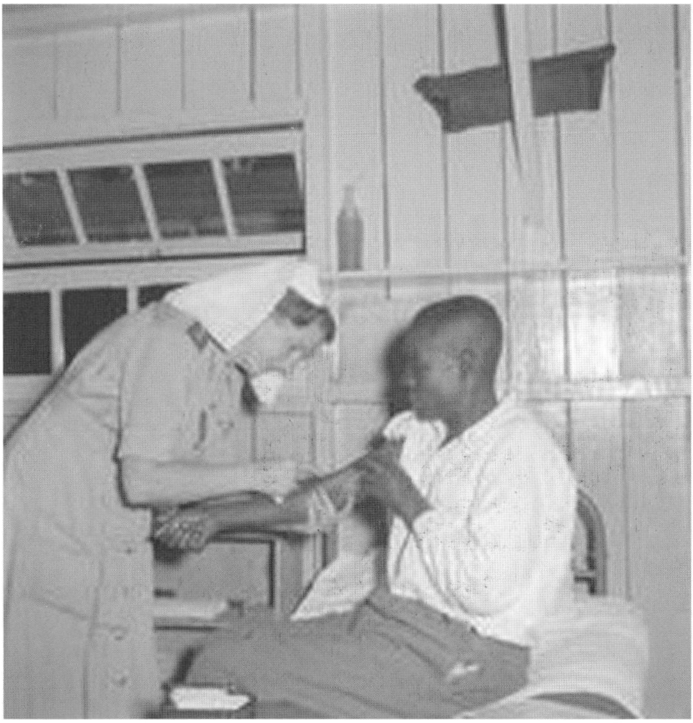

A QARANC officer treats a patient. Army nurses were found in those provincial hospitals with a military ward.

A wounded soldier is unloaded from the only Sycamore helicopter deployed to Kenya.

A feature of National Service was exploiting those with a skill or trade, in this instance, a barber or a soldier who convinced his colleagues he could cut hair.

Sgt Kenneth Yates, 1 Black Watch, and his wife, Madeleine. A veteran of World War Two and Korea, he was wounded in the legs when his lorry crashed in an ambush. Wooden plates were inserted into his shattered knees. (*Courtesy of Christopher Yates*).

Christmas lunch in a forest camp (*Hampshire Records Office*).

The 'School Run' bus for many Service children was a Bedford One-Ton Army lorry. The young girl is Lynn Munro. (*Courtesy of Lynn Wood*).

RASC drivers refill water bowsers from a river.

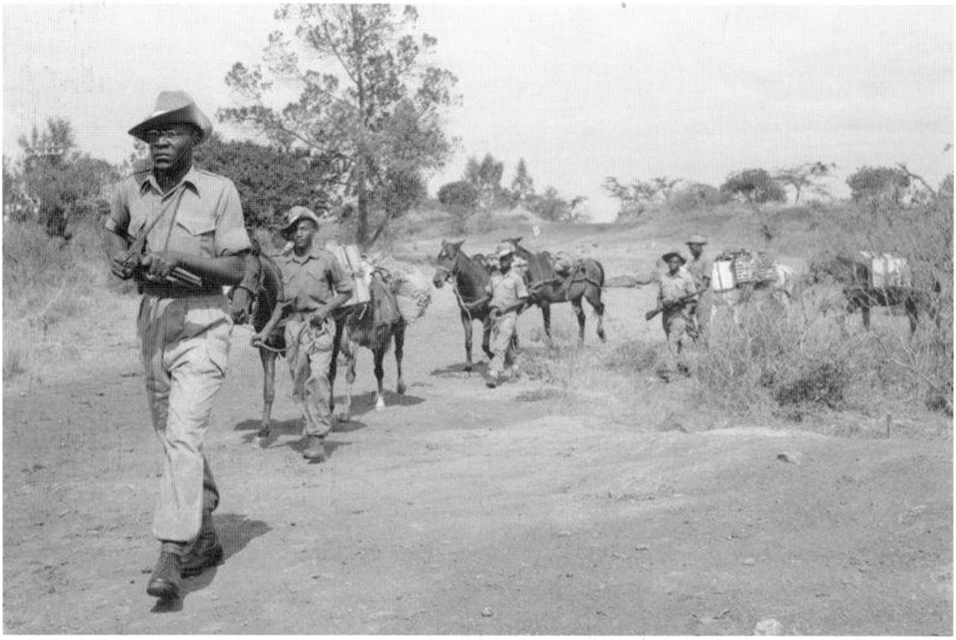

A section of 67 Animal Transport Company, East African Service Corps. Mules and ponies played a crucial role suppling operations between 12,000 and 14,000ft. They often proved far better at negotiation than their handlers.

August 1954. General Erskine (wearing goggles) watching Sergeant Peter Newman and his Buffs patrol conducting operations against a suspected Mau Mau hide near Embu. It was the first time that the general had been able to watch operations. In the foreground in his distinctive field cap is Lt Col Gracey, the CO 1 Buffs.

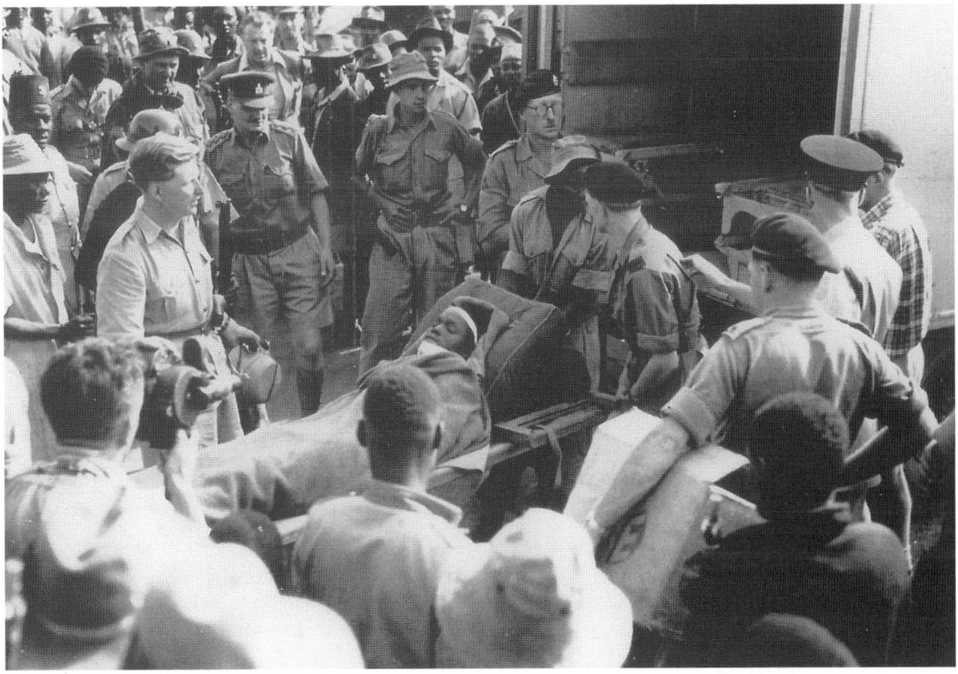

16 February 1954. The wounded General 'China' is loaded into an ambulance at Nyeri for transfer to Nairobi. (*Courtesy of the Military Intelligence Museum*). 1954.

Operation Anvil. A Royal Inniskilling Fusiliers patrol checking identity cards in Nairobi in a period of increased internal security threat.

Ptes Horsely and Green (Royal Army Veterinary Corps) and their Labradors. Both were attached to 1 Rifle Brigade. (*Courtesy of the Hampshire Records Office*).

Late 1954. A patrol equipped with a 7.62mm SLRs. The photo gives an impression of the gloom and density of the bamboo belt.

Home Guard depart from a village in response to a sighting of Mau Mau.

Home Guard and a police officer escort four captured Mau Mau.

Gray Leakey, accompanied by family outside Buckingham Palace, after collecting the VC awarded to his son. Leakey was murdered by the Mau Mau on 13 October 1954.

Nairobi, April 1955. 1 Rifle Brigade march past Governor Baring on leaving Kenya. Military ceremony was deemed important in maintaining civil morale.

Guard 'had been seized by the KAR', Petro advised Collins, who told him not to investigate until B Company had completed its operation. Early next day, the Karigine commander advised Petro of the events the previous day.

Next morning, the two subalterns decided to send three patrols into the forest led by themselves and the 4 Warrant Officer Platoon Commander, Hussein. A fourth patrol of eight askaris and eight porters commanded by Corporal Killis was tasked to fetch water. Hussein left first, followed by Innes-Walker, Howard and Killis, in that order. In spite of Lieutenant Colonel Evans' orders, the three fighting patrols lingered in the Reserve, where some askaris stole money. At about 11.00 a.m., two brothers were in the Mogokulo homestead when about seven African men were escorted into the village. Three people, including one of the brothers, were then conscripted to help search for Mau Mau. The second brother hid. During the afternoon. a man collecting water was returning to the village of Karege when he heard shooting and hid in a coffee *shamba* (enclosure) owned by a teacher. He saw an askari armed with a rifle and fixed bayonet pointing at a group of men taking their shirts off; after being instructed to pick up their bows and arrows, spears and pangas, they were marched into the forest. A soldier who had stolen money from a hut returned to collect the hut's owner, who was sitting outside it with his wife. As Corporal Killis' patrol approached the *shamba* on their way to draw water from the river, they heard a shot from the house where the teacher lived. When the patrol re-entered the forest on the way back to their platoon base, they passed two askaris escorting ten armed men they recognized as being from the Reserve; but when a porter suggested they should be released, the two soldiers replied that they were Mau Mau. As the fighting patrols returned to camp, at about 3.30 p.m., automatic and rifle fire was heard; then Hussein's patrol returned carrying bows and arrows, pangas and a number of severed hands, claiming they had killed several Mau Mau who had failed to stop after being challenged.

Meanwhile, District Officer Collins was investigating the claims. When he met the two KAR platoons reporting they had killed twenty-two Mau Mau, he asked if the victims were actually Home Guard; this was denied. During the day, District Officer William Raymor wrote to District Commissioner (Meru) Arthur Small saying that he believed fifteen Home Guard had been killed by 5 (Kenya) KAR and that post-mortems might be needed. Headmen in the area were also demanding an investigation. District Officer Collins arrived in Chuka to find the town agitated. When Chief Karawa said that several Home Guard had been shot in the Protected Area about a mile from the Coffee Factory, a Home Guard detachment sent to investigate found twelve bodies in a clearing about 100yds from one of the KAR patrol bases. The following morning, Collins received a letter from Second Lieutenant Innes-Walker confirming the earlier report that the two platoons had not run into any Home Guard and that they had killed twenty-two Mau Mau over the previous two days. Next day, Collins and Petro went to the site and found eleven bodies. A twelfth was found near the camp, as was the body of the teacher in the Reserve. Collins reported his findings to Small, and thereafter the matter was referred to the Kenya Police. That afternoon, Assistant Inspector Dennis Prior was taken to ten bodies, which Petro confirmed to be Home Guard; the hands of six had been amputated. On the 21st, Dr Clive Irvine was part of a group that identified and then buried the murdered Home Guards. His conclusion was that most of the first group of ten had been bayoneted and the second group had been shot, as had the teacher. Of the twenty-two dead, one could not be identified. Nineteen left widows, among whom three were pregnant. Forty children were left without fathers. The Government refused to make the affair public.

Suspicious that there had been a serious incident of some sort, Brigadier Cornah ordered that a Brigade court of inquiry be held at Embu on 22 June presided over by Lieutenant Colonel Collins, the 7 KAR Commanding Officer. Witnesses placed blame squarely on the shoulders of the KAR, with District Commissioner Small writing that the Home Guard had been murdered. In his 2005 thesis, Professor Daniel Branch suggests the 'most likely immediate cause' was the KAR belief that Chief Petro had shown disrespect by not providing the three goats requested. In his study, *Fighting the Mau Mau*, Huw Bennett suggests the practice of units competing for the highest number of kills was the primary factor, citing the fact that in his orders to B Company Major Griffiths had instructed that any Kikuyu was to be killed; if the dead person was a government employee or employed by a civilian firm, a panga was to be placed in his hand; and if Home Guard, then his brassard was to be removed. While soldiers from time immemorial have kept details of their kills, as did fighter pilots and ships hunting submarines, in Kenya no distinction was made between Kikuyu and Mau Mau: the bounty for the first kill was usually about £5, which had to be proved either through identification by a police officer or a loyalist or by the provision of an amputated hand for fingerprint analysis. There were no rewards for taking prisoners. Griffiths was paying £5. 5s for every kill. By mid-1953, competition was at its height, with units keeping scoreboards; for instance, at the time of the Chuka massacre, 5 KAR was chasing the 2/3 KAR score of over 100 kills before it deployed to Malaya.

The inquiry's findings were never released, not even to senior Provincial officials; nevertheless, General Erskine wrote to the Chief Native Commissioner and Member for African Affairs on 14 July that no blame could be attributed to the Home Guard. It then became clear that Major Griffiths had coached Second Lieutenant Innes-Walker and that he, in turn, had coached his warrant officer and his patrol.

Such was the impact of the murders that within the week the morale and effectiveness of the Chuka Home Guard collapsed, while support for the Mau Mau skyrocketed and the town became an insurgents' stronghold, with most government officials leaving for fear of attack. In an attempt to keep loyalists on side, in mid-July District Commissioner Small awarded the relatives of the murdered Home Guard £125 (about £2,500 at 2016 values) in compensation. Those involved in the murders were placed under open arrest in Buller Barracks.

As the Royal Military Police Special Investigation Branch began their criminal investigation, their inquiries proved to be so complex and wide-ranging, covering assaults and various other forms of indiscipline, that the detachment was reinforced from the UK. Although corporal punishment in colonial armies had been banned as late as 1946, clips around the ear and jabs with rifle butts on civilians and soldiers were justified by one KAR company commander as being no worse than what he had experienced at school. And herein lay the problem: Kenya had been largely settled by former public school boys brought up on corporal punishment by prefects. Afrikaners in the Kenya Regiment achieved a special notoriety, and the Kenya Police Reserve and the Kikuyu Home Guard gained unenviable reputations as the worst offenders when it came to beating prisoners, so much so that a Parliamentary delegation commented that the scale of brutality and malpractice was threatening confidence in the application of law and order. Early convictions included offences such as:

- Burning the ears of Mau Mau suspects with cigarettes.
- Pouring paraffin over a prisoner and setting him alight.
- Beating a prisoner to death.
- Roasting a prisoner over a fire.
- Committing perjury to secure a death sentence.
- Beating a European who complained of the treatment being given to a prisoner.
- Injuring a prisoner during an interrogation that lasted five days, so that he died.

But before General Erskine could move, he had to re-impose military discipline. In response to a question in the House of Commons in December 1953, the Judge Advocate-General reported that between 20 October 1952 and 1 July 1953 there had been 37 courts martial judging 57 offences, the largest category being allegations of theft. Eleven prosecutions were brought under the 1881 Army Act, Sections 18 (5) and 40, which essentially refer to ill-discipline, in particular assault, but the circumstances were not described. In April 1953, the Swahili newspaper *Baraza* commented that the KPR contained young men who could be described as sadists and who boasted about beating up prisoners. Two Afrikaner Special Branch officers were notorious for committing assaults during interrogations. While the police were bound by legislation, the Home Guard were settling old scores with the Kikuyu, and assaults were sometimes condoned by KPR officers. The lower courts had a reputation for not challenging the collection of evidence. The Minister for Law and Order, John Whyatt, who had experience in Malaya, insisted on either prosecution of or disciplinary measures against any police officer who committed offences while on duty. He was supported by Assistant Commissioner of Police Kenneth Hadingham, who controlled police operations in Nyeri District, and later by the Head of CID, Duncan MacPherson, who arrived in 1954 from the Royal

Hong Kong Police and, as a soldier, had been captured when Hong Kong surrendered to the Japanese in 1941. But Whyatt did not receive the full backing of Governor Baring, who claimed that adherence to the law was secondary to defeating the Mau Mau. In the event, not one person convicted of killing a colonist was ever pardoned or reprieved, while about one third of those convicted of killing Africans were. Judge Arthur Cram, who spent four years as a prisoner-of-war in Germany, arrived with conventional views and left calling Kenya a 'Gestapo state'.

Research by Huw Bennett found that before Erskine arrived there were no instructions for the treatment and disposal of prisoners – remarkable, but symptomatic of the fact that in the Kenyan Armed Forces an officer's word would suffice. Although he realized that summary justice in Kenyan units was resulting in mistreatment and was adversely affecting discipline, Erskine still had the Mau Mau to defeat and needed the support of the Security Forces on his terms. He needed British units to set an example in abiding by international and national law and to recognize that the defence of 'following orders' lodged at the 1946 Nuremberg trials was not acceptable. He therefore circulated a confidential memorandum to all officers in the Army and Police reminding them that a high standard of discipline was expected; he also issued an instruction dated 23 June for all new arrivals:

> It must be clearly understood that the Security Forces under my command are disciplined forces who know how to behave in circumstances which are most distasteful.
>
> I have the greatest confidence in the Army and the Police to uphold their honour and integrity while dealing with the present situation.
>
> I will not tolerate distasteful breaches of discipline leading to the unfair treatment of anybody. We have a very difficult task and I have no intentions of tying the hands of Security Forces by orders and rules which make it impossible for them to carry out their duty – I am a practical soldier enough to know that mistakes can be made and nobody need fear my lack of support if the mistake is made in good faith.
>
> I most strongly disapprove of 'beating up' the inhabitants of

> this country just because they are the inhabitants. I hope that this has not happened in the past. Any indiscipline of this kind would do great damage to the reputation of the Security Forces and make our task settling Mau Mau much more difficult. I therefore order that every officer in the Police and the Army should stamp on at once any conduct which he would be ashamed to see used against his own people. I want to stand up for the Honour of the Security Forces with a clear conscience – I can only do that if I have absolutely loyal support and I rely on you to provide it.
>
> Any complaints against the Police or Army which come from outside sources will be referred to me immediately on receipt and will be investigated either by the Police or by the Army as the Attorney-General and I may, in consultation, direct. There will be full mutual co-operation between the Police and the Army in regard to all investigations and in no circumstances will either deny information or assistance to the other.

East Africa Command instructed that every KAR platoon should have two officers. A month later, GHQ issued Operational Intelligence Instruction No.4 that capturing units should retain captured and surrendered Mau Mau for tactical questioning for 24 (or 72 at most) hours before formally transferring them to the police. The instruction also reminded interrogators that violence seldom produces accurate information. A month later, GHQ Training Instruction No.7 stipulated:

> Under no circumstances will bodies be mutilated, even for identification. Bodies are to be taken to police stations and where the terrain makes this impossible, fingerprints are to be taken.

Thereafter, patrols were issued with fingerprint kits, although they were almost useless in wet conditions. But the colonial powers, civilian and military, regarded Erskine as a threat to their aspirations of retaining Kenya as a white colony. They resisted his measures by sending to the sympathetic Major General Hinde, citing the case of Major R. Sinclair-Scott, of 2/3 KAR, who was alleged to have assaulted an African in January 1953 but escaped punishment because there was no law prohibiting assaults on prisoners. In fact there was a prohibition in Common Law, as well as in Article 3 of the 1949 Fourth Geneva Convention that extended basic rights to protecting non-combatants in internal conflict. Collectively, the KAR felt the inquiries were a waste of time. The Kenya Regiment believed that criticism and 'legal quibbles' hampered operations and that courts martial only confused the rationale of the rules of engagement.

Chapter 8

Consolidation 1953

In July, General Erskine prepared for his third phase by handing over internal security in Fort Hall District to the civil authorities, in order to release the Army to dominate the two Prohibited Areas. But he was hindered by the ramifications of the killings in Meru District. In mid-August, Major Griffiths was transferred to the East Africa Depot and Training Centre and General Erskine relieved Brigadier Cornah and Lieutenant Colonel Evans of their commands. Brigadier J.R.H. Orr took command of 70 (East African) Brigade. Commissioned into the Indian Army, he had seen service in North Africa with the 11th Prince Albert Victor's Own Cavalry (Frontier Force) and then transferred to the Mahrattas. After Partition, he was accepted by the Royal Welch Fusiliers and seconded to the KAR. When General Erskine sought assurances from the two brigade commanders that abuses were not occurring, Orr reminded 70th (East African) Brigade on 8 September that prisoners were to be treated within the law and that killing competitions were to cease. A fortnight later, he issued orders that prisoners were not to be mistreated in the pursuit of intelligence.

So far, operations had largely been unproductive and the intelligence produced had been inaccurate. There were thought to be about 5,000 Mau Mau in the Mt Kenya Prohibited Area and 6,000 in the Aberdares, and while insufficient weapons and the difficulty of procuring food supplies were hindering recruitment, the Passive Wing was passing intelligence of military operations from the assembly of troops. The Militant Wing responded by melting deeper into the forest, knowing that the troops opposing them were not as skilled in forest warfare, were confined to the paths, were noisy when patrolling and then returned to their camps once the patrols had left. Erskine realized that the Mau Mau could not be defeated by military operations alone and wrote to Field

Marshal Harding on 15 August: 'Unless we deal with the fundamental causes which allowed the Mau Mau to grow and prosper, we shall get further trouble in a different form.' Erskine still had too few troops, and when he asked for another brigade, in September, 49 Independent Infantry Brigade began arriving from England with 1 Royal Northumberland Fusiliers and 1 Royal Inniskilling Fusiliers, the first of two Irish battalions to serve in the Emergency. The Brigade had been on the Western Front during the First World War and during the Second had fought in the 1940 Norwegian Campaign, defended Iceland and then landed in Normandy. Its insignia was a polar bear. In 39 Brigade, 1st Black Watch replaced the Lancashire Fusiliers, and 70 Brigade was joined by 3 (Kenya) KAR returning from Malaya. With the equivalent of a division, Erskine could now apply further pressure on the Mau Mau as follows:

- 39 Brigade: East Aberdares, Fort Hall, South Nyeri and Thika
- 49 Brigade: West Aberdares and the Rift Valley
- 70 Brigade: Mount Kenya, Embu, Meru and Nanyuki

When the Devons returned to their hunting ground between the Gura and Mathioya rivers in mid-August, C Company attempted to shield its deployment by moving to Topsham's Farm in lorries; after an evening meal at Konyu, they then marched overnight to Burnt House and immediately sent a platoon to the Zuti Roundabout. On the right of the Battalion were the Buffs and to the south were the Black Watch.

The Black Watch, commanded by Lieutenant Colonel David Rose, arrived fresh from Korea, where between November 1952 and May 1953 it had fought the Chinese at the Hook in a series of vicious winter battles, trying to gain territory before a proposed truce. It had boarded HMT *Empire Fowey* bound for UK but was diverted to Mombasa. The ship had been built in 1936 as the *Potsdam* for the Hamburg-America Line and, after being seized by the British in 1945 as a prize, was refitted as a troopship in Northern Ireland by the Ministry of War Transport and managed by P & O. Among those on board was Major (Archibald John) Earl Wavell, commanding D Company. The son of Field Marshal Archibald Wavell, also Black Watch, he had lost his left hand in Burma in 1943 and had been awarded the Military Cross. Derek Halley was called up in 1952 and had fought at the second Battle of the Hook. Jack Erskine was the son of a Black Watch soldier who had moved the family to Yorkshire, where Jack became an apprentice blacksmith and farrier. On being called up, he insisted on joining the Regiment and served in Korea as an Oxford Carrier Armoured Personnel Carrier driver. The Battalion travelled by train to Gilgil. The skirl of the pipes and drums, and the bands of other battalions, were regularly heard at company locations and were popular at country club events. The fact that the Regiment had men who danced reels greatly impressed the Maasai. A Company was based at North Kinangop, C Company on the Maasai Reserve near the Mau Escarpment and D Company at Meru.

In the meantime, the Kenya Regiment was developing a scheme that would epitomize the Emergency. Derek Erskine had arrived with his sister soon after the First World War and opened a fruit and vegetable shop. After independence he would be knighted for his contribution to Kenya as a non-racial society and he was among the first whites to apply for citizenship. In 1953, his son Francis, a captain, persuaded General Erskine to allow loyal Kikuyu masquerading as Mau Mau to eliminate guerrilla leaders. A key aim was to persuade an intermediary sympathetic to the Mau Mau to facilitate meetings. The concept became known as 'pseudo-gangs'. The first gang, consisting of a disguised European officer and two loyalists, was formed at Squair's Farm. Europeans in the gangs stained their white skin brown, darkened the sclera of their eyes with a solution and wore wigs, cloth hats and ragged, unwashed and greasy clothing such as raincoats or Army greatcoats. An ability to scratch convincingly was also deemed useful.

As the insurgency intensified in 1953, the JAPOIT wobbled under the pressure and this was resolved by attaching Army intelligence officers to Special Branch. Probably the best known was Captain Frank Kitson (Rifle Brigade) who was appointed as the Kiambia District MIO in July 1953. Special Branch in Kiambu consisted of a European police inspector and two African constables. Kitson recalled:

> I had absolutely no idea what it was all about when warned for duty in Kenya and had only gleaned a little understanding of it by the time I arrived one month later. I had been sent as one of seven

> or eight officers to reinforce the intelligence branch of the Kenya Police. Having had no knowledge or experience of anywhere beyond the confines of Europe, I was doubtless considered to be well suited for the task.

He was then quickly given Thika District, an area of forty farms growing coffee, citrus fruit and pineapple, served by an inspector and a constable. He was given a house, which he fortified, at Kamiti on the district border, a Land Rover and several Field Intelligence Assistants (FIA) from the Kenya Regiment; the latter he whittled down to Private Eric Holyoak, who had just turned eighteen and was regarded as too young for front-line operations, and a KPR constable. While those involved in intelligence often exude an air of necessary mystery around their activities, the application of common sense, initiative, inquisitiveness and motivation are crucial. In its simplest form, intelligence aims to transmit information about an enemy in time for a commander to fight a battle. Acceptance or rejection of it is a command responsibility. With little practical experience of the intelligence process, Kitson applied common sense by familiarizing himself with his patch and building a network of informants among police stations, district administrators, Army bases, chiefs, colonists – indeed, anyone prepared to pass the time of day with him. By Christmas, he had three FIAs in Kiambu District and two in Thika District and was briefing District Operational Committees. Kitson initially believed that his intelligence organization was 'marginally useful', which is hardly surprising given the short time he had been in Kenya.

The Kenya Intelligence Committee followed the Special Military Intelligence Unit (Malaya) by replacing the JAPOIT with the Operational Intelligence Organisation Unit to improve intelligence flow for the Army. Within four months of the system being introduced in Malaya, the SMIU had discovered the location of Ching Pen, the communist leader, forcing him to seek safe haven in Thailand. Seven Military Intelligence Officers (MIO) eventually arrived, each supported by an FIA from the Kenya Regiment. In addition to supporting Special Branch, they also liaised with other intelligence assets, including Field Security counter-intelligence, document intelligence, interrogations and air photographic interpretation, and relevant information was disseminated in single-subject Intelligence Reports, multi-page Intelligence Summaries and specialist Supplementary Reports. The Intelligence Corps provided two MIOs, with Major A. Parry proving successful in Nanyuki. A 'three-legged' structure was adopted, with intelligence committees at District, Provincial and Executive level.

In mid-1953, when Erskine rested the Kenya Regiment because it had been on continuous active service since October 1952, it moved to Naivasha, where it was reduced from seven companies to four, the members of the disbanded companies redeploying as liaison officers, interpreters, intelligence staff, scouts and guides among the British battalions.The Kenya Regiment commanding officer, Lieutenant Colonel Guy Campbell, later wrote in his *The Charging Buffalo* (1986) that, 'The Kenyan's incentive was that he was fighting for his home, way of life and the country he loved.' The Mau Mau would probably have accepted their sentiments were the same. He also claims that the strength of the regiment should not have been reduced because it could have brought the Emergency to an end quicker by harrying and destroying the gangs. He does not suggest how the backbone of the Mau Mau, the Passive Wing, could have been destroyed.

By the end of 1953, the Administration had recognized the value of clandestine operations, and the police formed Special Force Teams to work with Special Branch in eliminating specific Mau Mau leaders and their gangs. The possibility of encountering Security Force patrols, and the inclination of the police to shoot first, led to Police HQ issuing these orders:

> No pseudo-gang should be carried out during the hours of daylight in settled areas of the Reserves, if the object could equally well be achieved by an operation carried out at night . . . In the event of pseudo–gang being encountered and unable to retire, the patrol leader will establish his identity by word of mouth or removal of his disguise.

David Drummond was born in Nairobi in 1932 and trained as a surveyor and engineer. Enlisting in the KPR in 1952, he was posted to Wanjoh District, where his fluency in Swahili and his bushcraft, learned from a Kikuyu hunter, were invaluable. Now known as 'Bwana Drum', he recruited a grocer as an informer, formed a Police Special Force Team and tracked a gang led by Harun Njeroge to forested high ground west of Nakuru. Taking advantage of a diversion caused by a young sentry being beaten on his backside for some misdemeanour, the team edged close to the camp, but were spotted. As a sentry raised his gun, Drummond shot him in the legs and then dived for cover as a grenade slowly toppled through the undergrowth but did not detonate. Harun was not in the camp, but Drummond learnt several days later that he was staying on the outskirts of Nakuru; he burst into Harun's hut, but his quarry floored him with a punch and escaped into the forest. Drummond married in June 1953 and, after receiving threatening letters from Harun, realized that his grocer was passing information to a Mau Mau running an extortion and protection racket. Drummond sent messages challenging Harun to traditional single combat, but they remained in Mau Mau dead letter boxes unanswered. After a short spell in hospital, Drummond was persuaded by Captain Cooper to join the Kenya Regiment Intelligence Force (I Force), a proposal he at first found preposterous; nevertheless, he warmed to the idea and, teaming up with another police reservist, Jim McNab, he recruited five former Mau Mau. On operations, one pseudo was charged with deflecting close attention to the Europeans; on one occasion, a girl made a heavy pass at Drummond, until put off by his escort, who told her that he had venereal disease. Drummond also targeted Captain 'Jimmy', who led 100 Mau Mau in Mt Londiani in the northern Rift Valley. By now he had so thoroughly adopted the 'jungle code' that he once allowed his own men to beat him for a security lapse. Information collected by I Force enabled Drummond and his pseudos to meet a Mau Mau foraging party, who took them to 'Jimmy's' camp, where they took an oath and joined his gang. But their disguise was breached when a pseudo-gang member mentioned a name that spooked the Mau Mau so seriously that they quickly disappeared into the forest.

Second Lieutenant R.J. Horton joined B Company, 4 (Uganda) KAR in Fort Hall District in August and for the next three months was deployed with two platoons at Fort Winchester, at the end of tracks through the bamboo belt of the Aberdares. He described the fort as a 'hillock cleared of bamboo surrounded by ditch of bamboo *punji* sticks [spikes]'. The bamboo belt was patrolled by elephants. Fort Winchester was at about

12,000ft, and soldiers first had to acclimatize to the thin air and cold nights. The mountains were sometimes bathed in sun, but low cloud, rain and drizzle meant the soldiers were cold and wet most of the time, the only protection being a ground sheet rigged as a tent over a shallow trench, and a greatcoat. The food was compo rations of bacon and hard, dry biscuits. In the centre of the position was a radio aerial strapped to length of bamboo providing the only link with the outside world. Re-supply was by KPRAW aircraft dropping supplies packed by the Air Despatch Detachment of thirty RASC attached to 37 Supply Depot EAASC at Karawa. After a visit from the Director of Supplies and Transport, the soldiers were attached to the KPRAW as despatchers. With the rear seats removed, the Tri-Pacers could deliver a total of 300lb, usually dropped as ten packages from a maximum height of 10,000ft. Despatch involved keeping the door open with the right leg and then placing as many packages on it before a shout or a shoulder tap was the signal to release the consignments. The aim was to deliver six packs per day. Two Cessna-180s could deliver 600lbs. When the weather was too poor for drops, the troops simply went hungry. Water was extracted from bamboo shoots. With a half-platoon providing the defence, the second platoon patrolled, often to the snow line. Since breathing was difficult at this altitude, turns were taken to carry radios and Bren gun. The platoons took part in several attacks. In one, a guide tethered to the wrist of an officer led the patrol through thick forest until it gave way to moorland. When shots were fired from bamboo ahead, the askaris spread out into the fire and movement tactic of the period, but by the time they reached the enemy position, the Mau Mau had melted into the forest with their wounded. The KAR lost the guide and a Bren gunner killed, and the officer was wounded. The Mau Mau camp was searched, and a home-made rifle was later handed to the Battalion Intelligence Officer.

Also crucial to re-supply at heights ranging from 12,000 to 14,000ft were the ponies and mules of 67 Animal Transport Company, East African Army Service Corps carrying loads reduced from 160lbs to 100lbs of food, water, ammunition, radios and their forage. As with the soldiers, it took several days for the animals to acclimatize to the height and the terrain. The accepted belief was that a loaded mule or pony could not negotiate a really steep slope, but in the western Aberdares a section reached in four hours the top of an escarpment that men were unable to climb without using their hands – admittedly, with the ends of the animals' horseshoes bent to form studs. In due course, a section of twelve animals was attached to each battalion. They travelled in four lorries with their saddlery and fodder for seven days. During September, the *Daily Herald* was one of several tabloids that resurrected the 'kills' issue by alleging that the Devons were being paid for every Mau Mau killed. The editor highlighted the fact that the Regiment was known as the Bloody Eleventh, but made no mention that this commemorated its gallantry at the Battle of Salamanca in 1812 during the Peninsula War. The socialist *Daily Herald* asked the parents of soldiers serving in Kenya, 'Is Your Son a Murderer?' The question has frequently resonated since. The pacifist MP Fenner Brockway raised the issue in the House of Commons. It seems most likely that the source was a Wessex Brigade second lieutenant attached to the Devons who had been convicted at a court martial of failing to carry out a patrol, and in revenge had circulated a copy of the Battalion periodical, *Semper Fidelis*, in which Lieutenant Colonel Gleadell offered £5 for the first Mau Mau to be killed. Not for the first and certainly not for the last time would attention-seeking editors in safe London offices demand sensationalism at the expense of reality. Several angry soldiers raised the allegations with Richard Crossman MP when he visited Kenya in January 1954; nevertheless, the damage done in Kenya to the credibility of the British Army has resonated in most post-1945 campaigns.

Screening is a standard counter-insurgency tactic. In Kenya, its purpose varied according to whether it was done by the Administration, the police or the military. The Administration needed information and evidence in order to prosecute those associated with the Mau Mau and rehabilitate those who either did not support or had rejected the organization; while military intelligence needed information of use to the conduct of military operations. A useful by-product was the recruitment of willing, and perhaps sometimes not so willing, individuals as agents and sources. The standard method of cordon and search was for the military to isolate the target area to enable the police, not infrequently helped by the Home Guard, village chiefs and hooded informants, to make their arrests. But some screeners achieved a reputation for brutality and failed to recognize that there was no need for assault during interrogation. Those selected for further questioning were usually moved to Government-run detention camps, where credible accounts of torture and mistreatment still resonate today. The Army sent a few Field Intelligence Assistants to act as collators and recorders alongside interrogators, who were known as 'crackers'.

To facilitate operations, the Public Works Department used prison labour to hack five tracks into the forest of the Aberdare Mountains in mid-August. Forward operating bases were established in a series of simple forts at both ends, enabling deep penetration patrols, food denial operations and obstruction of the connection between the Militant Wing and Passive Wing in the Reserves. After the tracks had proved their value for the first time on Operation Primrose between 10 and 27 August, Erskine instructed that twenty more be built. This resulted in 39 Corps Engineer Regiment with 72 and 72 Squadrons and 74 Field Park Squadron arriving from Ripon to speed up the process. Lieutenant Colonel C.J. Godfrey was appointed Commander, Royal Engineers. In due course, the Royal Engineers would be involved in constructing 260 miles of road in the Aberdares and 403 miles in the Mt Kenya Prohibited Area. They also provided field engineering support to the tented camps.

Thomas Askwith, a double rowing blue and competitor in the 1932 and 1936 Olympic Games, arrived in Kenya in 1936 as a District Commissioner. Appointed in 1945 as Commissioner of Community Development and Principal of Jeanes School, Kabete, a training establishment for African colonial development officers, he recognized the inevitability of social change in Africa and so promoted community development, encouraged women to take up roles in society and argued strongly against segregation. The Emergency came as no surprise to him, because he had predicted that economic and social pressures would generate a generational split among the Kikuyu. Baring sent him to Malaya in June 1953 to visit detention and rehabilitation camps and assess their impact on the community. When he returned to Nairobi in August, Baring appointed him Permanent Secretary in the Ministry of African Affairs, with a remit to adopt a similar system. Two months later, Askwith submitted a socio-economic and civic reform strategy based around a continuous process of screening and collection of intelligence that he named 'The Pipeline'. The system allowed for Mau Mau suspects to float between three grades of detention camp, most of which were outside Central Province:

- 'Black' (Z1): known or proven association and hard core. Interned in detention camps.
- 'Intermediate or Grey' (Y1): possible association. Although oath-takers, compliant and could be sent to work camps in their local districts before release. Rehabilitation included lectures by Christian organizations teaching moral values.
- 'White' (Y2): no known association with the Mau Mau and suitable for repatriation to the Reserves.

Askwith planned for the Pipeline to handle 20,000 suspects. Detention camps were the responsibility of the Commissioner of Prisons, with one objective being 'moral education'. Formal training began in 1955. Under Emergency Regulations, a variety of offences committed in camps, such as theft, spitting or disrespect to staff, could result in solitary confinement and a reduced diet. Mutiny or assaulting staff could result in corporal punishment (twelve strokes) or solitary confinement on bread and water. Prisoners could also be made to work. Most of the fifteen detention camps were located outside Central Province and were managed by temporary district officers. A substantial number of the 14,000 warders had formerly served in pioneer battalions in Egypt. Little thought was given to the siting and layout of the camps, and this led to overcrowding, insanitary conditions, malnutrition and disease. The organization of forced labour was near-chaotic. During prisoner transfers, food, water and sanitation were either limited or non-existent. Hola Camp held the most militant. The internment of several thousand women and girls in Kamiti Camp led to dozens of babies being born in captivity. Appeals for clothes and bedding to replace dirty sacking and blankets were frequent. Unaccompanied boys were held in Wamumu Camp, although thousands seem to have been detained in adult camps. As the conditions and regimes in the camps became progressively more brutal, Askwith became highly critical of them and was eventually dismissed when he suggested the government should act more humanely.

Meanwhile, the battle-hardened Black Watch were finding that the Mau Mau avoided contact by melting into the forest. Animals also posed a problem. Corporal Halley leading his section on a three-day patrol came to a clearing containing about twenty elephants and half a dozen calves. Paying no attention to their African tracker, who spoke only Swahili, the soldiers began to cross the clearing; a female then charged when they approached several calves, and they were chased down the slope into the shelter of the forest.

It soon became apparent that the Harvards were unsuitable for close support because they lacked the power to climb out of difficulties and were therefore unable to attack small groups of Mau Mau spotted, for instance, by the KPRAW. In October, Prime Minister Sir Winston Churchill instructed the Chief of the Air Staff to offer Middle East Air Force an Avro Lincoln B-2 bomber squadron to support operations in Kenya. In early November, General Erskine received a glowing report from General Templer in Malaya of the value of air power in a jungle setting. Within eight days, on 5 November, No.49 Squadron, a bomber squadron since 1938, arrived at RAF Eastleigh with eight Lincolns, 24 aircrew and 37 ground crew, having flown from RAF Wittering on the first of two monthly rotations involving Nos.100, 61 and 214 Squadrons. The Lincoln was similar in appearance to the Lancaster and had the ability to carry up to 14,000lb of bombs; it was equipped with two M2 50 Browning machine guns and either an M2 or twin 30mm Hispano cannon in the dorsal turret and had an aircrew of seven: a pilot, flight engineer/co-pilot, navigator, wireless operator, front gunner/bomb aimer, dorsal and rear gunners. The counter-insurgency role of bombers was to impose such conditions on the ground that staying in the forest was not an option, specifically by:

- Reducing the morale of the Mau Mau.
- Spreading disaffection and inducing desertion.
- Driving the insurgents from the forest into the open.
- Breaking up gangs.

Command and control of the Air Wing remained at the Joint Operations Centre at GHQ. Blind bombing was restricted by the rainy seasons and was restricted to daylight. Ignoring the extensive experience of the KPRAW pilots during the Second World War, No.49 Squadron commented that since none were serving pilots the RAF were thus ‘in the invidious position of having to rely entirely on this organisation for the success and conduct of its operations’. Although the ‘find’ and ‘fix’ elements of a system that became known as ISTAR (Information, Surveillance, Target Acquisition and Reconnaissance) existed, the RAF struggled to 'strike' because high-level intelligence co-ordination was lacking. It was not unknown for information collected by Army patrols or during interrogations to take up to two months to reach the bombers, by which time it was inaccurate. Initially, there was no air photographic capability, and planning was therefore reduced to using maps. Fortunately, the Mau Mau had no air defence, and no losses suffered by the RAF could be attributed to enemy action.

Erskine discarded the largely unproductive forest sweeps and used bombers to drive the Militant Wing from their camps into the Reserves. Bombing usually took place either in the early morning before the afternoon build-up of clouds and turbulence, or at night. Typical bomb loads were five 1,000lbers and nine either 500lb bombs or 350lb cluster bombs. The 1,000lbers could create craters 12ft deep by 25ft wide, damaging anything with 80yds of the centre and hurling spoil up to 100yds away. But the unreliability of some bombs sent to Kenya meant, initially, that the Lincolns flew to RAF Khormaksar in Aden to bomb up and bomb, before returning to RAF Eastleigh. Typically, a marker aircraft, often from the KPRAW, would pinpoint the target. Although bombing jungle in Burma and Malaya had not proved particularly successful, because shattered trees still provided shelter, negotiating wrecked forest became difficult and the risk from stampeding, injured and distressed animals increased. On Boxing Day 1955, 49 Squadron dropped a string of bombs on a Mt Kenya Mau Mau hideout from 13,000ft because Army patrols were operating above that height. Below was a Royal Inniskilling Fusilier company commanded by Major Terry Troy in ambushes designed to catch Mau Mau using game tracks as they fled from the chaos:

> The soldiers lying in wait were suddenly and frighteningly faced by very enraged animals charging down the game tracks as they fled the bombing. Impressed as they were by the accuracy of the RAF bombing, the soldiers' language, as they hurled themselves off the tracks deep into the surrounding undergrowth, was highly expressive.

In December, Erskine assured Churchill that the Lincolns had become vital to military operations and that intelligence was indicating that bombing had:

- Lowered insurgency morale.
- Forced insurgency gangs to relocate from the forest.
- Raised Security Force morale because the fight had been taken to the deepest and most difficult to reach parts of the forest.

As part of Psychological Operations (Psy Ops) strategy, voice aircraft (planes equipped with loudspeakers) and word of mouth began spreading the notion that any Mau Mau wishing to surrender should present themselves at a Security Forces base carrying green branches. This became known as the Green Branch strategy.

The MI6 Information Research Department was responsible for the development of Psychological Operations in the Commonwealth after the Second World War, as a counter-measure to the spread of aggressive Soviet and Chinese Communism. The US Department of Defense defines Psy Ops as:

> Planned operations to convey selected information and indicators to foreign audiences to influence their emotions, motives, objective reasoning, and ultimately the behaviour of foreign governments, organizations, groups, and individuals. The purpose of psychological operations is to induce or reinforce foreign attitudes and behavior favourable to the originator's objectives.

Today, the British Ministry of Defence defines it more simply as a method of persuading 'the enemy, or other target audience, to think and act in a way which will be to our advantage'. There are essentially two types:

- 'White' Psy Ops state the facts. This is the preferred option because untruths can discredit.
- 'Black Psy Ops' broadcast believable information.

In the language of Psy Ops, the good guys (colonists and loyal Africans) were 'white' and 'enlightened', while the bad guys (the Mau Mau) were 'dark', 'secretive' and 'degraded'. Inevitably, the press cashed in by juxtaposing white heroism with black savagery. The media initially focused on Kenyatta's pre-war visits to the Soviet Union and the widely-held, but mistaken, belief that he led the Mau Mau. Once the error was recognized, operations focused on discrediting the Mau Mau as barbaric pagans who used bestial oaths to enforce secrecy and obedience. To some extent, it was colonist Psy Ops that undermined indigenous practices. The *New York Times* reported the Mau Mau to be frustrated and savage people mentally and economically unable to adjust to the swift pace of civilization. Propaganda newspapers such as *The True News* branded the Mau Mau as thugs, murderers and bandits. Methods of delivery in Kenya included the distribution of wirelesses to village chiefs, a Valetta freighter conducting leaflet drops and the East African Communication Flight Auster AOP-6 and a Pembroke fitted with loudspeakers as voice aircraft. Generally the Voice aircraft flew at about 2,000ft broadcasting pre-recorded messages in a variety of African languages. During an engagement in Thika District in which a Pys Ops loudspeaker van attracted considerable fire, a prisoner told Captain Kitson that troops had stumbled on a Central Committee escort handing over several recruits from Nairobi to the Militant Wing. There had been no intelligence about the transfer and thus the interception was sheer good luck.

October saw a significant rise in violence and intimidation in Central Province by marauding Mau Mau gangs. On one occasion, Captain Kitson watched as a gang evaded a police and Black Watch cordon by filtering through a thick coffee plantation. The following day, another gang retreating towards Fort Hall lost ten killed. One of several prisoners cracked under police interrogation and divulged substantial information about the Aberdares Mau Mau. During the course of these operations, Sergeant George Hales, a Fort Hall FIA, and a group of Kikuyu soldiers in civilian clothes on patrol outside the Aberdares Prohibited Area were chatting to several African farmers, when about 200 insurgents led by General Kago emerged from the forest. An inspirational leader, Kago had defied the defensive strategy ordered by Kimathi. Knowing that he would be killed if he was spotted, Hales dodged behind a bush; in his absence, the insurgents believed that his men were also Mau Mau and came over for a brief amicable conversation before returning to the forest. Hales and his patrol then hurried to the nearest security post and arranged for Kago to be pursued. At the time, Captain Kitson was searching for methods of collecting information, and when he heard of the encounter he was struck by the ease with which Hales and his men had escaped detection; unaware of the Kenya Regiment pseudo-gangs, he began investigating the use of a similar system to collect intelligence.

Studies in Malaya and Kenya concluded in November 1953 that Militant Wings gangs were detecting and avoiding patrols and ambushes because of troops' poor track discipline, the noise they made in the forest and the lack of trackers. Captain Kitson claimed that 'of all the specialist activities relevant to the prosecution of a counter-insurgency campaign, none is more important than the provision of trackers'. This was particularly relevant in Kenya, where good tracking became a battle-winning weapon. The report led to East Africa Command persuading the Game Department and new National Parks Department to release several game wardens on Emergency Service to lead African scouts and trackers enlisted into the KPR. Trackers were divided between forest dwellers, such as Kikuyu and Ndorobo, and savannah peoples, for example the Samburu and Maasai. Among those recruited were Game Warden George Adamson of *Born Free* fame, who worked with two British battalions in the Aberdares in December 1953 and January 1954 before returning to northern Kenya to lead a detachment of mounted police and trackers supporting KAR operations intercepting Somalis smuggling weapons to the Mau Mau. Fred Bartlett tracked Mau Mau collecting supplies from squatters on farms. Game Warden Jack Sim led 'Sim Force' of ten Kenya Regiment soldiers and several Game Department trackers. The Kenya Regiment had already formed the 'Tracker, Kenya Regiment' of about 1,500 trackers split between forest and savannah tribes historically hostile to the Kikuyu. About 20 per cent were loyalist or turned Kikuyu, Embu and Meru. Major Rodney Elliott formed the Tracking School at Nanyuki to test the skills of potential African trackers and to give British officers sufficient knowledge to enable them to manage trackers on patrol or in quick reaction forces organized by Company HQs. Elliott was a wartime Parachute Regiment officer now employed by the Game Department. He had returned to Kenya from grouse shooting in Scotland and formed a tracker section of forest-dwellers that regularly followed Mau Mau in the Mt Kenya Prohibited Area. A 55-year old former farm manager, Sergeant Jim Tooley (Kenya Regiment), who had been raised among the Kipsigis and had learnt to hunt, trap and collect honey, recruited some of his trackers from Mau Mau prisoners. Erskine promoted the use of trackers by instructing the three brigade commanders that, since ambushes and patrols were having limited success because they were being detected, it was now time to find the Mau Mau and attack their camps; therefore each British battalion was to form a 30-strong tracking platoon segregated by tribe, except on operations, by July 1954. However, British officers in the KAR battalions believed that their soldiers naturally possessed tracking skills. Elliott proposed that Tracker Combat Teams (TCT) should consist of a three African trackers, a British officer, a Bren team, a rearguard of three soldiers and an experienced NCO to take command if the officer was killed or badly wounded. Each man was equipped with two No.36 grenades. Included in the team was a tracker dog, an infantry patrol dog and their Royal Army Veterinary Corps handlers. In dry conditions, tracker dogs can follow spoor that is days old; however, their efforts were so intense that their concentration only lasted about half an hour and they then needed a twenty-minute rest. At best, dogs can track for six hours in a twenty-four period. Several factors limit their performance:

- Heat and low humidity, causing scent to evaporate quickly.
- Scent being carried away downwind.
- Heavy rain dispersing scent.
- Extremely rugged terrain, which exhausts dogs.
- Dry ground, which does not preserve scent.

Infantry patrol dogs can give early warning of people in the area, usually by listening for them and/or detecting scent carried on the wind, then ‘pointing’ by raising the head, wagging the tail and displaying a keenness to investigate. One factor that had to be taken into consideration when using dogs was food. Eventually, British infantry companies were supported by a tracking section of one or two Kenya Regiment NCOs and six African trackers. The Service records of trackers were later destroyed to prevent revenge attacks on them.

After the Army Legal Service had concluded there was evidence of crimes involving Major Griffiths, a psychiatrist sent by the War Office to investigate if a recurrence of 'battle fatigue' was a factor concluded that, while he was 'not a normal man', he was fit to stand trial. Believing that convicting an officer would send a clear message to East Africa Command and to loyalist Kikuyu that Security Forces' ill-discipline would not be tolerated, Erskine informed the War Office on 23 October that he intended to court-martial Griffiths for his involvement in the murders of the two forest workers. Three days later, Griffiths was promoted to substantive major. In November, he was acquitted because some evidence was less than frank and there had been 'improper admission of hearsay defence' in the identification of a victim. Although this was a victory for those objecting to the tightening of discipline, Erskine nevertheless kept the defendant in Kenya while alternative charges were investigated. Meanwhile, the British press, from the comfort of their Fleet Street offices, were printing lurid accounts of score cards, bounties for 'bagged' Mau Mau and amputation of hands to aid identification. Colonist concerns focused on the belief that inquiries would demoralize and jeopardize the loyalty of officers and soldiers; therefore, they believed, there was no reason to change the strategy of bludgeoning the Kikuyu into submission.

On 3 December, an inquiry investigated the murders by WOPC Hussein's patrol, while the SIB opened an investigation into beatings by 7 KAR. Two days later, after a conference of Army and Police ranked lieutenant colonel and above and their equivalents, Erskine asked the War Office to appoint a formal court of inquiry into the conduct of the Mau Mau campaign. In his letter to the War Office, Erskine made this candid admission:

> There is no doubt that in the early days, i.e. from Oct 1952 until last June, there was a great deal of indiscriminate shooting by Army and Police. I am quite certain prisoners were beaten to extract information.

On the 10th, two Kenya Regiment sergeants were jailed for assaulting an African and burning his house, a sure sign that Erskine was enforcing military discipline.

After weeks of hostile questions in Parliament, the Government announced two days later that Lieutenant General Sir Kenneth McLean would chair the inquiry and that it would focus on three principal issues: rewards for kills; scoreboards of official and unofficial kills; and the promotion of unit cohesion by the number of kills. McLean had enlisted as a private during the First World War and was commissioned into the Royal Engineers in 1918. During the Second World War, he was heavily involved in Operation Overlord, the D-Day landings in Normandy, and then held senior staff appointments in Occupied Germany, HQ Far East Command, HQ Middle East Command and, since 1951, as the War Office Chief Staff Officer. He was nearing retirement. Secretary of State for War Anthony Head hoped that the inquiry would result in 'a clean-up rather than to cover up'. General Erskine warned that all ranks were to co-operate. Meanwhile, Major General Richard Goodbody (late Royal Artillery), who commanded 56 (London) Division TA, had arrived in Kenya to prepare for the inquiry and was collecting information from 5 and 7 KAR.

On 12 December McLean opened his inquiry at Buller Barracks and over the next twelve days heard evidence on oath from 147 witnesses, mostly officers ranked from second lieutenant to major. Lieutenant Colonel John Windeatt, commanding 1 Devons, told the McLean Inquiry that he considered 'a lot of fuss was being made out of nothing'. McLean concluded that while the Chuka affair may have constituted irregularities in procedures by some units, the conduct of the British Army in Kenya 'under difficult and arduous circumstances, showed that measure of restraint backed by good discipline which this country has traditionally expected'.

When intelligence emerged in December that Field Marshal Dedan Kimathi intended to meet General Kassam Njogu (Patrick wa Njogu) in a cave in the North Mathioya valley at the foot of Mt Kinangop, HQ 39 Brigade developed a plan for the Lincolns to bomb the valley and for a Devons patrol and a guide/informer to lead Second Lieutenant Peter Roberts to the cave to collect intelligence. As the Lincolns appeared, on a clear morning, a KPRAW Tri-Pacer dropped a phosphorous grenade as a marker. But Roberts had encountered extremely bad going and was well short of the cave, and to Brigadier Tweedie's displeasure it was not until next morning that the patrol reached the area, only to find that their route through the valley was blocked by rocks and rubble thrown up by the bombing. A Black Watch patrol later captured two Mau Mau, who said that the cave had been hit and several insurgents had been killed.

Meanwhile, the failure to trap the marauding Kago was affecting morale in Thika District. The Black Watch were working with the KPR. Shortly before Christmas, Security Forces were pursuing about sixty Mau Mau who had beheaded a headman near Thika. On 23 December, Major Archibald Wavell summoned the Pipes and Drums to help, and by next day, Christmas Eve, the gang had been trapped in a copse. Piper Harry Ellis recalled:

> All he [Wavell] had was a revolver and he said, 'Right, we're going down into a thicket down there, a sort of a valley. And we're going down. We've got a gang of Mau Mau trapped. The police have got them trapped. We're all going to go down.'
>
> We got in the back of the truck with our rifles. And we were sent up on the railway to look down. And he moved forward with all the – about ten guys – just with a pistol. That's all he had. We moved forward and I heard a Patchett [submachine gun] you know, tat, tat, tat, that's what a Patchett sounded like and I saw him falling. Later on, they came round with the food, it was in the morning by this time, and they brought the food along the railway track. 'What's happened?' 'Major Wavell's been killed.' It was so demoralising you know. A great soldier like that. But very brave.

After dark, Police Reserve District Commander Peter Dean, who was commanding the operation, used burning petrol to flush the gang into the open but was shot when he was silhouetted by the flames. During the night, the Mau Mau found a weak link in the cordon, killing two sleeping police officers and disappearing into the security of the forest gloom. When two hides of the gang were located on Boxing Day, Harvards dive-bombed and machine-gunned them, and this was followed by troops conducting a sweep into the forest. Twenty-three Mau Mau were killed. Meanwhile, a police raid in Nairobi had found printed orders from Dedan Kimathi ordering increased attacks over the Christmas period, with a bounty of £7.10 shillings offered for each European killed and £3.9 shillings for each loyal African. Nyeri was tense after reports of infiltrations from the Aberdares. The Tanganikya Police detained 640 Kikuyu in its Northern Province following a Mau Mau attack on a loyalist Kikuyu family.

There is no doubt that the first ten months of the Kenya Emergency constituted an unsavoury period of British post-war military history and opened the door to criticism that has resonated since. There were several reasons: Middle East Land Forces took little interest in operations, largely because it was focused on the departure from Egypt and events elsewhere in the Middle East, to some extent not surprisingly since there were other more pressing matters affecting British global strategy; it had been agreed that East Africa Command would have little influence on operations in Kenya; and, fundamentally, the absence of a Director of Operations meant that unit commanders essentially set their own principles and standards, based on the idea of wiping the Kikuyu from the face of the earth. There was also no sign that the strategy of isolating the Kikuyu was disrupting the Mau Mau; indeed, the Chuka massacre had served as a recruiting sergeant for insurgents.

By 1954, the Security Forces had killed about 4,500 Mau Mau, 492 wounded captured and 2,400 arrested or detained at the cost of 383 Security Forces and about 1,000 loyalists killed. The two Brigades had just about adapted to the enemy and to the forest and were tss and captured about 1,000

Chapter 9

Opening the Offensive, 1954

As part of the strategy to release the Army to concentrate on attacking the Mau Mau in the Prohibited Areas, Major General Hinde recommended in January 1954 to General Erskine that the security of loyalist Kikuyu, Embu and Meru could be improved by erecting a chain of Home Guard posts. After a visiting Parliamentary delegation had recommended that the Home Guard be expanded into the Kikuyu, Embu and Home Guards, Erskine transferred Colonel Morcombe's organization to military control, and it therefore came under military discipline. Some farms in the Rift formed Farm Guard, usually commanded by a farmer appointed as a temporary district officer. Most farms were equipped with rocket flares to signal an emergency. The forts and their quick reaction forces gave farmers a sense of security that had been lacking since the Emergency began. Farmers were instructed not to grow crops within three miles of the mile-wide restricted zone, and were required to confine their cattle in enclosures at night.

When Second Lieutenant M.J. Van Brugen, then serving with the Royal Inniskilling Fusiliers as part of 49 Brigade, deployed to the White Sisters Mission in Thika District, he and his platoon were instructed to build a network of forts. District officers pooled labour so that each fort took about three weeks to complete. The forts were designed to be mutually visible, about half a mile from each other and with a good view over ground and clear fields of fire. The roughly 3ft mud walls were lined with barbed wire and overlooked by a 40ft observation tower. The forts were surrounded by a moat about 7ft wide and 10ft deep littered with bamboo *punji* sticks and crossed by a drawbridge. Inside, there were several *sangars* (temporary fortified positions). Accommodation included a command post, a dormitory of 40 beds in sections of ten, an enclosure for prisoners, a kitchen and a trench latrine. Communications included telephones and electrically-fired flares. Trip flares were more reliable but tricky to defuse, though when detonated their light and noise could be easily detected. In the event that a sentry saw a flare, he would phone the fort commander giving the compass bearing from which the farm under attack could be identified, using a chart listing farms in the sector. Generally, three Home Guard sections were on immediate notice to move, with the fourth in reserve. The permanent staff of usually former servicemen administered the fort, arranged rosters, exercised defence and managed the armoury of firearms, mainly shotguns. A *boma* (stockade) capable of housing cattle overnight was built near most forts. Training was organized by a British officer, with an infantry section for demonstration purposes. Training usually began after work, at about 3.00 p.m., and was usually limited to three hours, although sometimes extended to about 8.00 p.m. for night training in patrols and ambushes. Although Van Brugen was given a Kenya Regiment sergeant as an interpreter, he found that his knowledge of Kikuyu was insufficient, but was then lucky enough to find a former KAR Home Guard who spoke Kikuyu, Swahili and English and was experienced in jungle warfare, sweeps, tracking and counter-ambush tactics. While ambush drills were generally discarded, because the Home Guard tended to fidget, they excelled at fieldcraft and, equipped with bows and arrows, spears and pangas, they could move silently through jungle and bush. While vetting suspected Mau Mau and those with doubtful loyalty, district officers conducted a recruitment programme in which having taken the Mau Mau oath was not necessarily a bar.

In early February, Brigadier Tweedie handed command of 39 Brigade to Brigadier the Lord Harry Thurlow DSO, CBE. Commissioned into the Seaforth Highlanders in 1930, during the Second World War he had served in Eritrea, Palestine and Libya and had commanded the 44th (Lowland) Brigade in North-West Europe. He had held several staff appointments before the posting to Kenya.

One of those who had joined the Buffs shortly before Christmas was Lieutenant Cecil West. An Old Etonian commissioned in 1949, he had just completed a mortar course. He had also attended the Brigade and Battalion Intelligence Officers course at the Intelligence School at Maresfield, where he learnt about intelligence processes but little else that was applicable to Kenya, because courses focused, not surprisingly, on the Soviet threat to Europe. On arriving in Kenya, he was posted to HQ 39 Brigade and then returned to his Battalion as the Intelligence Officer when his predecessor returned to UK. West reorganized the Section of a sergeant, corporal and two privates, introduced Duty Intelligence NCOs and ensured that members joined operations. Sergeant Mabb, of the Royal Army Education Corps, who shared the Intelligence tent, ran the Battalion library, and mysteriously 'lost' most of the 'blood and thunder' books in favour of Greek plays and Oscar Wilde.

On 6 February, Corporal Sleeman of the Devons was in a Harvard on a bombing mission north of Gura River when the pilot, Flight Lieutenant Alfred Pullmam, was unable to pull it from its dive. The plane crashed but did not explode. While Pullman was killed, Sleemen was thrown clear and sustained an injury when bamboo lanced his leg. He was rescued by a Buffs patrol.

After a Royal Engineer survey patrol was attacked one early evening near Wamagana, Special Branch at Giakanja advised the Buffs of probable Mau Mau activity along the Kagumo River between Gacatha and Wamagana, a dozen miles south of Nyeri. Lieutenant Duncan Lees, the Battalion Duty Officer, acting on police information, assembled five men from Mortar Platoon and approached a suspect village in a Land Rover. Lees sent in his patrol from three directions, however their search was inconclusive. Driving to Gacatha, he selected seven Kikuyu Home Guard and then headed in a south-easterly direction and returned to the Kagumo Valley, where the Home Guard became suspicious of several women apparently washing clothes in the river. The patrol reached a 60ft waterfall, which Lees decided to investigate. Sending Private Harrison and some Home Guard to the head of the waterfall as fire support, he and the remainder scrambled down 60 feet of near-sheer cliff and started investigating the pool for tracks. While checking the small beaches, Lees pulled aside some creepers to reveal a small cave, and when someone inside shouted, as the Bren gunner sprayed the cave, he joined his men taking cover behind a large tree. Soon after he had sent a Home Guard to collect Harrison and his men, a Mau Mau armed with a homemade shotgun appeared at the mouth of the cave. Lees ordered the Bren gunner to open fire and instructed the man to come out, but as he scrambled out into vegetation, he was shot. A second man armed with a rifle was shot also trying to escape. A third man equipped with a shotgun ignored invitations to surrender and began swimming across the pond; but as the Bren gunner loaded a new magazine, he failed to ensure that it was properly fitted and it fell off. As one Home Guard threw a spear, Lees drew his .38 revolver and fired all six rounds at the insurgent, who kept swimming, until the blast of a grenade propelled him on to the shore.

Harrison's section then arrived and took up positions to cover the cave. A torch was obtained from Battalion HQ and, since there had been no activity from inside for some time, Lees and Harrison crawled into the cave and found a dead Mau Mau. Further in, a wounded man admitted that there were two others with him and passed their weapons to Lees. The Home Guard extracted the three survivors, who were handed to Special Branch. Also captured were six homemade rifles, two revolvers, knives and parts of a homemade weapon, twenty-nine rounds of .303 ammunition, six rounds of 9mm, thirty rounds of .22 and a shotgun cartridge, a mirror, a torch, scissors, clothing including hats decorated with paper medals, canned food and some medical equipment, including anti-malarial paludrine. The prisoners admitted that General Kahiu, who led a 100-strong gang in the Aberdares, was their leader and that he had left the forest the previous day on his way to meet General 'China', with the intention of returning to the forest on 8 February. Their Passive Wing guide was one of the three killed.

During the month, Company Sergeant Major Burton of B Company, 1 Devons, and a 2in mortar crewman Private Roy Sarahs were involved in an operation in which company mortars bombarded tracks along the forest edge to force the Mau Mau into the open or make them use tracks covered by ambushes. As they were moving to a new position, they strayed into a zone of booby traps laid by the Assault Pioneers and detonated one. Burton was knocked out, and although Sarahs was severely wounded in the legs, he recovered Burton's Patchett from undergrowth. Both lay undiscovered until after dark, when a platoon commander collecting his teams found them. After they had been loaded into a vehicle to be taken back to the Company base at Munyange, the platoon commander radioed a KPRAW aircraft overhead which turned out to be piloted by Jimmy Dodds, who immediately arranged for the Battalion medical officer, an ambulance and a blood transfusion team to meet the casualties; however, Sarahs died on his way to hospital. Dodds had just supplied an A Company patrol in a Moorlands observation post watching for evidence of Mau Mau avoiding patrols by leaving the forest. Several were seen and one was killed by a Bren gun firing at 800yds. Jimmy Dodds DFM was the RAF's most successful Hurricane sergeant-pilot, with fourteen 'kills' and six 'probables' in North Africa. Commissioned in 1942, he flew communications and training aircraft in Egypt and then returned to Britain to fly Tempests and Meteors. After leaving the RAF, he was employed as a charter pilot in Nairobi and was seconded to KPRAW in 1953 with the call sign 'Eagle Green'.

General 'China' and six other Mau Mau were planning to collect weapons from a drop in an abandoned house near Kiawargi in Nyeri District when, during the morning of 15 February, General 'Tanganyika' (Muriuki Kimotho) reported that General 'Kaleba' (Gatici Kabutu) had been ambushed. Armed with his Sten and accompanied by several of his men, China set off to help and was walking along a track through a banana plantation when he met a (Kenya) KAR ambush commanded by Lieutenant Wallace Young from his base at Kiawarigi, about ten miles east of Nyeri. A fortnight later, Young described the ambush at China's trial:

> I directed my Bren burst toward the banana plantation and fired two bursts at five men dressed in black coats and khaki trousers. One seemed to stumble. Five minutes later, I saw what I thought to be a man at the edge of the plantation. I fired two more bursts and then decided to sweep the area.

Two askaris found China collapsed and losing blood from a wound in the face and took him to a homestead, where they dressed his wounds and put him in a sling. As they neared the platoon base, having advised him to claim that he had surrendered as opposed to admitting being captured, China struggled to his feet and staggered toward the camp. It was about 11.00 a.m. Recognizing China from his days as an employee of the East African Railways and Harbours Administration, Young re-dressed his wounds, ordering that he was not to be harmed, then searched him and found in a pocket a small notebook that 'China' later said he used on visits to the Reserve. China later claimed that it was Young who had shot him. A headman gave Young another notebook he had found at the ambush. The prisoner then lost consciousness and was first driven to Katerina Hospital, where Lieutenant Walker RAMC stabilized him before transferring him to Nyeri Civil Hospital; he was then sent, that night, to the King George VI Hospital in Nairobi, where he woke up chained to a bed. News of his capture spread fast, and inevitably colonists started clamouring for his execution.

General China was the most important prisoner captured so far, and the next morning Assistant Superintendent Ian Henderson, of Special Branch visited him. The son of a colonist who had arrived in 1922, he grew up among the Kikuyu in Central Province and joined the Police in 1944. Thoroughly conversant with Kikuyu culture and language and with an interest in the flora, fauna and lepidoptera of the country, by 1953 he had been in Special Branch for eight years. Despite the advice of the two askaris who had captured him, China knew that he faced the death penalty. There was no reason why wounded prisoners could not be interrogated, and from the two captured notebooks Henderson knew the prisoner had plenty to divulge; all he had to do was prompt him. As was normally the case with Mau Mau prisoners, China talked freely and with political conviction, which greatly reduced the chance of deliberate lying. After a total of 68 hours of interrogation spread over four days Henderson summarized, over 44 pages, the information received:

- A description of the organization and leadership of the Mau Mau.
- The Mt Kenya Militant Wing consisted of 7,500, of whom 4,600 were active while the remainder were in reserve in the Reserve.
- 12 per cent of the active were armed with conventional weapons, 26 per cent with homemade weapons.
- Mau Mau organization tended to follow that of the British army, i.e.:
    - Battalion – 350 men plus divided into companies. Nine battalions centred on Mt Kenya.
    - Company – 160 to 350 men divided into platoons.
    - Section – 50 to 160 men.
    - The name of the commanding officer of the Hika Hika Battalion, its area of operations and the

number and types of weapons. He named the officer commanding the Rumuri Company. It had six sections. In the Kuhanga Section were eight 'prominent' Mau Mau.
    - 375 Company/*Hika Hika* (Hurry, Hurry) Battalion had 600 men and was known as the suicide battalion because it was used to conduct attacks where loss of life was likely. China could not explain why it had been inactive for the last eight months. It was the only company allowed to smoke *bhang* (cannabis) and also keep money gained during attacks.
- Distances and difficult terrain meant that commanders could not meet on a regular basis and therefore they had considerable freedom of action. His Mt Kenya Committee of nineteen senior officers, including himself, and a secretary controlled overall operational policy.
- No attacks were conducted unless the local *muhiriga* (chief) agreed. He insisted that Mau Mau abide by standards of human decency.
- The Mau Mau Intelligence and security Special Police had informants in government, the police, army and prisons.
- His group had four wirelesses which were controlled and handled by English speakers, who intercepted police communications and also listened to local radio for news.
- Counter-measures were taken to degrade British propaganda.
- He had last met Dedan Kimathi on 4 January.
- Kimathi was not highly regarded by senior Mau Mau and had lost much of his prestige among the rank and file because of his inactivity. When China had shown him prototypes of two homemade firearms, Kimathi had rejected them out of hand.
- China had been determined to maintain links with the Passive Wing and local support in Reserves. He claimed that 200 Mau Mau could travel the four miles from Ndia to Tumutumu in broad daylight without Security Force interference.

- Food was always available from the Reserves and from shops.
- The Home Guards were notorious for abuse and corruption.
- China insisted that he would fight for independence, his land and the release of Kenyatta.

China refused to supply any details about the Embu Battalion commanded by General Njogu. East Africa Command assessed the information as being reliable and accurate and described the interrogation as being a 'provocative discussion on Kikuyu political aims and their methods of achievement'. Then 124 copies of Henderson's report were circulated to Governor Baring, the Chief Secretary and the Attorney-General, 45 copies were passed to General Erskine and the remainder went to the Kenya Police and to several administrative officials in Central Province. For the first time, the Security Forces had a synopsis of the Mau Mau in general and detail of the Mt Kenya Protected Area and its sympathizers therein.

Baring and Erskine now had every intelligence officer's dream: not only a compliant, top-level prisoner supplying substantial information, but someone they could exploit to persuade other senior Mau Mau to surrender. In the absence of a political channel after the jailing of Kenyatta, China was the only credible intermediary. There had been doubt about his credibility because he had not been carrying a green leaf when he surrendered; however, as Lieutenant Young admitted at his trial, carrying one was not compulsory. With his life in the balance, China could see he was of use to Baring and Erskine and agreed to help arrange peace talks, initially on condition of safe passage and acceptance by the Administration that the Mau Mau was a movement with a cause. To maintain the masquerade, he was convicted after a two-week trial in February of possession of a weapon and two rounds of ammunition and sentenced to death, a sentence he immediately appealed against. The same night, dressed in a policeman's uniform and masquerading as 'Constable Wambu', China was smuggled to a cell at Nyeri Police Station, where he was guarded by KAR soldiers.

General Erskine had been planning Operation Anvil, a massive cordon and search of Nairobi to dig out and isolate militants , but he still needed troops and police for operations in the Rift Valley and Central

Provinces, support to the Prison Departments managing the detention camps and to arrange a ceasefire. Using as a benchmark the bombing in Palestine of the King David Hotel in July 1946, after which Tel Aviv and parts of Jaffa were isolated in Operation Shark, he planned a house-to-house search of Nairobi for terrorists and arms, accompanied by a major identity check operation. The proposed exploitation of China gave him valuable breathing space.

Since he had established a relationship with China, Henderson was tasked to manage Operation Wedgewood, the name given to the surrender negotiations with effect from 13 February. China first wrote twenty-six letters to Mau Mau leaders inviting them to negotiate surrender with government officials. These were posted in Mau Mau dead letter boxes and inserted into the Passive Wing courier network. As the news of his capitulation and surrender negotiations spread like wildfire through the forest, concerns emerged that the Home Guards would retaliate and that his detention would be extended. On 6 March, General 'Tanganyika' expressed interest in surrendering. He had left the Mathira Reserve in 1953 and, aligning himself with the *Hika Hika* Battalion, had attacked farms and homesteads. As the negotiations gathered pace, among the first leaflets dropped was one showing General China being treated for wounds. His claim that he had been shot in the neck was obviously not true. Voice aircraft appealed:

> Today your food is being brought; it is the gift of bombs. Surrender today, carrying a green branch. Take the road leading to —— with your arms and you will be welcomed by the Devons.

Henderson gambled on China's integrity by allowing him and Tanganyika to return to the Mt Kenya Protected Area and promote surrenders. However, Dedan Kimathi felt that he was being marginalized, and even though he had denounced Tanganyika at a forest meeting for considering surrender, he focused on the 79 Articles of the Charter that he presented to the Central Committee in 1953:

> My soldiers will never leave the forests until the British Government accepts our demands:

1. Disarm its forces unconditionally.
2. Release all political prisoners
3. Recognise our country's independence.

These are our terms for negotiation.

In mid-February, General 'Gatunga' was captured by a Home Guard patrol in Embu District during a fierce clash that saw him severely wounded. Gatunga was the *nom de guerre* of Joshua Douglas, a respected Christian teacher among the Kikuyu in Fort Hall District. Nevertheless, he targeted Christians who refused to take the Mau Mau oath and conducted several well-planned attacks on loyalist leaders in Embu District he had known as a teacher, announcing his arrival with a bugle call. Like China, he kept meticulous details in five notebooks, one damning entry noting the serial number of a personal weapon taken from a teacher and stalwart member of the Home Guard he had ambushed on 25 January.

The British Government was becoming increasingly impatient over the inability of Baring to unearth a solution; indeed, Prime Minister Churchill came to consider the Kikuyu as not primitive and cowardly but people 'of considerable fibre, ability and steel'. While Michael Blundell told Churchill in 1954 that a settlement could only be reached once the Kikuyu were defeated militarily, Churchill regarded the intransigence of 'difficult' colonists as part of the problem, as did General Erskine, who wrote to his wife:

> I hate the guts of them all . . . They are not prepared to do anything to help themselves . . . Kenya is the mecca of the middle class . . . a sunny place for shady people.

Since Service wives were not initially permitted to accompany their husbands, he not taken his wife to Kenya; consequently the regular letters he wrote to her give a personal insight into the country. Colonial officials and colonists frequently criticized General Erskine for being soft on the Mau Mau, an accusation he relished brushing aside. The critics failed to recognize that, like many senior officers of the day, this battle-hardened soldier believed his duty was alongside his soldiers. The new Secretary of State for the Colonies, Oliver Lyttelton, visiting Kenya, proposed that the 'Member' system be replaced by an Executive Council of four elected Europeans, two Asians and a nominated African and that it focus on developing a multi-racial constitution. In response to repeated colonist representation in favour of a small inner circle to direct operations, Baring replaced the unwieldy Colony Emergency Committee with the twice-weekly War Council of the Governor, the Director of Operations and colonist representation through Michael Blundell.

Meanwhile, evidence from several witnesses who had turned Queen's Evidence during the MacLean Inquiry allowed the Army Legal Service to bring charges of grievous bodily harm against Major Griffiths. Although he pleaded that his askaris had committed the offences, he was convicted on 11 March, sentenced to five years imprisonment in an English prison and cashiered. The evidence of some of those involved remains protected under the terms of the Freedom of Information Act.

In the absence of air photographic intelligence, No.49 Squadron and KPRAW had developed the tactic of a pair of Lincolns rendezvousing with a Pacer indicating two targets. The first Lincoln would drop ten 500lb bombs on each target. The Pacer would then mark two targets for the second bomber, then both aircraft would conduct low-level strafing attacks, something which the Mau Mau feared more than bombing. However, the Mau Mau soon learned to recognize the sight of a KPRAW aircraft circling overhead and to understand that this indicated the probability of bombing. The RAF experiments with alternatives settled on using Army anti-aircraft radar sets, which permitted blind pattern bombing without the need for visual targeting, so the bombers could fly higher.

Two Meteor PR 10s updated the existing coverage. 'A' Flight, No.100 Squadron rotated with No.49 Squadron in January and then, in March, handed over to No.61 Squadron, whose base was at RAF Upwood. When 'A' Flight returned to Wittering, it bid farewell to the piston-engined Lincolns and welcomed the Canberra B2 jet. The new squadron quickly lost a Lincoln and its aircrew when it flew into high ground during a night operation. Although HQ Middle East Air Force refused to deploy its small air photographic interpretation asset to Kenya, nevertheless in March Air Commodore Walter Beisiegel, a well-known pre-war cricketer, was sent to evaluate the necessity for a Joint Air

Intelligence Centre. His recommendations led to Major C.A. Lowe (Intelligence Corps) arriving from the Joint School of Photographic Interpretation on 3 August to take command of a small photographic interpretation detachment. Among his staff were Captain J.A. Corcoran (Royal Artillery) and Lieutenant A.G. Inskip (Intelligence Corps). Major Lowe recalled:

> The enemy in Kenya is a particularly difficult one from the PI point of view. The only signs of movement and occupation of territory are tracks and huts. Even on the ground these signs are not easily visible; for a large part of the Mau Mau use game tracks and their huts and 'hides' are usually hidden in dense forest, and well camouflaged into the bargain. From the air photographs we are trying to find, therefore, enemy track activity in a country, which is covered with tens and thousands of game tracks, and enemy dwellings hidden in dense forest and usually constructed of or camouflaged with the natural vegetation growing in the area. (*APIS. Soldiers with Stereo*)

During the negotiations, in late February, General Kago infiltrated into Fort Hall District and planned to attack a Roman Catholic mission occupied by two priests, who had refused protection; however, he was short of weapons. Although he lost one man captured by the Security Forces, he ambushed a police vehicle on 5 March, killing District Officer Jim Chandler, although the police escort escaped with their weapons and equipment. On the 27th, Kago and members of his gang masquerading as police and Tribal Police attempted to persuade Home Guard in a fort to help pursue a gang; but when one was recognized as Mau Mau, a fierce battle saw the fort overrun and all but two Home Guard killed. Kago's men were ransacking it when a police patrol arrived, and over three days the gang fought their way across Fort Hall District, losing 23 men to the Royal Inniskilling Fusiliers, police and Home Guard on the first day.

Meanwhile, the Buffs were conducting cordon-and-sweep operations north of the River Gura and killed eight Mau Mau in two days of clashes in mid-February; five more were killed on the 28th by HQ C Company on the Nyeri to Nairobi road. On 3 March, when two platoons were sent to intercept a gang of 25 heading for the Aberdares, Sergeant P.A. Newman deployed his platoon along the road and was walking between two posts, listening to the radio traffic on his No.88 radio, when he came under very close range fire. He retaliated by quickly firing all ten rounds in his .303 rifle's magazine and was reaching for more from his bandolier when two Mau Mau armed with pangas ran towards him. A former instructor at the Buffs depot, he charged the two men, bayonet fixed, and killed both. Two of the eight Mau Mau killed and four captured were credited to his platoon. The battalion lost its only man killed in action when Lance Corporal Michael Warrener was part of a Mortar Platoon operation sent to flush Mau Mau from a maize field south of Nyeri. He was badly wounded in the knee and although his leg was amputated, he died on 10 March. Kago was shot on the 30th by a Tribal Policeman and again the Mau Mau lost another inspirational leader. This was during a two-day battle, during which a 40-strong gang led by Brigadier Gumakomba was trapped by A Company, police and the Kikuyu Home Guard, under command of the Devons, south of Nyeri. Soldiers guarded a nearby European school during lessons a mile from the action.

The surrender initiative scored another success when General 'Kaleba', who had succeeded General China on Mt Kent, apparently surrendered while thumbing a lift from an Army lorry. When he mentioned, under interrogation, that if the Mt Kenya Mau Mau negotiated a ceasefire then some in the Aberdares would follow suit, GHQ concluded that Operation Wedgwood was undermining Mau Mau solidarity. After China had urged Mau Mau leaders to send two representatives from each of the Prohibited Areas to talks scheduled to be held on 30 March in Nyeri, the Mau Mau negotiators demanded their leaders be released and independence and land reform be put on the agenda. The Administration insisted on surrender first and then floated the idea of creating an independent Kikuyu enclave in Embu and Meru Districts. The offer was rejected by the Mau Mau, who insisted on independence.

Meanwhile, General Erskine advised his senior officers that since Operation Wedgewood was producing good intelligence he did not intend to apply brakes to military operations, in spite of the possibility of a ceasefire. In preparation for a ceasefire, Brigadier Orr planned that the management of surrenders to 70 Brigade should take place in forests out of public view; while troops would guard those who surrendered, the Police would conduct searches and interrogations and organize administration. China wrote to highly suspicious Mau Mau leaders assuring them he was being fairly treated and that his death sentence had been commuted to life imprisonment, but the unwise public parading of him by Special Branch damaged loyalist morale, even after assurances that militants would not be permitted to return to the Reserve. Nevertheless, a ceasefire was agreed on 30 March, with Baring releasing Tanganyika as a sign of good faith. A second meeting was set for 10 April, but when the Mau Mau negotiators returned to the forests, there were suspicions among the leaders about the integrity of the talks, and they were arrested by the hard-line General Gatamuki. This deepened the split among the Mau Mau. Meanwhile, a 7 (Kenya) KAR reconnaissance patrol reported on 5 April that about 100 insurgents were camped just *inside* the Reserve boundary, and therefore *outside* the agreed surrender assembly area. By the next day, about 1,000 insurgents were camped near Konyu, with a further 600 expected from Meru and Embu Districts, led by Kabela. Although it was clear the 100 were waiting to surrender, Brigadier Orr ordered the 7 KAR to conduct a sweep along the forest boundary, and in the clash that followed the next day, 25 Mau Mau were killed, five wounded and seven were captured, including Gatamuki. The waiting Mau Mau took fright as the noise of the battle rolled through the valley and, believing the Administration had created an elaborate trap, they dispersed into the forest. Orr told journalists that he was pleased with the action, while Erskine regarded it as 'bad luck'. On 19 April, three Harvards crashed; all the crews survived.

Operation Wedgewood was concluded ten days later, and China was transferred to Lokitaung Prison, where he joined Jomo Kenyatta, Bildad Kaggia and Fred Kubai. To prevent him from escaping, he was shackled, as were the other prisoners, with a short chain fastened to his ankles, was kept in solitary confinement and carried out hard labour for a year. After a year of imprisonment, China was released from solitary by Lieutenant Colonel Paddy de Robeck, the new District Officer and prison commandant. Ten years earlier, they had fought together in Burma.

Chapter 10

The Initiative Seized

By 1954, the colonists were beginning to ask to discuss their future and were splitting into factions. Michael Blundell formed the multi-racial United Country Party (UCP), while the Federal Independence Party (FIP) chaired by Major E.P. Roberts opposed multi-racial government. A third force headed by the Earl of Portsmouth, who was president of the ailing Electors' Union, aimed to preserve European power by burying the other two parties. But the post-1945 colonists were very different from the pre-war rugged pioneers. Many were in business, living in Nairobi and Mombasa and rarely venturing into the bush. Added to the mix was an emerging African and Indian middle class. When Portsmouth proposed a four-month political truce on 4 October, two questions were on the table: should the colonists assemble as a united white front? Or should they agree to fracture into different parties, including one supporting a multi-racial government? An attempt by Roberts to pave the way for increased representation by his party failed, and a call by Blundell for a six-month ban on political disagreements was also defeated. When the conference rejected Blundell's 'face realities' motion, Portsmouth had won; nevertheless, the parties agreed to find a solution on the back of the truce. The disagreements led to three farmers in Londioni suggesting regional autonomy for separate areas governed by Europeans, by Africans and by the Colonial Office, as well as a multi-racial region. This was something of an acknowledgement by the colonists that the survival of Kenya as a white colony was unlikely.

The failure of a political solution meant that a golden opportunity to develop a settlement had been lost; thus the only option open to General Erskine, at last, was to escalate Security Forces operations and defeat the Mau Mau. Using intelligence gained from 'China' and during

Operation Wedgewood, the police began to regain control of Central Province, arresting suppliers and recruits and undermining the Passive Wing, and the Army and RAF drove the Mau Mau deeper into the Prohibited Areas. Piper Alexander Farmer was serving with the Black Watch Pipes and Drums at Gilgil and, when not performing at functions, was supplying half-sections to guard farms that the Battalion Intelligence Section believed to be under threat. When Captain McKillop, the KPR liaison officer attached to the Battalion, reported that a track was regularly used by the Mau Mau, Drum Major Roy Dear led a section to lay an ambush. Farmer, who was armed with a Sterling, which had recently replaced the Patchett, wrote in the May 2011 Edition of the *Red Hackle*:

> The site selected was a slight swale on a slope facing downhill. To our right, the forest and a small path headed across our front and disappeared into another part of the forest . . . Night fell and it was cold . . . we settled down as best as we could with taking turns on the Bren. I was lying almost under the Bren so that the gunner just had to drop his hand to my shoulder. When he saw, or heard, whatever was in front him, he should have nudged me, but didn't. Instead of being jerked out of a fitful doze . . . I woke to the chatter of the Bren and a handful of hot empty cases down my neck. Everything was just a blur, everyone on their knees, blazing away at a group of screaming, shouting, terrified Mau Mau who were approximately 45–50 yards away.

The clash lasted about a minute, and shortly after dawn Farmer and two other men moved into the kill zone, where they found a dozen bodies and, among discarded equipment, two modified .303 rifles, suggesting the gang were a supply group. Next morning, a Black Watch subaltern arrived with a Battalion TCT, who followed a blood trail until it petered out not far from a remote farmhouse on a hill owned by an elderly white couple. They gave the soldiers a most welcome home-cooked meal.

General Erskine eventually launched Operation Anvil at 4.30 am on 24 April. Its aims were to degrade Central Committee influence, undermine recruitment and disrupt Mau Mau lines of communications.

His intention to deport all Kikuyu, Embu and Meru from Nairobi into detention camps or to the Kikuyu Reserve was rejected, on the grounds that the city's economy and administration would be adversely affected. While two British brigades, a KAR battalion and several hundred Home Guard isolated Nairobi by placing vehicle and pedestrian checkpoints on every road, path and track, the Devons redeployed to the Rift Valley. Overhead, a section of four No.8 Squadron twin-boomed NFB-9s detached from Aden provided low-level 20mm fighter ground attack and fired about a hundred 60lb rockets. Several hundred regular and reserve Kenya Police conducted methodical sector-by-sector, house-by-house searches, while Special Branch screening and search teams checked identifications and rounded up suspects, in particular from the Kikuyu, Embu and Meru suburbs. About 30,000 suspects were screened, of whom about 16,500 were transferred to detention camps at Langata, Mackinnon Road and Manyani and about 2,400 were exiled to the Reserves. Informants disguised in rice bags identified suspects, although some undoubtedly fingered individuals against whom they harboured a grudge. During the third week, militant enclaves were again searched and occupants issued with identity cards less susceptible to forgery. At the end of the operation, Erskine reported to the War Office in his review of the Emergency that since his arrival 165,000 suspects had been sent to detention camps; many remained there for several years pending criminal charges. While information leaks had alerted the Militant Wing, Operation Anvil crippled the Passive Wing.

Commissioner of Police O'Rourke had reformed the Kenya Police by established the training school, the KPRAW and the Dog Section, had modernized Special Branch, introduced modern communications and improved terms and conditions. Although he had predicted the emergence of the Mau Mau, the Colonial Office and Administration held him responsible for the massacre at Navaisha and were determined that he should be replaced. But it took a year to find a police officer with colonial experience in the person of Arthur Young, the Commissioner of the City of London, who had served in the Gold Coast and Malaya, where his belief in community policing had stabilized police operations. He was also aware of the disciplinary issues the Kenya Police faced. With a reputation as 'the policeman's policeman', he was fair but intolerant of failings in himself and others. Before he left in April, O'Rourke wrote to Hugh Fraser, Parliamentary Private Secretary to Oliver Lyttelton, that the Kikuyu Home Guard was largely out of control, fighting each other as much as the Mau Mau, and therefore ought to be disbanded.

With the Army largely tied down in Operation Anvil, air power had maintained the pressure against the Prohibited Areas. Three weeks after the conclusion of the operation, General Erskine welcomed a strategy developed in Malaya by Lieutenant General Briggs, who had isolated Communist terrorists by resettling 500,000 largely Chinese squatters into fifty-five New Villages. In a scheme known in Kenya as 'Villagisation', the plan was to compel Kikuyu, Embu and Meru squatters in Central Province to leave their homesteads and assemble in fortified villages. In spite of anxieties that they would reject the transition from their traditional way of life, this proved not to be the case; but once again, feeble colonial administration led to needless overcrowding, inadequate health provision and poor sanitation. Nevertheless, by the New Year, the villages were developing into secure, self-sufficient enclaves. To add to the incentives, Roger Swynnerton of the Department of Agriculture had developed a 20-year plan to undermine political subversion by creating African-owned enclosures of about ten acres in Central and Nyanza Provinces capable of supporting a family with food and generating small businesses selling and investing in high-value crops, such as tea and coffee, something thus far restricted to colonist farmers. As the pressure mounted on the Passive Wing, the Indian High Commission implied, in June, that Mau Mau leaders wished to re-open negotiations; however, the Administration rejected the proposal on the grounds that the Militant Wing lacked credibility, even though a trickle of surrenders was forcing the Administration to reject annihilation of the Mau Mau in favour of moderation.

With the two British brigades focusing on supporting the Home Guard and Provincial administrations, the Devons moved to Kiambu in late May with instructions to eliminate the gangs operating among the farms and plantations, taking over responsibility for fifty-eight Kikuyu Home Guard forts and KPR stations. In total, there were now 20,000 Home Guard manning 550 forts. When farmers near Nyeri complained about rustling, Colonel Melvin Cowie, the Head of the National Parks

Department, helped the Kenya Police form five tracking teams specifically to recover livestock, each consisting of professional hunters and their black trackers – at a loose end during the safari off-season. They recovered 336 out of 473 cattle reported stolen in May. This led to the National Parks, the Game Department and nine colonists over military age being enlisted into the KPR to form tracking teams to recover stolen stock and prevent rustling by Mau Mau and their food suppliers. They sometimes worked with military patrols on Operation Cowboy.

Erskine had become sufficiently confident of the RAF to use them as the advance guard for his offensive planned for early September, when the 'long rains' soaked the forest. Known Mau Mau camps were to be bombed, with the aim of driving the enemy into the Reserve so that they could be dealt with more easily. In the absence of air photographic intelligence, No.49 Squadron and KPRAW had developed the tactic of a pair of Lincolns rendezvousing with a Pacer indicating two targets. The first Lincoln would drop ten 500lb bombs on each target. The Pacer would then mark two targets for the second bomber, and then both aircraft would conduct low-level strafing attacks, something which the Mau Mau feared more than bombing. However, they soon learnt to recognize the sight of a KPRAW aircraft circling overhead indicating the probability of bombing. The RAF experiments with alternatives settled on using Army anti-aircraft radar sets, which permitted blind pattern bombing without the need for visual targeting. Safe bombing height was between 3,000 and 4,000ft, with radar used at night or during cloudy weather at 10,000ft leading to target error of about 250yds.

Between August 1954 and June 1955, flying at 30,000ft, two No.13 Squadron Meteors PR 10s with full internal and external fuel tanks took vertical photographs of the two Prohibited Areas. Lowe wrote:

> The RAF rely on us for about 80% of their information for bombing purposes and appear to be very well satisfied with the information they get. The whole of the Mount Kenya and Aberdares have been mosaicked, and of these 300 about 200 have been reproduced in quantities to issue to infantry companies. We found, plotted and reported 150 DZs for supplies for Op Hammer

> One . . . we liaised with 39 Corps Engineer Regiment in planning tracks through the Mount Kenya forest, we gave 156 Battery targets for their guns. (APIS. Soldiers with Stereo)

The Harvards of No.1340 Flight were also providing crucial support by dive-bombing targets. With six of its aircraft and eight pilots always available for operations, in September the flight flew 504 sorties, dropped 3,974 bombs, fired 187,240 machine gun bullets and clocked up 532 hours flown. By November, the KPRAW Communication Flight was also operating two Cessna 180s and a Chipmunk flying a daily mail run to the Air Wing bases. The two Ansons had been replaced by two Pembrokes, also used as a Voice aircraft and for supply drops. Two Cessnas and two Tri-Pacers were on order. There were seventeen full-time pilots and eight part-timers, who put in one day's flying each week. Most sorties lasted about 40 minutes and therefore it was not uncommon for pilots to fly up to four times daily, weather permitting. By the time that No.214 Squadron, which was commanded by Squadron Leader K.R. Bowhill, arrived from RAF Upwood, bombing had become effective. When a target was selected, ground forces were withdrawn to allow the Lincolns to conduct pattern bombing. The squadron dropped nearly 1,500 tons of high explosive with the number of strikes rising from 40 in June to 180 in November. Most bomb-loads were fourteen 500lb bombs and 1,000 rounds of .50in ammunition. In June, in the 'Mushroom procedures', Brigade HQs could instruct aircraft to attack targets in the Reserves. The fuselage of the Tri-Pacers had been equipped with racks for four 19lb fragmentation bombs. During each strike, the crews took photographs of the target for Bomb Strike Analysis by Lowe's unit.Taking advantage of the shock of an attack, Psy Ops Voice aircraft and leaflet drops encouraged surrenders. At the same time, troops littered the forest with patrols and ambushes. There is no doubt that air power was having a significant role on demoralizing the Mau Mau, particularly when raids were directed at the same target over several days and sometimes weeks. One valuable source of air intelligence was the interrogation of surrendered Mau Mau:

> Gatheru Wairgu – surrendered 5 September 1954. In July, he was at a meeting called by Dedan Kimathi on the Aberdare Moorlands.

> Approximately 1,000 Mau Mau were there when the area was attacked by nine Harvards. The meeting broke up and he states casualties were high. In January 1954, he was bombed on the (River) Chania. Of 154 in his gang, he states that 105 were killed. On 3 September 1954, he was with a gang of seven which was bombed. No casualties were inflicted but as a result of the attack, he and two others surrendered.

The military intelligence network had blossomed. All MIOs, now numbering six officers and about twenty FIAs from the Kenya Regiment, attended the Training Centre, whose programme included the management of intelligence pseudo-gangs. Kitson, now a major, covered Central Southern Province of the districts of Kiambu, Thika, Nairobi and Fort Hall. With Mau Mau influence predicted to extend to Southern Province, this was also included in his remit. Special Branch and the MIOs ran extensive screening operations in which the police and Army cordoned areas in the Reserve where the Mau Mau were active and then arranged for informers disguised in rice bags to identify militants. If more than two informers identified the same person, the suspect was taken away for interrogation. This proved a reliable method of arresting Militant and Passive Wing activists. Kitson insisted that notes taken in interrogation be filed into a collation system, from which information was converted into reliable intelligence of sufficient quality, for instance, for Meteor PR 10s to conduct air photographic reconnaissance. When a target was selected, ground forces were withdrawn to allow the Lincolns to conduct pattern bombing, the results of which were subjected to bomb damage assessment.

When Inspector Drummond heard that Harun was back in circulation, they agreed to meet. Although the Mau Mau were becoming wary of strangers, Drummond accepted their offer of a meal and he, McNab and their eight pseudos arrived at Harun's camp. Drummond stabbed the sentry and hid the body in undergrowth. During the meal, Harun challenged the pseudo-gang to rifle drill and they sloped and ordered arms, then pointed their weapons at their hosts and fired a volley. Although wounded, Harun escaped in the confusion but was captured a week later by Drummond and a police patrol, convicted and hanged. Drummond eventually killed Captain 'Jimmy' and tracked his gang to

Menengai Crater, about ten miles north of Nakuru. McNab was later killed near Naivasha. Drummond was awarded the George Medal for this and other acts.

Although Erskine had instructed the brigades to form TCTs by July, only Brigadier Taylor had assembled his five TCTs into the 49 Brigade Tracker Combat Group (TCG) under the command of Captain Venn Fey. The other two brigade commanders employed the TCTs separately. After observing trackers at work during Operation Anvil, British officers in 70 Brigade KAR realised that *askaris* did not possess natural tracking skills and therefore formed TCTs. Since there was a shortage of officers, sergeants were permitted to lead the TCTs. Fey was born in 1919 and had grown up among the Kikuyu. His grandparents were the first settlers on the Kinangop. During the Second World War he served with the East African Forces and then sent his family to England in 1947 because he rejected the idea of Kenya as a white colony and sympathized with Kikuyu resentment. Selling their farm after the Emergency was declared, the family moved to South Africa. Fey was in Scotland recovering from a nervous breakdown when Major Elliott, who knew him to be an expert tracker, persuaded him to accept a commission in the Kenya Regiment. Fey sought out his childhood friend, a Ndorobo honey-collector named Gichumu, and deployed three TCTs around Fort Jericho west of Mt Kinangop and two in Kiambu District.

When Elliott said that the September rains would mean the wet ground would ease tracking, three 49 Brigade TCTs concentrated at the bamboo headwater of the River Thika found evidence of hides, even though Lincolns had bombed the area three weeks earlier. By mid-October the TCTs had killed, wounded or captured twenty-seven insurgents. The success of the Brigade led to General Erskine insisting that 39 and 70 Brigades each form a TCG by the New Year. The 49 Brigade TCG was resting when intelligence reports emerged of Mau Mau seen lurking in the forest edge near Fort Hall. The Royal Northumberland Fusiliers and 6 (Somaliland) KAR TCTs, supported by three Home Guard trackers, attacked their camp, killing several Mau Mau.

On the recommendation of Captain Jack Bonham, a recently retired hunter, the Kenya Police increased the strength of their eight tracker teams to two colonists, two trackers, four constables, a vehicle and a radio. By mid-December, five teams were based at Nanyuki and three at Nyeri, but the police did not like the idea of civilians heading teams and sought police officers contracted from British constabularies to attend the Battle School Tracking Course before taking a leading role. Inspector Derek Franklin, leading one of the teams, believed his main role was to keep the Mau Mau on the move and thus force them to scavenge for food:

> Our efforts to combat the threat were largely ineffectual. It was more a case of following up after an incident, sometimes following tracks for half a day or more, but never achieving a satisfactory contact.

On 27 June 2009, on the BBC Radio 4 show *Saturday Live*, Tim Symonds recalled arriving in Kenya aged seventeen determined to broaden his horizons and spend a year working on a farm. He knew little about the Emergency, but at breakfast he would scan the skies for circling vultures that could indicate a kill or rustled livestock. Seeing aircraft dropping leaflets, he was told by his employer that most Mau Mau could not read and would give the leaflets to others who could. He also saw several insurgents emerging from the forest clutching green 'surrender' branches. After about a year, Symonds joined the KPR, first becoming a tracker team leader and then transferring to a 'pseudo gang', in which role he wore a filthy set of old torn clothes that might once have been First World War battledress. When he washed the clothes in the detergent Tide they gave off a strange smell, and he was issued with another wardrobe of smelly, shabby garments. During one mission in the bamboo belt he captured a 50- or 60-year-old insurgent named Obama, who spoke perfect English.

In June, after Operation Anvil, several Nairobi militants began destabilizing Kiambu District with attacks. In July, the RAF Police Eastleigh was involved in an ambush near Nairobi, which resulted in twenty arrests and weapons captured. In mid-August, the Devons moved to Embu District for operations on the lower slopes of the Mt Kenya Prohibited Area and to train the Embu Home Guard. After a B Company patrol clashed with Mau Mau rustlers about three miles inside the forest, Major Martin Hastings, the Company Commander, led a patrol which he had divided into three: Reconnaisance, consisting of a Home Guard Combat Unit led by District Officer 'Spike' Powell; Assault, himself armed with a Patchett, two riflemen and a Bren gun team; and Support, Corporal Barrington's eight-man section. Overhead was a KPR Pacer flown by Major Michael 'Punch' Bearcroft. He had lost his right hand in a motor cycle accident and used a hook with interchangeable attachments. With a map resting on his knee, he used his left hand to jot down messages, operate his No.88 wireless and shove out supplies, pulling the safety pins of smoke markers and hand grenades with his teeth and dropping them out of a window while in a steep turning dive that took him to treetop height.

The patrol entered the forest soon after dawn on the 27th and reached the scene of the clash by mid-morning. A Kikuyu tracker followed footprints, which included those of women and children, for eight miles to the edge of a small glade in which there were several small huts. Hastings posted sentries, and soon after ordering his men to rest, male voices and breaking twigs were heard. Alerting his men, he sent the Home Guard to investigate. Then a shot rang out. About ten minutes later, Powell returned with the news that the enemy were aggressive. Assuming that the gang did not know of the presence of soldiers, at about 3.30 pm Hastings and the Assault and Support Groups had just crossed a stream flowing through a clearing when a dog ambled from the forest and then his tracker, pointing to several figures in the forest taking cover behind a fallen tree, whispered 'Mau Mau'. Hastings ordered the Assault Group to form into extended line and, as he led them in a charge towards the enemy, he was wounded in the chest. As the soldiers dived for cover, Powell realized the patrol was in danger of being pinned down and attacked the enemy flank with the Home Guard, killing two Mau Mau armed with .303 rifles who turned out to be brothers, Brigadier 'Saiko' and Colonel 'Sonkey'. Both were members of Njoro's gang of about 140 militants acting as a rearguard. In a night of heavy rain, Corporal Barrington organized relays of stretcher-bearers to carry Hastings to a rendezvous with Bearcroft, who flew him to BMH Nairobi next morning.

Meanwhile, Mau Mau prophets, in particular one named Mama Mwangi (Mama Future), were demanding the blood of a white man to unlock the fate of Waiyaki and enable the Mau Mau to continue the fight. Arundell Gray Leakey, an active member of several counter-intelligence committees, was chosen as the sacrifice. Leakey owned a large farm five miles north of Nyeri on the slopes on Mt Kenya. Mary, aged fifty-seven, was his second wife, his first having died before the Second World War. His son Nigel had been posthumously awarded the VC during the Second World War. He had been accepted as a Kikuyu 'blood brother', spoke their language fluently and was known as *murungaru*, in Swahili 'tall, straight'. While he had genuine sympathy for the Kikuyu, his writings lent strength to the popular belief that Mau Mau was an evil organization that was savage, anti-white and anti-Christian, an attitude that had attracted several death threats. He did not believe that the Mau Mau would harm him or his family and so rarely armed himself. He was a diabetic, reliant upon medication. General 'Tanganyika' selected General 'Kaleba' to lead the raid. Leakey had disturbed several Mau Mau on his property in October and had told them to leave. During the night of 13th, the Leakeys were having supper when about thirty Mau Mau burst into the house. Mary and her daughter, Mrs Diana Hartley, aged thirty-seven and a mother of two, barricaded themselves in a bedroom, where Mary suggested they climb into the loft using a trap door. However, when Diana was unable to lift her mother, Mary told her to stay quietly up there and think of her children. The Mau Mau broke into the bedroom and, finding Mary hiding behind a basket, demanded money from the safe. After about an hour of silence, Diana apprehensively lowered herself from the loft, only to find the strangled body of her mother in the garden and two Kikuyu servants, one a Christian, hanged and disembowelled with *pangas*. Of her stepfather, there was no sign, in spite of extensive searches, in particular by the Kikuyu Home Guard. Louis Leakey later warned colonists that although they might believe their African servants to be loyal:

> It is no good counting on them being able to help if you are attacked or counting on them to rush a warning to your neighbour. The Mau Mau intelligence service knows if your servants are loyal, or which of them are, and will try to kill or abduct them before they attack you.

In the aftermath of the murder, nine elderly colonists were moved from their farms near Nyeri because they were believed to be on sacrificial lists. Most suffered considerable financial loss. 'Kaleba', who had promoted himself to field marshal, was widely held to be responsible, but the search for him after the Operation Wedgewood negotiations was fruitless until 3 October, when a Special Branch officer named Superintendent Bernard Ruck, who had just been awarded the first of two George Medals, interrogated a surrendered insurgent, who said that 'Kaleba' was in a cave in the Mount Kenya Protected Area and wished to surrender. During the negotiations he had double-crossed Administration negotiators by not surrendering, so surrender was not now an option; capture, however, was. September had proved to be the busiest month for bombing, and No.49 Squadron returned for its second tour.

In October, the Buffs and Devons were warned they would rotate with two light infantry battalions. The Rifle Brigade had been formed in 1800 as skirmishers and rearguards in the Napoleonic wars. The 1 King's Own Yorkshire Light Infantry (KOYLI) had emerged from the amalgamation of the 53rd Foot and 105th Madras European Light Infantry in 1881. The rotations began on 9 October, when a Britavia Airways Hermes flew the Rifle Brigade Operational Training Party of eight officers and five other ranks from Blackbushe Airport to RAF Eastleigh, where they were welcomed by senior officers and several former Rifle Brigade serving with the Kenya Regiment. Somewhat dazed by the long flight and their 12-hour reception, the Party was then driven to the Buffs Battalion HQ at Fort Hall, where tents had been erected in the shade of blue gums in a space fringed by tall forest-flame trees. To the south-east the ground fell away, green and undulating, towards the plains, while to the north-west the snowy peak of Mt Kenya rose out of dark forest. Under instructions to gather as much information as possible, the KPR flew several flights over the Northern Aberdares during which the pilots demonstrated their versatility in dropping supplies and low-level flying through river gorges. The Advance Party also attended the Battle School and then joined patrols in the soaking forest gloom, each man carrying 70lb of equipment. The main cause of anxiety was short-range encounters with wild animals in the bamboo belt. Several days were spent with a 7 (Uganda) KAR company patrolling above 12,000 feet, during which the only person to see the enemy was Lieutenant John Cornell, the Intelligence Officer, who fired three shots at a solitary Mau Mau. In the only clash involving members of the Advance Party, the trackers detected evidence of Mau Mau while following a wide and not too steep track; there was an outburst of firing at the head of the patrol:

> Almost instantaneously, we were all blazing away at the undergrowth. We had surprised two sentries, one of whom we killed; the other escaped, as did the rest of the gang, who, according to our tracker's estimate, numbered about thirty men and ten women. Their hide which was barely fifty yards from the sentry post, consisted of nine large lean-to shelters made of branches and leaves, and showed evidence of hurried evacuation. The ashes of the fires were red hot, and amongst the 'booty' we recovered were three home-made rifles and one roll-book. Pursuit was judged to be hopeless, since the rain would make tracking by our African or by the dog impossible. It must now be confessed that this decision was greeted with some relief by the novices of the party, who knew just enough about these kinds of operation to realize the implications of chasing Mau Mau, who move through the forest at about ten miles per hour when in a hurry.

An officer offered this assessment of the Emergency:

> From the military point of view the situation is unlike anything the British Army has had to face in recent years. The nearest parallel is Malaya, but the parallel is far from exact. The Mau Mau are fortunately very short of 'precision weapons' and ammunition. The great majority are armed with homemade rifles, whose only value is to intimidate ignorant natives and, possibly, to boost the morale of their owners. It is hardly surprising therefore, that so far from being aggressive, they do everything in their power to avoid contact with troops or police. Their forest craft is, of course, superb, and they can move across country at anything up to ten miles per hour. This means that a tremendous effort has to be made

by British troops for very small results. Dozens of ambushes have to be laid and dozens of patrols sent out before a contact is made, and even then much skill is required if the enemy is to be killed or captured in the ensuing 'engagement', which is all over in about ten seconds.

It can be easily imagined that endless patrolling through thick country, carrying anything up to seventy pounds, can become monotonous if few results are obtained; and the same applies to ambushes, where members have to remain still but alert for long hours. It is hardly surprising that some of the troops who have been operating under these conditions for eighteen months without a break have become stale. Casualties so far have been understandably light. The great majority are caused by careless handling of arms by young and inexperienced soldiers. The soldier's greatest fear out here is attack by big game; these certainly can be frightening, particularly when they have been stirred up by bombing and patrolling; but instances of men being wounded by game are rare. Bottom on the list come the Mau Mau. One battalion which has just left the country suffered only one fatal casualty from the enemy in eighteen months.

Politically, the problem is confusing. Everyone is agreed that it is a political problem, but here agreement stops. The situation is certainly improving, but it is not easy to see how it will finally be solved.

During the evening of 23 October, Second Lieutenant Alan Liddell, B Company, 2/3 (Kenya) KAR platoon commander, was in the Battalion Officers' Mess at Karatina when Ruck entered and reported that an informant had said that 'Kaleba' was lying up with several Mau Mau in jungle north of Nyeri and that he needed support from an Army patrol. Liddell was selected, and assembling a WOPC, about five *askaris* and a radio operator, joined Ruck, the informant and his escort of a police constable, trekking in the chilly darkness along the railway for about three hours. Turning east, they crossed rivers and ridges, until at about 3.00 am the informant pointed toward a hill, which they climbed using all the cover they could; then in the gloom of the dawn the informant indicated the mouth of a cave surrounded by bush. Seeing no sign of a sentry, the patrol crept close and, hearing snoring from inside, rushed in and overpowered the occupants. Illuminated by Ruck's torch were three men and a woman, and among the clutter of belongings and weapons recovered were Gray's revolver and some of his clothing. While 'Kaleba' was calm, the other two men and the woman were clearly shocked. He was flown to Nairobi in a Communications Flight Cessna and was later hanged for the murder of Leakey. Of Leakey himself there was no sign. A search of books and documents revealed a letter to 'Kaleba' that read: 'G Kubai could come because we are making arrangements for the sacrifice.' Another letter to Field Marshal 'Kaleba' was signed by 'Wagikungu':

> To the leaders who sent their askaris to go to the European called *murungari*, and who caught him and participated in the deed, I want every leader to submit names of their askaris who were seen to take part.

When Leakey was captured, he was taken away without his medication. David Reed, then employed in Barclays Bank in Nairobi during a two-year fellowship from the Institute of Current World Affairs, wrote on 6 December:

> After a long search, security forces found his body in a grave in dense forest near Mount Kenya. There were no signs of violence. The authorities said that the 70-year-old man must have been buried alive as a sacrifice to the resting place of Ngai and Mount Kenya as a holy mountain.

The existence of Operation Wedgewood had not been widely disclosed, and thus colonists were shocked when 'Kaleba' said at his trial that he had returned to the forest during the surrender negotiations and insisted that he was a prisoner-of-war. But this did not prevent three Kikuyu assessors convicting him of possession of a .45 revolver and thirteen rounds of ammunition, and he was sentenced to death. A week after 'Kaleba' was captured, a member of the KPR, who was in civilian life an assistant farm manager, was fined £50 for shooting two Africans in the legs while questioning them, in his belief that they were connected with the Mau Mau. His lawyer pleaded 'nervous exhaustion'. To add to the tension in Nairobi, a plague of snakes, including cobras, puff adders, night adders and Gunther's garter snakes, took refuge in gardens after losing their territories to urban development.

Diana Hartley later married Eddie Knodi, a chef at Nairobi's Norfolk Hotel, and was involved in trapping animals until she was mauled to death by a lion in November 1960 when she unwisely entered his cage. She had just delivered two cheetahs to the set of the film *Hatari.*

Two days later, the Security Forces scored another success. On 17 September, forty insurgents led by David Mathu had freed about 200 prisoners in an audacious raid on Lukenya prison camp, about 20 miles south-east of Nairobi; most had committed minor offences. When others refused to leave, the Mau Mau threatened them with death and then left with several weapons from the armoury. Shortly afterwards, Captain Nyagi Nyaga, a battalion commander from the Aberdares, visited Mathu and Mwangi Mtoto at their camp on the southern fringes of Naroibi to collect arms and ammunition and was given seven shotguns, clothing and money. Mtoto's camp was attacked on 12 October and he was among the six Mau Mau killed. Among the prisoners was Mathu. Five weeks later, on 25 October, an informant reported that Mau Mau had been seen on a sisal plantation in a camp underneath a spreading tree in Dandora Swamp eight miles north of Nairobi and east of the junction of the Ruaraka and Nairobi rivers. A Royal Northumberland Fusiliers platoon found the spot and, noticing avenues cut through the papyrus, encircled the camp and then advanced. A ferocious battle followed, and the soldiers were forced to withdraw. Reinforcements, which included Kikuyu Home Guard, police officers from Thika and a second platoon, then arrived. After the Mau Mau rejected an offer to surrender, before dawn the platoons used their 2-inch mortars to plaster the camp and then at mid-morning slowly skirmished through the swamp and, against determined resistance, drove Mau Mau towards Home Guard 'stops'. By the end of the day, thirty Mau Mau had been killed and fifty captured, among them 'hardcore' prisoners liberated from Lukenya Prison, men at risk of the death penalty, and women and children. One prisoner was identified as Nyaga, who admitted that his gang had left the Aberdares to collect arms, ammunition and supplies from Mtoto and Mathu for his battalion. Interrogations confirmed that Operation Anvil had severely disrupted the ability of the Passive Wing to supply the Militant Wing.

Meanwhile, the Buffs were continuing to patrol the forest. One C Company patrol led by Lieutenant M.J. Cheney (Royal Tank Regiment) had just reached the bamboo belt when he shot two Mau Mau in a clearing. When the patrol came under bren, sub machine gun and rifle fire, he counter-attacked, shooting another Mau Mau, and found an abandoned hide with six fires burning and the remains of forty cattle but no sign of Mau Mau, except their shouted threats from the bamboo. The patrol searched the area and found another hide of two neat huts and six under construction. Elephant spoor prevented tracking. On 25 October, Erskine was visiting the battalion as it was conducting a sweep near Embu. Major B. McGrath, the A Company commander, had been controlling operations from a KPRAW Tri-Pacer but had become violently airsick and was landed without seeing anyone. Bursts of firing and shouts then indicated that troops and Home Guard had disturbed Mau Mau, and three bodies, a wounded man strapped to a stretcher and one begging to be spared from the Home Guard were brought from the bush. It was the first time that Erskine had been at the kill of Mau Mau.

When on 9 November, Lieutenant Robin Shearer, the Devons Intelligence Officer, advised Lieutenant Peter Burdick, the B Company second-in-command at Kiburu, that the Embu Home Guard and the Police had clashed with about 200 Mau Mau on the banks of the River Tana, most of the Company were deployed elsewhere. The only soldiers available were clerks, storemen and sentries, and the only vehicle a Bedford 3-tonner used by a visiting RAOC Mobile Bath Section, with its driver. In the last major action of the Devons' deployment to Kenya, Burdick arrived at the Police Post to find the chaos exacerbated by 'Kenya cowboys' (KPR officers recruited in the UK) threatening to go off on their own unless 'someone gets going, man!' When an inspector said that he was going to approach from the north and that Burdick was welcome to advance along the river bank, he realized the policeman was ignoring the philosophy of a co-ordinated plan. Using a map that turned out to be inaccurate, Burdick guided the RAOC driver and the patrol in the lorry to the sound of the battle. Overhead, Michael Bearcroft was struggling to persuade the disparate Security Forces to converge on a copse of stunted bush where Mau Mau had been seen. Burdick ordered his men into extended line anchored on the river and, after clearing the copse, then instructed a Home Guard unit to move to his left and give covering fire, while B Company quickly advanced to the next river bend, where two Mau Mau were killed. When Bearcroft reported a mass of Mau Mau crossing the river, B Company advanced and threw grenades into the mass, while the Home Guard opened fire. Meanwhile, Sergeant Osborne MM and a D Company platoon joined the advance, and the Mau Mau melted into the forest slopes overlooking the river. As dusk fell, Bearcroft left, low on fuel, leaving B Company to ambush several tracks and Burdick to face a furious commanding officer, who had missed the battle and was cursing the Survey Department for producing an out-of-date map. More importantly, he brought rations and water. After a chilly night, A and D Companies conducted a sweep next morning, then Burdick and his platoon climbed into the Mobile Bath Section lorry and returned to Kiburu.

On the second anniversary of the declaration of the Emergency, the War Council acknowledged:

> While recent successes against the terrorists justify cautious optimism, there is nothing in the military situation which suggests an early end to the Emergency . . . Operations now being conducted by the Security Forces and others planned are designed to kill or capture the leaders and to inflict casualties on the members of their gangs so as to reduce their fighting potential and destroy their morale.

Among civilians, thirty Europeans, twenty-five Asians and 1,200 loyal Africans, of whom 450 were Kikuyu Home Guard, had been killed by the Mau Mau; while 487 members of the Security Forces including thirty Europeans, two Asians and 455 Africans had been killed by enemy action, friendly fire incidents and accidents, including aircrew losses. Neither sex nor age spared anyone from murder. The killings of Walter and Dorothy Bruxner-Randall at their coffee farm near Thika on 15 March were followed swiftly by that of Andrew Stephens, aged four, decapitated while riding his tricycle at Atwell's Estate on 18 April by a recently sworn Mau Mau who had promised to decapitate an European. Dr Charles Pentreath, aged eighty-three, was clubbed to death in Kiambu District. Basil McNichol, a railway employee, and his wife Doris, a barber's shop receptionist, both in their thirties, were trapped in their cottage and sustained serious burns. The latter case led to an Emergency law that anyone found in possession of 'incendiary material without reasonable excuse' risked fourteen years on conviction. The estimate of 6,700 Mau Mau killed was suspected to be lower than the actual figure, while 433 had surrendered under the 'green branch' initiative, mostly food suppliers. It was recognized that the nerves of some Security Forces had been frayed by having seen too many atrocities. The Kikuyu Home Guard, it was said, 'are not eager to take prisoners'.

East Africa Command assessed in November that since Mau Mau had been largely broken into small, widely dispersed groups, conventional forces should hold the ground while 'specialist forces' should deliver the final blows. The combination of the elimination of pseudo-gangs, bombing and ground forces operations, leading to an average of 600 Mau Mau casualties monthly in the last quarter of 1954, soon undermined enemy morale and improved the collection of intelligence. History is full of examples of such units, now generally referred to as 'special forces', an early example being the Greek Trojan Horse inside which a few soldiers were inserted into the seemingly invincible city of Troy. A definition of special forces could be 'selected units tasked to conduct difficult missions outside the parameters of conventional forces'. While their inherent capabilities give them opportunities not available to conventional forces, they have their limitations, notably their misuse by commanders and over-confidence in their abilities. Critical to their success is detailed intelligence, signals and logistics. The British Army had a proliferation of special forces during the Second World War, all of which had either been merged or disbanded by the 1950s; indeed, the nature of conscription meant selection and training were restricted by time constraints. From their experiences during the Second World War, most commanders embraced the notion of using special forces but knew that units would have to be found from within East Africa Command. The Kenya Regiment elimination and Major Kitson's intelligence pseudo-gangs were proving their worth. The other option was the trackers. General Erskine therefore summoned Kitson and Captain Fey to a meeting which resulted in the five British and six KAR battalions and the East African Armoured Car Squadron each forming a Forest Operating Company of three TCTs commanded by a British officer. Since the Kenya Regiment would be heavily involved in supporting the proposed twelve companies, it was to provide one company. While Fey, promoted to major, introduced the concept to commanders on operations in the Aberdares, prospective TCT commanders attended the East Africa Command Battle School at Nakuru.

The bulk of 1 KOYLI and 1 Rifle Brigade arrived at Mombasa on 26 November on the HMT *Georgic* after a two-week voyage from UK and then boarded a train for the 36-hour journey to Nanyuki, where they linked up with their Advance Parties. On board were 400 semi-automatic FN 7.62mm Self-Loading Rifles (SLR) on trial and soon to replace the .303 Lee Enfield Mark 4 as the standard British rifle. After three weeks of acclimization and forest warfare training, 1 KOYLI relieved the Devons while the Rifle Brigade took over the Buffs' operational area south of Mount Kenya. In one of the first sorties, a 7 Platoon patrol spotted a Mau Mau, but a jammed sten gun allowed him to escape. The Buffs Advance Party, which included three families, returned to Blackbushe Airport in a Hermes. The Main Body returned to Nairobi on the train that had brought the Rifle Brigade, to the usual ceremonial march past and farewell parties. Both outgoing battalions also linked up with their families. The *Georgic* collected two battalions from Egypt and arrived in Liverpool on 19 December. When the Buffs returned to Old Park Barracks, it numbered 41 officers and 665 soldiers, of whom 12 officers and 171 soldiers had arrived in Kenya on deployment. About 360 were Regulars.

The British Army has a long tradition of taking families with it on campaigns and would continue to do until the 1990s. Those wives and children who elected to join their husbands faced the possibility of retaliation. Several were murdered in Cyprus and Aden, and also in West Germany by the IRA. In Kenya, families lived in hostels, hotels such as the Outspan in Nyeri and Brackenhurst in Limuru for officers, and in hirings. While the local overseas allowance was generous, bills were high. Families were fully supported by the Welfare Branch at GHQ and regimental welfare systems that covered the costs of voyages and flights, access to military hospitals and dental services, local education or boarding schools in UK. Operational limitations usually meant that the men in rifle companies saw their wives about once a fortnight; their departure in 'passion trucks' to see their wives was known as 'padding' and the married quarter as a 'pad'. The Branch also organised Command concert parties, often with local talent.

In February 1954, Mrs Munro, her five-year-old son and four-year-old daughter, Lyn, joined her husband, Staff Sergeant William Munro RAOC in Kenya. He had arrived the previous October. After spending several months in Hill Hotel, a transit hostel in Nairobi, they moved to an isolated bungalow on the outskirts of Nairobi owned by Mrs Keer, a widow who had returned to England when the Emergency was declared and had rented her property to the Army, complete with her staff and a German Shepherd called 'Skipper'. Lyn recalls:

> Most of the grounds were overgrown, but the grass was kept short around the house to discourage snakes. The garden boys were paid for each snake they killed and used to hang the bodies over a wall near the front door to be counted. However, my mother, who had a phobia of snakes, was so freaked out by coming face to face with anything up to a dozen snakes as she got out of the car that the boys were told to leave them in sacks out of sight. We always closed the shutters on the windows before dark in case the Mau Mau set light to the curtains. This was said to have happened to another Army family. If we returned home after dark, we had to stay shut in the car until my Dad, who was always armed, had had a look round and unlocked the front door. Then we had to run quickly into the house and the door was locked after us. When my Dad was on duty in the evenings or overnight, which seemed to happen quite a lot at this period, my Mum sat in the lounge with a loaded rifle across her knees; she had been in the Army for several years before she married, so she knew how to use it.

When families went on safaris, they usually travelled in convoys and sometimes took their houseboy, because many local people had not seen their own country and its wildlife. On one trip, Munro and his family were standing of a steep river bank watching hippos and crocodiles when it gave way. Munro would have fallen into the water had their houseboy not grabbed his clothing. Several days after this incident, the Mau Mau had held an oathing ceremony and forced many local Kikuyu to swear allegiance, including the houseboy, who had sworn to behead a white man before the next full moon. In 1955, the Munros moved to a flat in Nyeri. Lyn again:

> Neither my brother nor I have many memories of our time in Nyeri, but photos show we seemed to be living in or near an Army compound, so a much safer location. There were a lot of trips to places like Buffalo Springs and Thomson Falls, and also holidays in Mombasa (where my brother was badly stung by a Portuguese man-of-war and I contracted yellow fever).
>
> The final two years of our time in Kenya were in Army Quarters in a camp [Rayner's Camp?] about five miles outside Nairobi, near the entrance to Nairobi National Park. As my mother had another daughter in October 1956, my brother and I were less closely supervised and were part of a gang of children on the camp, which had a tall barbed-wire-topped perimeter fence and so was probably considered a safe play area by parents. In truth, the fence was easily breached and we spent a lot of time outside camp limits, especially in the land surrounding the neighbouring reservoir, which was posted with notices saying the water was unsafe for swimming (some disease that required 21 injections in your stomach!). On our rambles we occasionally encountered pug marks and droppings from big cats, especially in the dry season when there was a shortage of water in the nearby National Park. My memories of encounters with local people are all positive: for instance, one of the native boys showed us how to make rope from sisal and use it to make baskets or bows and arrows. In our final year, when my brother and I used to take the bus into Nairobi for Saturday morning cinema, we used to travel on the top deck with the Africans because it was cheaper (I presume they had no choice where to sit: apartheid?). There was never any

resentment shown to us for being there: everybody was very friendly.

In all my years in Kenya, including the closest we came to the troubles in the early years, I can never remember feeling frightened: we thought it was all very exciting. My brother remembers it as a very carefree time. The grown-ups seemed to be enjoying themselves too, especially in the later years: polo matches, horse racing at Nanyuki, parades with military bands, parties and dances.

Looking back on it, I cannot understand why the military put a young family in such an isolated location. The key to that decision may have been my father. He loved Kenya and its people, and in the early years of his tour was tempted to settle out there. Many of the white-owned farms were available at a low price because of the unrest: I can remember being taken to see two coffee farms he said he was considering buying. However, when he returned to Kenya on a 6-month unaccompanied posting shortly before Independence, he noticed that the attitude of many of the native people had become much more antagonistic, so he was glad he had not been able to go ahead with his relocation plans.

On 27 November, GHQ East Africa published the 167-page *A Handbook of Anti Mau Mau Operations.* While not as detailed as the twenty-three chapters of *The Conduct of Anti-Terrorist Operations in Malaya,* it provided a much-needed operational framework for Kenya.

With most of Kenya relatively secure, on 11 December General Erskine launched his largest operation so far, Operation Hammer, to 'seek out and destroy the Mau Mau in the two Prohibited Areas and Settled Areas'. With the Kenya Police maintaining law and order in the lowlands, the brigades in large sweeps controlled by Major-General Hinde from an Advanced GHQ at Nyeri, were to clear the moorland and then sweep through the bamboo and forest belts and flush Mau Mau towards 'stops' manned by the Home Guard and Tribal Police along the forest edge. Three days later, Erskine added a dimension to his specialist forces by instructing the battalions to raise 'Trojan Teams' to work with Special Branch, through District MIOs, following up intelligence reports. Generally, teams consisted of a Swahili-speaking Kenya Regiment NCO, five soldiers and an interpreter, all with an aptitude for commando operations. The Administration also formed its own 'Trojan Teams' of surrendered Mau Mau organized into five Special Police units.

Meanwhile, Baring faced a crisis when Commissioner of Police Young resigned. Although he had considerable counter-insurgency experience as part of General Templer's top level committee in Malaya, he had not been invited to sit on the War Council. He had tried to improve the operational and ethical level of the Kenya Police by recommending that it adopt British constabulary standards, in particular relating to interrogations and criminal investigations; however, the declaration of the Emergency had seen a rapid expansion of the police which resulted in lapses in the quality of training and personal conduct and consequent distrust from local communities. He was critical of the detention camps and predicted to Baring on 22 November:

> The horror of some of the so-called Screening Camps now present a state of affairs so deplorable that they should be investigated without delay, so that the ever increasing allegations of inhumanity and disregard of the rights of the African citizen are dealt with and so that the Government will have no reason to be ashamed of the acts which are done in its own name by its own servants.

At about the same time, Dr Louis Leakey wrote an angry letter, published in the *East African Standard*, criticizing a decision that Kikuyu graded as 'white' in the screening system be held in rehabilitation camps; he demanded that they be released quickly with an apology and their *kipendis* returned to enable them to work. In another letter to Baring three weeks later, Young described the Kikuyu Reserve in Central Province as governed by 'the rule of fear' and the misuse of power, and claimed that repression and excesses were considered to be normal. But Deputy Governor Frederick Crawford wrote to Sir Oliver Lyttelton in January 1955 that Young's recommendations were 'as unrealizable as trying to turn the Royal Irish Constabulary into the Winchester Police in the middle of an Irish Rebellion'.

Young later wrote to a colleague that the methods he had developed in Malaya had led to his resignation in Kenya. When the Northern Ireland Troubles broke out in 1969, he was appointed to head the new Royal Ulster Constabulary, but his efforts to convert it into an unarmed British police force met similar resistance to that he had encountered in Kenya. Within the year he had resigned.

Chapter 11

The Defeat of the Mau Mau 1955

In the New Year, Arthur Young was replaced as Commissioner of Police by Richard Catling. Joining the Palestine Police in 1935, Catling rose to Assistant Inspector-General during the Palestine Emergency and then transferred to the Malaya Police. His experience of counter-insurgency led him to conclude that political negotiations were crucial. He therefore visited Kenyatta in prison, who complained that it was difficult to grow vegetables. Catling came from a Suffolk farming family and sent Kenyatta a packet of spinach seeds suitable for growing in the sun-baked ground, Kenyatta later joked that it was 'the Commissioner's spinach' that kept his fellow prisoners going. Catling also set about improving police morale, which had dipped under Young, by adding several Cessna-180s and a Chipmunk to the KPRAW. During the Emergency, seven police aircraft crashed with the loss of six pilots. When he learnt that 64,000 people were in detention camps, a number which Templer thought excessive when compared with a total of 500 throughout the Palestine Emergency and 1,200 in Malaya, Catling attributed the figure to District Commissioners keeping the peace by locking up troublemakers. He instructed Special Branch to review the number, but damage had already been done to the crucial task of keeping loyal Kikuyu on side. The Malayan mantra of 'winning hearts and minds' simply did not operate in Kenya.

The Rifle Brigade joined Operation Hammer One in January when B, C and I Companies were tasked to clear a 15-mile stretch of the Aberdare forest from the moorland around Mt Satima eastwards towards A and S Companies, who provided 'stops' near Ngobit and Mweiga. Royal Engineers built the Wander Track in the C Company sector, while B

Company cut a track to a feature nicknamed 'the Tortoise'. The Rifle Brigade marched along muddy tracks to their tactical areas on the moorland, each man carrying two blankets and other equipment in a bergen. But for two days it rained without stopping, soaking everything, and at night it was freezing, causing the death of two mules. Lieutenant Mike Tippett shot a rhino that had just gored a Kenya Regiment sergeant. Riflemen benefited from double rations and a tot of rum. On the 6th the weather cleared and C Company had its first contact when a patrol clashed with a Mau Mau supply party in swirling mist and killed one. During the final phases of the Operation, the Battalion negotiated the deep ravines running across the Reserve and then halted on Cole's Plain on the western slopes of Mt Kenya. A, B and C Companies moved to Bartlett's forest station, while I Company joined Battalion HQ at Nro Moru after the Royal Northumberland Fusiliers had learnt from the captured Mau Mau leader, Mackenyanga, the location of Dedan Kimathi's camp, killing or capturing insurgents within 1,000yds of the hide.

The KOYLI Lieutenant Colonel Nicholas Pope established his Command Post at Fletcher's Farm. His brother had been the 1 Devons Animal Transport Officer in Burma and was farming near Molo. Pope decided not to interfere with company operations and, guarded by the Bugles, regularly fished for trout. At least one company commander authorised a grenade to be tossed into a river to feed his men with fish. The operation was a considerable shakedown for inexperienced soldiers, exposed not only to frightened wild animals stampeded by the bombing but also the consequences of operational errors. At the Battle School soldiers were taught not to fire instinctively. Second Lieutenant J.A. Hare had deployed his platoon around a village under curfew that was strongly suspected of supplying the Militant Wing with food. After dark, he was re-positioning one of his soldiers when a Bren gunner opened fire at the movement and wounded Hare in the eye, which he lost. One cardinal rule in ambush operations is not to move at night.

On 18 January the War Council launched a second attempt to attract mass surrenders by declaring a two-week ceasefire and amnesty. When Baring announced the initiative at a public meeting, and the police in North Kinangop District then discovered that hard-line colonists were undermining the strategy by threatening retribution to anyone who surrendered, he issued Emergency Regulations making it an offence to produce and display anti-surrender notices. Baring had originally intended to launch the scheme in March; however, weak Home Guard morale was leading to desertions and disbandment, with reliable members transferred to the Tribal Police and Watch and Ward schemes. As part of the Psy Ops to induce surrenders, Special Branch sent surrendered and captured Mau Mau into the forest to induce further surrenders, in particular of Kimathi. During the first six days leaflets were dropped from aircraft and inserted into the Mau Mau courier network. Voice Aircraft also spread the word. Leaflets included an offer of fair treatment, food, and medical attention. The text on the reverse included the following:

> To all the Mau Mau leaders and their followers
> NEW DIRECTIVES CONCERNING THOSE WHO INTEND TO SURRENDER.
> This is the time to save your soul!
> As you know, the government has put great effort in the fight against the Mau Mau and it will continue to pursue and kill those who refuse to surrender.
> THIS IS THE TIME TO SAVE YOUR SOUL.
> The government has continued to issue directives like this to the leaders and followers of the Mau Mau.
> If you surrender today and give up all your weapons you will indeed save your soul.
> YOU WILL NOT BE PROSECUTED BECAUSE OF THE MISDEEDS OF THE MAU MAU, NOT EVEN ONCE, IF YOU AGREE TO HONOUR THIS OATH. THIS APPLIES AS OF 18 JANUARY 1955. THIS IS A PROMISE TO YOU THAT YOU CAN NOT BE KILLED OR HANGED DUE TO YOUR PREVIOUS INVOLVEMENT WITH THE MAU MAU AFTER YOU AGREE TO SURRENDER, ON THE CONDITION THAT YOU DO NOT REJOIN THE MAU MAU AFTER 18 JANUARY 1955.

Another leaflet read:

> The Kenya Government has offered all the fighters a chance to come out of the forest and return to normal peaceful life. His Excellency the Governor of Kenya Sir Evelyn Baring has given a general amnesty up to today, 18 January 1955. Save your life now! Surrender with all your fighting weapons and you will not be prosecuted. You will be detained and receive good medical treatment, food, clothing and general care.

But only sixty-eight insurgents surrendered in the first fortnight, all low ranked, and so on 4 February the Administration introduced greater urgency by declaring that the surrender offer would elapse on 10 July.

Major Wainright, the NdIa District Officer in Central Province, wrote to his successor in 1956:

> [Kamiuru] has been the worst village in the division for a long time now. General Chui, the toughest of our terrorists, also came from Kamuina and it was he who kept the villagers on the side of the Mau Mau. They have been given every punishment I could devise.

'Chui' had surrendered after his family was arrested and he was first sent to Manyani Detention Camp for hardline Mau Mau, then transferred to Kamiti Work Camp, which was later nicknamed 'Satan's Prison', where he was held between 1954 and 1958. The inmates built the airport at Embakasi, later renamed Jomo Kenyatta Airport. On 24 January 'Chui' and three insurgents agreed to encourage surrenders. But the number of 'friendlies' going in and out of the forest confused D Company, 1 KOYLI based at Deighton Downs airstrip, east of the northern Aberdares, and when the Kenya Police advised that fifty Mau Mau were hiding nearby, a patrol was sent in to flush out the insurgents, with orders to shoot any emerging from the forest. Private P. Kirton was part of the cordon when a colleague shouted to him to shoot a Mau Mau walking towards him. In a dilemma and with everybody shouting at him, Kirton let the African approach to within 20yds and asked him if he was Mau Mau. When the man replied, '*Mingy Mau Mau*' (Plenty Mau Mau), Kirton cocked his rifle, but the man dropped his spear and burst into tears. Kirton later learnt from a police inspector that he was an informer.

The War Council also formed a Psy Ops committee drawn from East

Africa Command and the Administration and including a missionary, which met twice a week to develop plans and oversee the printing and distribution of leaflets to announce, through broadcast vans visiting the Reserves in Central Province and aircraft flying over the Prohibited Areas, the intention to confiscate the property of known Mau Mau. African media outlets published government notices, and the radio broadcast announcements of Security Forces successes and information on well-known surrenders and ridiculed the effectiveness of and disagreements within Mau Mau leadership. An example of a safe conduct pass circulated in June is as follows:

> 12 FACTS THAT ARE TRUE
> (1) It is known that most of you are willing to surrender, but the agreement to surrender dating 18 January will expire 10 July 1955.
> (2) You have only 7 days left to act upon the agreement that will save your souls and your land.
> (3) You will be hunted and killed wherever you are if you do not surrender yourselves.
> (4) The government is acting in good faith. Those people who surrender themselves before 10 July 1955 will be rewarded in addition to securing their land and their property.
> (5) If you do not surrender your people will starve and your children will face unending suffering.
> (6) 877 smart people surrendered since 18 January1955.
> (7) 1,281 Mau Mau insurgents have already been killed, and 625 have been arrested. In addition hundreds of thousands more in the reserves and homesteads have concluded that after 16 January there will be no hope to survive for those who do not surrender.
> (8) Your leaders have lied and mislead you. They are the reason why the previous oaths for surrender failed.
> (9) Be warned that your leaders who disagree among themselves may sacrifice you in their bid to save themselves.
> (10) Those sympathizers that were assisting you in the reserves and the homesteads have lost hope and given up, and have decided to save themselves.
> (11) You have no future in remaining in the forest, only suffering and death and your descendants will forget you.

(12) When you are being misled by those that assist you, lied to by your leaders, cursed by your tribal family, and lied to god, the only possible choice is,
SURRENDER AND YOU WILL BE SAVED

The reverse bears an old Kikuyu proverb: those who wait will never get to where they were going, but will race in vain to get where they want to go and end up disappointed. In the East Africa Communications Flight the two Ansons had been replaced by two Pembrokes, reinforced by two Austers and an Auster-6 Air Observation Post used as a Voice aircraft.

At the end of January, 49 Brigade experienced several rotations. First, 1 Royal Irish Fusiliers, commanded by Lieutenant Colonel G.J. Hamilton DSO, landed in Mombasa from garrison duties in Korea and a month later took over part of the Rift Valley from the Black Watch. Two days later, HMT *Dunera* with 1 Devons on board left bound for Southampton amid a hair-raising fly-past by a 49 Squadron Lincoln and two Harvards. In 1979, Colonel Westropp recorded in his *Devonshire Regiment August 1945–May 1958* that in the 'very delicate subject of "kills"', the Battalion had killed 119 Mau Mau and captured fifteen, all accounted for either in the Prohibited Areas or One Mile Strip where 'shoot to kill' was legitimate. They had seized eight rifles, one shotgun and one pistol. Of their eleven fatalities, four were killed on operations and a further two died on operations, including an attached Army Catering Corps; one died from wounds, one was accidentally killed, two died in motor accidents and one of disease. All were junior ranks. Seven men were wounded, including a major, a CSM, a Kenya Regiment sergeant and Corporal Sleeman. The Battalion joined 129 Lorried Infantry Brigade in West Germany.

Operation Hammer ended on 11 February and while expensive in terms of achieving just 99 confirmed Mau Mau killed, 32 captured and 11 surrendered, a total of 161, intelligence indicated the insurgents were on the defensive and frequently on the move. The 49 Brigade TCTs commanded by Captain Fey patrolling about two miles ahead of the main force accounted for twelve Mau Mau, including five in a single day, almost 10 per cent of enemy losses. Nevertheless, General Erskine felt confident enough the next day to return the responsibility for internal security in Fort Hall and Thika Districts in Central Province, all but

Narok District in Southern Province and the Rift Valley except Laikipia and Naivasha, to the Administration. On the same day, 'Chui' emerged from the forest with a letter addressed to Baring and Erskine from Aberdares leader Kahinga Wachanga seeking negotiations. So far, the amnesty had resulted in 979 surrenders.

On the 19th a No.49 Squadron Lincoln had just completed a mission over the Kipipiri Forest when the pilot, Flying Officer Alan Hunt, flew low over the Police Officers' Mess at Githunguri, where he knew several RAF colleagues were spending the afternoon. However, on the third pass he misjudged the height of the hill on which the Mess stood, and when a wing clipped the building, five aircrew and four civilians, including a child, were killed in the resulting crash. Tail-gunner Sergeant Stanley Bartlett was thrown clear but later died at BMH Nairobi.

Erskine launched 39 and 70 Brigades of eight battalions in Operation First Flute on 22 February in heavy rain against the 3,000 Mau Mau assessed to be on the western slopes of the Mount Kenya Protected Area, while 49 Brigade kept the pressure on the Aberdare Protected Area. The strategy was the same as for Operation Hammer. In addition to No.49 Squadron, a flight of four No.21 Squadron Canberras from RAF Scampton supported the operation using intelligence supplied by Major Lowe's PI Detachment to attack targets. The first task for the companies was to carve a track through the forest and then carry sufficient equipment for each company base, an exhausting and arduous trek with the ever-present threat of ambush and belligerent animals.

Crucial to operations throughout the Emergency was the support provided by the Royal Army Service Corps and East African Army Service Corps. Lieutenant T.E.L. Strange arrived in Kenya from Egypt in 1953 commanding a platoon of 77 Company (Motor Transport) and its National Service drivers. Company HQ was at Kahawa, about eight miles east of Nairobi. Generally the platoons were deployed as independent units for about six weeks. In thirty months the platoon covered over one million miles moving troops and supplies. Strange recalled:

> Our lack of experience in the driving conditions soon became very obvious, particularly when the 'rains' started. The rate that vehicles were written off was alarming but this not entirely the

> fault of our drivers; on corrugated 'murrain' roads, the old three-ton trucks would literally be shaken to pieces. (*The Story of the RASC and RCT 1945–1982*)

After each deployment the drivers returned to Kahawa, where the unit REME Light Aid Detachment and second level 47 Command Workshop could be faced with damaged superstructures, fuel tanks and spare wheel carriers, bent prop-shafts and, in one instance, a rhino horn embedded in the petrol tank and floorboards of a lorry. By the end of 1955, the Directorate of Supplies and Transport at HQ East Africa was controlling at Kahawa 77 Company RASC and 37 Supply Depot EAASC, the latter issuing 4,800 rations to British troops and 2,500 to Africans. In August, 77 Company had taken over the air despatch role from the Depot by forming a composite platoon at Nyeri to pack supplies into containers of sawdust, wood shavings and hessian strapped on to pallets, and 982 rations were being delivered daily. At Buller Barracks in Nairobi was 92 Company (Motor Transport), EAASC, and at Nanyuki, 70 Supply Depot EAASC, which usually supported 70 Brigade, was supplying 11,600 rations daily to British troops and 18,400 to Africans. A major controlled Barracks Services and a warrant officer commanded the 16 Army Fire Brigade detachments.

When the Rifle Brigade formed its Forest Operating Company, Lieutenant Colonel Pope told Major A.J. Wilson MBE MC on 28 February that his B Company should reform. Difficulties in recruiting local African trackers led to Sergeant Tooley trawling the detention camps, but he found that Special Branch had talent-spotted the better candidates for their pseudo-gangs. Nevertheless, he selected 73 candidates, of whom 37 passed selection at the Battle School. Wilson spent three weeks with Major Fenn during which he identified two principal requirements:

> (a) To be sufficiently skilful at tracking and patrolling to get a reasonable number of contacts.
> (b) To be certain of killing once contact had been obtained.

Wilson continued:

Each platoon was divided into a Patrol and a Tracker Combat Team, each of approximately 8 to 10 men, and commanded by either an officer or sergeant. A Tracker Combat Team was distinguished from a Patrol by the possession of a tracker dog, but was in other respects identical. Those men in each platoon not absorbed in patrols or tracker teams were employed to protect forest bases or as porters. The Company thus consisted of six tracker teams and patrols, supported by a `passive wing' under CSM Fosker, whose job it was to deliver rations to the patrols in the forest wherever they might find themselves.

Tactics were based on a close study of our opponents. By this stage of the Emergency, Mau Mau had completely lost the initiative, and gangs concentrated all their efforts on avoiding contact with the Security Forces. In order to contact them at all it was essential for our patrols to be able to live in the forest for long periods at a time without Mau Mau being aware of their presence. Gangs had to be hunted down by methodical patrolling across the grain of the country to find trails used by terrorists. The trails were then ambushed or more usually followed up, the African trackers attached to each patrol searching each exit from the track for signs of a terrorist hide. To be successful, rigorous routines and patrol discipline were necessary. Rouse was at 0600 hours daily, and patrols had to be on the move by 0630 hours to take advantage of early morning moisture which reflects tracks more clearly. A half-hour halt for lunch with biscuits and chocolate only to eat. No tea in the evening till 18.45 hours, when it was sufficiently dark to be able to make a fire in the bamboo, whose smoke would not be visible to a terrorist OP. Such a regime at heights of between 8,000–11,000 feet made considerable demands on the riflemen, and required a really high standard of physical fitness. All this would have been fruitless without an equally high standard of marksmanship at fleeting targets at ranges between 50–200 yards.

In the preparatory phases, A and C Companies and sixty Meru wielding *pangas* cut two jeep tracks to the moorland. These could be used by 3-

ton lorries, but the going was bumpy and slow, and the tracks were sometimes made impassable by rain.

Overlooked by the stern flanks of Mt Kenya, the Forest Operating Companies established camps on the moorland and over the next ten days were supported, often in spite of cloud, by air-dropped supplies that included radio batteries and self-heating soup. By this time, a Composite Platoon of thirty air drop packers had been attached to the East African Army Service Corps. A Verey flare fired by I Company, the Rifle Brigade, managed to set the tussock alight. The rifle companies began a programme of patrolling from the forest edge to the snowline at about 15,000ft, typically three-day patrols and ambushes followed by three days' rest. Both 1 Glosters and 1 Royal Irish Fusiliers complained that their trackers were 'NBG' (No Bloody Good). The sweep phase was conducted down through the bamboo and forest to infantry and Home Guard stops. So far as 1 KOYLI was concerned, B and D Companies were in the moorland, while A and C Companies formed the stops. Iven Woolf of the Forces Broadcasting Service joined a patrol. He had served as a Special Operations Executive wireless operator during the Second World War and had found when he arrived in 1954 that broadcasting between Nyeri and Nanyuki was fraught. When the patrol clashed with several Mau Mau, Alan Grace, the Forces Broadcasting Service archivist, recalls:

> [Woolf] switched on his tape recorder. Back in the studio, he realised his tape had recorded the encounter (in which several terrorists had been killed) and included women's voices, therefore it had to be vetted by Major General John Heyman, the Chief-of-Staff. At first Heyman was adamant. The programme could not be broadcast. Iven Woolf argued about the importance of the broadcast and in the end, it was allowed to go out minus the women's voices. Apparently the Army did not like the idea of the public knowing there were women terrorists.

The Rifle Brigade Forest Operating Company moved to Squair's Farm on 1 March where some adopted an 'Iron Curtain' approach to the colonists, while others encouraged familiarization with coffee and 'sundowners'. The Officers' Mess was a comfortable farmhouse. The nearby 'Erskine Highway' track ran north and south along the forest fringe. The Farm had been used by the Army since the beginning of the Emergency and consequently boasted more than its quota of '*choos*' (Swahili for latrines) and 'foul ground' notices. The Riflemen were told that the chore of filling in a full *choo* could be eased by covering it with a bamboo platform and a thin layer of soil, although it was not unknown when the rains came for the platform to collapse and expose a minor Grand Canyon of human excreta, a sight and odour not welcomed by neighbouring farmers. One apparently tried to profit by driving two thin cows into the *choo* and then attempting to sell them as prize Ayrshires. Investigations into who had designed the bamboo platform focused on the Black Watch when a filthy McVitie and Price tartan biscuit tin was found in a *choo*. After a break of two days, on 7 March the first patrols began, and after a clash involving Sergeant Arnold's TCT, the tracker dog detachment commanded by Second Lieutenant Charles Baker-Cresswell (Royal Northumberland Fusiliers) followed the spoor the next day. His father had commanded the destroyer that captured a German Enigma cypher machine from U-Boat 110 in 1941. The patrol debrief concluded that fourteen bullets missing their target at a range of 200yds was a result of the trajectories of both seldom coinciding. Next night, Lieutenant Rogan Maclean and 6 Platoon rescued the pilot of a Harvard that had crashed during the day, then somewhat smugly advised the newly-arrived Sycamore helicopter pilot that the casualty had been in Nyeri Hospital for eight hours. The rescue was mentioned in a Parliamentary statement by the Under-Secretary of State for Air on 20 January 1955. The Bristol Sycamore HC-11 XE 309 helicopter had been available for operations since December 1954, largely to evacuate casualties from above the forest line. Sycamores first entered service with No.275 Squadron in April 1953, mainly on search and rescue and casualty evacuation. They later proved their worth transporting troops and supplies into terrain inaccessible to fixed wing aircraft and vehicles. Meanwhile, when intelligence indicated that the Mau Mau had established an organization in Thika District, the FIO, Warrant Officer 2 John Miller, Kenya Regiment, led a pseudo gang to collect intelligence on it. Masquerading as Mau Mau, he held several meetings with a senior committee, eliminated a senior leader and recovered weapons. In mid-

March, he arranged for the police to attack a meeting he had arranged with several Mau Mau. It accounted for fifteen terrorists. For his courage, in situations always risking compromise, Miller was awarded the Distinguished Conduct Medal.

On 1 April 1 Glosters had arrived from England and after the month of acclimatization and training rotated with the Black Watch in 49 Brigade. The Battalion had reformed after its gallant stand at the Battle of the Imjin River in Korea in 1951 after which its commanding officer was awarded the VC. Battalion HQ was at Gilgil with the companies spread on several farms around Kipipiri and on the western range of the Aberdares. B Company, 1 Glosters recorded:

> Heavy patrolling has been carried out in the aptly named 'badlands' west of Gilgil. The Company met with some success, Lieutenant Rudgard's patrol finding some terrorist equipment including a medical haversack which contained, amongst other things, a tin of Eno's Fruit Salts! Lieutenant Brasington's patrol found a hide with the fire still smoking, but in both cases the Mau Mau were not tracked. The 'badlands' are floored with volcanic lava and tracking is all but impossible. Corporal Lyall, who has the distinction of being the first Gloucester to wound a Mau Mau whilst in the advance party, shot a large buck which was cooked on return to the Company camp, and Corporal Mellor scared the wits out of a herd boy who was in a place forbidden to all Africans. At the time of writing Lieutenant Rudgard's platoon has gone to West Kipipiri to help farmers wire their labour in.

Operation First Flute was concluded on 7 April with 189 enemy killed, 43 wounded and 45 surrenders. In his post-operation 'Lessons Learnt', Brigadier Taylor opined that 24-hour cordon-and-searches were now a waste of time and should be replaced by longer patrols to dominate the forest. Erskine was pleased with both operations because they proved that, as in Malaya, defeating insurgency takes time and effort. However, adverse editorial and colonist criticism of Erskine led to lapses in troop morale and anxiety among military planners. By mid-April, while he was confident that 'Chui' could induce more surrenders, he nevertheless planned to sweep the Aberdares with the three brigades in Operation

Gimlet to further fracture the gangs in the central Aberdares should 'Chui' fail. At the same time, an attempt by a pseudo-gang to persuade Stanley Mathenge to defect was undermined by Kimathi. Any trust between the two men was thus further eroded.

Now 1 KOYLI returned its sector near Nanyuki, where C Company assessed the SLR. Support Company helped Royal Engineers build a new Battalion HQ at Ngobit Camp 25 miles to the west, complete the officers' and sergeants' messes, a sports ground and a NAAFI canteen. Water from the muddy, meandering River Uaso Nyiro was placed in tanks, allowed to settle and then purified under the direction of Medical Officers, before issue. Within days of returning to camp after Operation First Flute, HQ 39 Brigade tasked the Rifle Brigade to tackle increased Mau Mau presence in the restless village of Chuka and to occupy the forest between the Nithi and Raguti rivers in Operation St Leger. Re-supply would be by air. While I Company discreetly entered the forest near Nyeri and then over the next three days climbed to the 12,000ft contour and turned east until it was above Chuka, KPRAW aircraft delivered supplies that included rations, radio batteries, mail, newspapers, rum, rifle oil and replacement jungle boots every three days. Meanwhile, the Command Post was set up at Itugururu, and parts of A and C Companies travelled openly by lorry to convince the population that a local sweep was imminent. Their appearance led to evacuation by frantic Mau Mau, but they were trapped by the remainder of A and C Companies with ambushes and patrol clashes and were squeezed by I Company, guided by a female former Mau Mau, into a large cordon. A patrol led by Corporal Hastie was somewhat startled by a poisoned arrow thudding into a tree, but I Company squeezed other escaping insurgents into ambushes. The operation concluded on 9 April. In the four months that the Rifle Brigade had been in Kenya, C and I Companies had been on operations for nearly three months, and A and B Companies a few weeks less.

By March, the Mau Mau had disintegrated into small bands, and consequently the need for bombing had diminished in favour of Voice operations; therefore the Lincolns, Meteor PR 10s and Harvards were withdrawn from operations, leaving the KPRAW to provide air support. There is no doubt that the use of air power had meant General Erskine did not to have to request another infantry brigade from an Army that was stretched from the UK to the Far East. But it was now clear that the destruction of the Passive Wing in Nairobi during Operation Anvil had also destroyed the supply chain to the Militant Wing and seen hardliners move into the Kiambu District, where most formed militant groups that became a nuisance in the city. Among the leaders was General Wairuinga Kurier, who had been the senior Mau Mau in Nairobi. He had converted several hundred renegades, bandits and those seeking revenge on loyalists into an effective, if sometimes dysfunctional, force. When a Mau Mau delegation committed to negotiations returned to the forest in mid-March and then asked for more time on the 29th, Special Branch drove the negotiators to the Protected Areas. Although the Mau Mau had lost the initiative, Dedan Kimathi was still committed to the fight and arrested the negotiators, including Henry Wachanga, a close ally of Mathenge, for treason, holding him for several days. The continued procrastination persuaded the War Council to consider withdrawing the terms, although General Erskine suggested that the Green Branch initiative should remain because it allowed for individual surrenders.

Taking advantage of the split between Kimathi and Mathenge hampering negotiations, when 49 Brigade launched Operation Hungerstrike on 25 April to deter livestock theft near Nanyuki, Rifle Brigade platoons based on farms conducted daytime patrols to prevent supplies being left for the Militant Wing and then guarded cattle and their herd boys at night. However, this did not stop a dozen cattle being spirited into the night only 200yds from HQ A Company.

Midway through the amnesty, on 2 May, Lieutenant General Sir Gerald Lathbury arrived in Kenya and succeeded Erskine as Director of Operations. Commissioned into the Oxfordshire and Buckinghamshire Light Infantry, he had served in the Royal West African Frontier Force and Gold Coast Regiment as a junior officer between 1928 and 1932. During the Second World War he commanded the 1st Parachute Brigade in North Africa and Sicily and was captured at Arnhem after being badly wounded. This did not prevent him escaping from hospital and reaching Allied lines. He had commanded the 6th Airborne Division in Palestine and had been appointed the Staff College Commandant in Camberley.

Further evidence of the split in the Mau Mau was mentioned in the Naivasha Operational Intelligence Summary 12–26 May: prisoner intelligence was suggesting that Stanley Mathenge had taken control of the Mau Mau and had ordered that all contact with the Security Forces be avoided and that no Mau Mau were to fight unless it was to acquire arms and ammunition. Food was to be stolen, and women and children were no longer to be harmed. Dedan Kimathi had vehemently disagreed and ordered that the fight should continue. While Mathenge used his military experience and leadership skills to hold his Mau Mau together, Kimathi controlled his group with a code of conduct that included thirty-eight capital offences. The disagreement was fundamental and drained Mau Mau morale.

In the same Intelligence Report, in an assessment of the effectiveness of bombing, three captured Mau Mau said that recent bombing had killed about 40 insurgents and that 42 others had disappeared. From documents found on a dead insurgent, the Royal Irish Fusiliers indicated that the 3rd Army had split into three: a detachment on Fey's Peak, another near South Kinangop and a third element to the its north, possibly on North Kinangop. The Mau Mau Fort Hall Brigade had been reduced to the nineteen-strong E Company. Stanley Mathenge almost wrecked the surrender negotiations ten days later with an inflammatory letter, but Brigadier Heyman warned Mau Mau negotiators that procrastination would result in the amnesty being withdrawn and gave them until 18 May to produce fifty surrenders as a sign of good faith. But they failed to provide the hostages, even though the period was extended by two days. Lathbury therefore decided to apply pressure before the 10 July deadline and launched Operation Gimlet. C Company, 1 Glosters, which was claiming to have killed more terrorists than the rest of the Battalion, recorded:

> [We] had to climb to the summit plateau of the Aberdares, 12,400 feet high, and to operate there for three weeks in a distinctly wet and chilly climate. The only enemy seen were herds of elephants, rhino and buffalo, which turned out to be far more dangerous than the elusive Mau Mau. Meanwhile Second Lieutenant Rudd and some of No.7 Platoon formed (he says) a highly successful reserve back at base and had all the fun killing a number of terrorists not far from Company H.Q.

The Battalion's Intelligence Section report noted:

> Our duties range from the interrogation of Mau Mau prisoners to convincing company commanders that the maps they want are out of print. We also collect extraordinary loot for the Regimental Museum.

There comes a time in most counter-insurgency operations when brigade, battalion and company operations become increasingly inappropriate and operations should be devolved to specialist forces. This time had now arrived. The War Council agreed at the end of May that Special Branch could form a special force of about fifty surrendered Mau Mau, who had to complete a month's course at the Battle School and thus become eligible to be sworn in as Special Police. The willingness to use former Mau Mau to work with the Security Forces can be attributed to several reasons. The swearing of oaths had lost much of its mystery and power. Military operations had driven the gangs from the relative comfort of their camps in the lower forest to a spartan life in the chill of the mountains. There was the fear of ambush, bombing and assassination by traitors. Between July and November, Special Branch accounted for 67 insurgents at no loss, through desertion and casualties, and had collected substantial intelligence, including camp locations in the Kinangop and Kipipiri areas.

General Lathbury also gained War Council approval to form five Special Forces Teams (SFT). Each SFT was to consist of ten 'turned' Mau Mau enrolled as Tribal Police commanded by a European and under the operational control of Commissioner Catling. Selection would be during a month's basic military training at the Command Battle School. With special forces now playing a bigger part in the fight, Catling issued a directive to preserve the operational security and safety of those involved:

- A warning order was to be issued by Police Divisional Operations of an intended operation.
- Patrol commanders were to check personally check with Security Forces commanders that they had received the warning order, were to be satisfied that the notifications were understood and were to confirm with Divisional Police commanders that the area of operations is clear.

- No operational area was to be declared open until the patrol commander was satisfied.

On short Special Branch reconnaissance patrols, patrol commanders were responsible for confirming clearances and ensuring that local Security Force commanders were aware. Since reconnaissance was crucial, it was to be conducted with officers who knew the ground well, and operational boundaries and limitations were established on the ground and note taken of possible locations of Mau Mau camps in such places as valleys and riverbeds; these details were transferred to maps for record purposes. Wherever possible, operations were to be conducted at night. Once all the information had been received, Divisional commanders were to issue clear and concise orders and circulate them to all Security Forces commanders directly or indirectly affected by the insertion.

On 10 June, the 900 men of 1 King's Shropshire Light Infantry (KSLI), the third light infantry battalion to serve in Kenya, arrived in Mombasa on HMT *Halladale*, having sailed from Liverpool, and rotated with the Royal Inniskilling Fusiliers in Muthaiga Camp, Nairobi as part of 49 Brigade. It had been on garrison duties in Korea and had just completed two years in West Germany. As usual, officers and NCOs attended jungle warfare training at the Battle School, while two companies attended the Battalion training camp at Kijabe in the Rift Valley. Platoons then joined other battalions to learn forest fighting skills; for instance, men from A Company joined a Royal Irish Fusiliers patrol in the second week of July which found several diaries and nominal rolls after disturbing a number of Mau Mau having breakfast.

A month later, the War Council withdrew the 10 July offer. During the amnesty, 979 Mau Mau had surrendered since 18 January, 448 since 21 May, compared to a previous total of 857 since the Emergency was declared. The War Council felt confident enough to return Embu and Meru Districts to civil administration. Constrained by the lack of an intelligence organization, Lathbury wrote to General Harding soon after arriving:

> Unlike Malaya, there is no Director of Intelligence and it has been the rule to retain parallel organisations within Special Branch to

> deal with political and military intelligence. There is also a great deal of friction between the Army and Police in this sphere. I have now combined the two Branches under the Director of Intelligence – a policeman – who virtually becomes the Director of Intelligence.

The man he appointed was Assistant Commissioner of Police John Prendergast, who had set up the SMIU and had been awarded the George Medal for controlling a Special Branch team during the surrender negotiations, during which he had entered the forest on over thirty occasions.

Although the Prohibited Areas Mau Mau were in disarray, both places contained hardliners and therefore on 15 July Lathbury launched the last two major military operations of the Emergency: Operation Dante directed against the central and southern Aberdares and Operation Beatrice on Mt Kenya. In the former, 49 Brigade, with 2/6 KAR and 156 (East African) HAA Regiment under command, were to sweep from the west and drive the insurgents to Home Guard 'stops' strung along the forest fringe on the slopes. The three brigade headquarters were thoroughly conversant with sweeps, and in the first phase long convoys climbed, without lights, along appalling tracks to debussing points. After battalion command posts were established, which Major Kitson visited to ensure that their Operations and Intelligence staff knew where he could be contacted, the companies disappeared into the dark forests with 2/6 KAR on the left and the Glosters, KSLI and the Royal Irish Fusiliers on the western edge of the Kiambu Reserve to their right. The new battalions had found it difficult to form Forest Operation Companies because the troops lacked confidence and commanding officers were keen to keep their rifle companies at full strength. The gunners, the Harvards and Lincolns, which Kitson described as 'ancient relics of Hitler's war', saturated known camps with high explosive. The bombers had entered service in September 1945.

The KSLI Command Post was based with Brigade HQ at Anderson's Farm at 5,400ft among bamboo huts and shelters, some equipped with fireplaces. The Bugles Platoon dug swill pits. Sergeant Blake had responsibility for eighteen pack mules and a section of two tracker dogs, while Sergeant Morgen and the water bowsers kept the HQs supplied with water; such was the uneven state of the muddy roads and tracks that the water sloshing around in the tanks was nicknamed ‘lemonade’. Snakes sheltering in tents proved to be a problem. Lieutenant Colonel Cuthbert Brooke-Smith, the Commanding Officer, decided to visit A Company on the morning of 18 July, and arranged for a message to be radioed in advance to the ambush commanded by Corporal Raymond Parker that he and his escort be guided to the position. But bad wireless operating conditions meant that the message was incorrectly received by Parker, and as a result no guides arrived. Nevertheless, Brooke-Smith decided to visit the ambush. However, he approached it from an unexpected direction and when his two African trackers were identified as Mau Mau, Parker fired a single shot, which was the signal for his Bren gunner, Private Egerton, to open fire. It was only when Captain Benson, the Intelligence Officer, shouted, ‘Stop! KSLI here!’ that Egerton ceased fire. Unfortunately, Brooke-Smith had been gravely wounded, but despite this he assured the ambush they were not to blame. In spite of the best efforts of the Battalion Medical Officer, Captain Pollock, and his sergeant, he died of his wounds. Parker and Egerton were later exonerated at a court of inquiry of any blame for the incident. Major A.J. Hardy MBE assumed command of the Battalion. Another friendly fire incident occurred when the A Company Commander, Major George Delme-Murray, who had won the DSO in Burma, used his Land Rover to collect Corporal Kettle’s section from an ambush position near Company HQ and took with him an escort of other members of the platoon. But all that Kettle’s men saw were eerie figures in the moonlight and consequently they sprung the ambush. As the Land Rover left the track and its headlights exposed several Mau Mau in the killing zone, Kettle’s men charged, killing an insurgent. Private Austin and Beddoes in 5 Platoon, B Company were collecting water just before dark when they became involved in a firefight with Mau Mau, during which Austin shot an insurgent and Beddoes was wounded. As they followed up the contact, they became lost and spent an anxious night in unfamiliar forest before finding their way back to Company HQ. Another 5 Platoon patrol collecting water clashed with eight Mau Mau and killed two, wounded and captured a third and wounded a fourth, who escaped. A 6 Platoon ambush opened fire on fifteen Mau Mau and killed a brigadier. Later, they killed an elderly food supplier described in the Battalion Intelligence Summary as a ‘hundred year old man with a six foot beard’.

C Company had spent the first six weeks at Muthaiga Camp as the Nairobi Company and although the Police had assured it that it would not be mobilized for at least four days, on the second evening it deployed in a cordon-and-search in Eastleigh after an Asian had been stabbed. It was involved in assisting in several similar incidents and adopted the standard urban tactic of two platoons throwing a cordon around the sector to be searched, while a third erected a barbed wire cage. Suspects were divided into tribes, with former Mau Mau informants helping to identify Passive Wing. On one occasion 8 Platoon searched the sewers. In July, the company joined the Battalion for Operation Dante and had several contacts. When the operation was completed, it remained in the area in a pleasant farmhouse, but had few contacts. Although the battalion set out to destroy Mau Mau groups, many militants broke through the cordon, but fourteen 'terrorists' were killed by the time the operation was concluded on 9 August. The KLSI Regimental Journal recorded:

> No other unit had so many kills. A great deal of patient discipline and skill had been required during long periods of waiting and watching, when many of the ambush parties saw nothing at all. But the terrorist groups had been split up into numerous small groups, and had been driven from their familiar haunts to become easy prey for later operations.

I Company, the Rifle Brigade was sent to Island Farms, in part of the Mt Kenya Prohibited Area that contained Royal Lodge. Each platoon formed two TCTs expected to live in the forest for seven days. The ground consisted of river valleys with thick undergrowth that significantly reduced visibility. When a 13 Platoon patrol commanded by Lieutenant Simon Horn found the tracks of a man who had recently collected water from a river, they carefully followed them, taking 45 minutes to cover 100yds; then, as two men ran from undergrowth, they opened fire and advanced to find a well-concealed cave big enough for five men and followed their tracks, but in vain. Another patrol found the bodies of two men. The clashes continued, and the company was given two prisoners who claimed to have knowledge of General 'Tanganyika'. One knew the location of a dead letter box in a tree, and a letter was left there inviting 'Tanganyika' to a meeting. He agreed to a meeting the following morning and said that he would be accompanied by General 'Chudigani'. When the prisoners then said they knew the location of 'Tanganyika's' hide, Horn was tasked to find him, while Sergeant Hickmott was to capture Chudigani and Kenya Regiment Sergeant Broadbent would ambush the dead letter box and capture insurgents who might use it as an RV. The prisoner chosen to lead Horn's patrol asked to have a rope tied around his waist because he had been in the forest so long that he automatically ran when he heard shooting. As Horn's patrol slowly approached the hideout at about 7.00 am:

> There was a scuffling in the bushes and two sets of head and shoulders were seen running. The patrol blazed off two FN magazines as if a rapid firing practice on the range and rushing forward found a hide for nine or ten men.

Tanganyika's bed and spear were found, as were two more bodies nearby. Using tracker dogs, Sergeant Hickmott found two hides but no insurgents. Sergeant Broadbent had just lifted his night ambush when three Mau Mau walked into the killing zone; one was killed and another mortally wounded by a Rifleman firing three snaps shots with his SLR. The ambush was re-inserted in the evening and opened fire on three terrorists, all of whom escaped. Two early mornings later, Lieutenant David Lyon and three NCOs from his 15 Platoon had just arrived to ambush another dead letter box when, within two minutes, they killed three insurgents arriving to collect items. I Company quickly dominated the Island Farms, and all was quiet until early November, when it joined two KAR battalions and six mortar platoons in Operation Hercules, resulting in nine Mau Mau killed and one captured. In the hope of catching insurgents returning to their hides after the operation, the Company laid a string of 48-hour ambushes, but without any success. During the five months' detachment, it had thirteen contacts, had killed twelve Mau Mau and wounded seven.

Major Kitson continued his intelligence operations after Operation Dante, collecting information about camps and recent tracks. When he reported that a dead letter box contained information that a supply group would soon be in the area, the Limuru District Officer suggested that if troops were finding it difficult to unearth Mau Mau in undergrowth, then an option was to remove it. Surrounding a small patch of forest with police officers and the Home Guard, he sent in 5,000 women, who hacked at the undergrowth and three Mau Mau. The Kiambu District Emergency Committee followed suit and collected 15,000 women protected by Home Guard. On 8 August the women slashed their way towards the dead letter box. Their first victim was a small buck. A Mau Mau shot by Tribal Police before the operation began was identified as Waruingi Kurier. Another insurgent shot dead by Home Guard and stabbed by some women inside thick forest was identified as a Passive Wing supplier who had written the letter found in the box. About 90 minutes later, three Mau Mau trapped in thick undergrowth opened fire and attempted to escape, but one was cornered by the Guard and the women. Kitson arrived just in time to rescue him.

In July and August, the SFTs attacked several Mau Mau camps and killed 65 Mau Mau; however, their effectiveness was diluted when the insurgents began avoiding association with anyone they did not know. Some SFTs had also lost their forest skills after a life of relative comfort in a detention camp and then a police station. Some colonists were uneasy that intelligence was being passed to the Mau Mau. While Kitson tended to recruit insurgents possessing a sense of adventure, Superintendent Henderson found that some unworldly Mau Mau feared progress.

As the threat began to diminish, the Army returned several districts in Nairobi and Kiambu, South Nyeri and Laikipia Districts to the Administration. Leaving D Company on the Mau Escarpment, 1 KSLI returned to Muthaiga to rest and refit. S Company relieved D Company and then stayed on until 24 August. On 1 September General Lathbury announced that 39 Brigade would thin out. The Royal Northumberland Fusiliers had left a fortnight earlier, followed by the KOYLI in the first week of November bound for Aden, except for D Company en route to Cyprus, and 39 Corps Engineer Regiment returned to Ripon, leaving 73 Squadron as an independent unit.

The Rifle Brigade joined 49 Brigade and, in November, relieved the Royal Irish Fusiliers in Naivasha, the only district yet to be returned to the Administration, while 4 (Uganda) KAR returned home. HQ 39 Brigade later served in Aden and, more famously, in Northern Ireland for the duration of the Troubles. These departures left about 5,000 British and 7,000 African troops in the field. While in Naivasha District, the

Royal Irish Fusiliers had divided the 1,600 square miles of their Tactical Area of Responsibility, a mix of the Aberdare Prohibited Area and settled Reserve, into four company sectors corresponding to four police divisions. A Company deploying to North Kinangop and B Company to South Kinangop in the Prohibited Areas sectors became skilled in the forest and gained a good knowledge of the terrain. The Forest Operating Company of three TCTs supported the rifle companies. In one operation, intelligence from a prisoner led to an attack on a Mau Mau camp which saw four enemy killed. The Battalion felt it never managed to achieve good relations with the local Kikuyu populations for fear of them breaching an oath.

In the third week of October, GHQ formed the Psychological Warfare Staff to focus on developing the Green Branch and other surrender initiatives by targeting areas where intelligence indicated a camp. When Lathbury changed his strategy in the same week to reducing conventional operations in the Prohibited Areas, Major General Michael Carver, his Chief-of-Staff, and Commissioner Catling agreed several principles for expanding the SFT concept.

The aims were to:

- Kill Mau Mau leaders.
- Gain the confidence of the Passive Wing.
- Improve the quality of intelligence, which had been eased by villagisation breaking the contact between the Passive and Military Wings.
- Develop contacts and sources.
- Deploy two Europeans to be in each team.
- Clear SFT operations with local Security Force commanders.
- SFT commanders to conduct detailed recces, agree boundaries with local commanders and detailed orders agreed.
- While contact with Security Forces patrols was to be avoided, if there was contact, it was to be verbal and face-to-face.
- All SFT operations to be conducted at night.
- Camps to be placed in locations where detection could be minimised.

- Camps to be protected by clearing patrols and local defence. Operations were to be conducted at nights.

There was a feeling at GHQ that the SFTs could develop into six private armies, each led by highly individual characters and with a tendency to bump off the enemy rather than to wait for greater success. Nevertheless, as conventional internal security operations continued in areas still at risk, Catling launched Operation Red Dog between 26 October to 1 November, in which SFT No.3 led by Lieutenant J.G. Harper collected intelligence on the activities and movements of General 'Tanganyika' in the settled areas and developed Passive Wing contacts and sources. Captain John Folliott, commanding SFT No 2, on a ten-day patrol from 10 November, confirmed the connection between Military and Passive Wings had 'practically ceased' and again highlighted the fact that soldiers in the forest were noisy. Captain Horace Clarke and SFT No.5 killed a general, a colonel, three lieutenant colonels and a regimental sergeant major in Operation Antbear between 9 and 13 December. SFT No. 6 was in reserve. On 21 December, recognizing that after the Mau Mau had been totally neutralized Kenya could develop a political process edging towards majority rule, Catling proposed to GHQ that the role of the SFTs should be ratcheted up to eliminating the surviving Mau Mau. GHQ were not convinced and demanded that the SFTs should still 'capture not kill terrorists . . . preliminary operations will be designed to secure information'. In essence, Intelligence was more important than body counts. With No.6 SFT still in reserve, SFT Nos.3, 4 and 5 deployed into Embu, Naivasha and South Nyeri Districts, while SFT Nos.1 and 2 were tasked to eliminate Kimathi and Mathenge in the eastern and north-eastern Aberdares in Operations Dodo and Albatross. SFT No.3 infiltrated Mt Kenya on Operation Mamba, while SFT No.5 on Operation Viking patrolled Wanjora. These two SFTs then conducted a joint patrol on the southern slopes of Mt Kenya in Operations Baboon and Gorilla. Although the patrols were often long, fruitless and littered with operational confusion, the new British battalions settled in. The SFTs collectively claimed on 3 February 1956 to have eliminated 100 insurgents, including two field marshals, six generals, a major general, two brigadiers and one colonel. That only two Mau Mau were captured flew in the face of the demand from GHQ for intelligence.

Chapter 12

Mopping Up and Independence

By 1956 the spirit of the Mau Mau had been terminally damaged. The movement now amounted to about 1,550 isolated insurgents confined to 6,000 square miles of forest and intent merely on survival, although they had become expert at bushcraft. The existence of the pseudo-gangs meant they trusted no one. Villagisation had undermined their supply lines. Only Naivasha District had yet to be returned to the Administration.

During the early morning of 30 December 1955, acting on prisoner intelligence, No.9 (Police) TCT led by Inspector Peter Hewitt, a former Fleet Air Arm rating and a 'Kenya Cowboy', attacked a Mau Mau hide among papyrus beds near a government veterinary station on the edge of Lake Naivasha, dispersing a gang of about thirty-five. As the insurgents scattered, a KPR aircraft sighted first a pair, then a party of ten, and a ground search of the hideout revealed pots and pans, *pangas* and clothing. When intelligence then indicated that Dedan Kimathi had summoned Field Marshal M'Baria Kania, who had stormed the Naivasha police compound in March 1953, and several other leaders to the northern foreshore to discuss future strategy, HQ 49 Brigade was presented with an opportunity to decapitate the leadership. In Operation Bullrush, HQ1 Rifle Brigade immediately instructed its C Company, then training at Mara N'Gisha, to mobilize as many soldiers as it could, including from S and HQ Companies. With its A and B Companies on forest operations and I Company on internal security in Nairobi, A and C Companies, 1 KSLI were placed the next day under command of the Rifle Brigade, as were two 1 Glosters companies, four Police General Service Units and several Home Guard detachments. Lieutenant Colonel Pope then threw a 12-mile cordon around an area of 35 square miles, of which 10 square miles was dense, luxuriant papyrus swamp, merging in some places into a 10ft high canopy that reduced daylight visibility to no more than a few yards. Small channels had been cut to farm the papyrus and to carry out the distinctly dangerous African practice of raiding wild bees' nests. Movement was largely confined to wading knee-deep through the stinking, leech-infested channels bisected by 6ft underwater runs carved out by hippopotamuses. Hewitt described negotiating the swamp as 'how a mouse must feel threading its way across an unknown lawn'. One difficulty, as with any cordon, was to give soldiers fields of fire without inducing friendly fire casualties. Lieutenant John Cornell, the Rifle Brigade Intelligence Officer described the strategy:

> The aim was to cut rides and by gradually sweeping inwards to drive the terrorists into a small area where they could be dealt with. The cordon was to be maintained and indeed became progressively stronger. The system for implementing this aim was as follows:
>
> - The cordon was all the time made stronger, both because the area was being reduced and the cordon shortened, by means of trip flares and wire.
> - Daily reconnaissances were made from light aircraft and, when available, the helicopter, to decide on the siting of rides to be cut. Rides were cut by some 300 prisoners obtained by the Administration from the Nairobi jail.
> - As new rides were cut sweeps were organised to clear the ground in towards the new rides on which stops were placed.
> - After the sweep was over, the stop line became the new cordon line and the old cordon line, which was used as a start line for the sweep, was abandoned.

On the first day, KPRAW aircraft and the Sycamore selected the direction of new channels to be cut. To ease identification, the channels were named after birds associated with the lake, such as 'Yellowbill', 'Pinkfoot', 'Teal', 'Mallard' and 'Widgeon'. At night, harassing fire and 2in and 3in mortars 'stonked' the swamp inside the cordon, aiming to reduce Mau Mau morale and convince them that the cordon was stronger than it actually was. Also, 2in mortar flares were extensively used to illuminate the cordon line. Every morning at first light, the cordon was checked for breaches. In due course, a launch skippered by a naval officer patrolled the lake.

As troops, labourers and prisoners hacked at the papyrus during the day, several men suffered severe bee stings. After three days, the KSLI companies returned to their bases. The first sweep by B Company, 1 Rifle Brigade and 2,000 Africans of both sexes from Kiambu took place on 4 January along 'Snow Goose' channel, but there were too few troops to cover such a large area. Two days later, the two KSLI companies returned to Lake Naivasha and A Company used several rafts built of oil drums and planks by Royal Engineers to patrol the channels. At least one was fitted with a small searchlight, but the infantry were not entirely convinced that the rafts had been sufficiently researched and tested for punting. C Company took up ambush positions on channels and tracks but were unable to prevent several Mau Mau using the cover of a thunderstorm to escape. Planning sweeps on a smaller scale, Pope and Cornell directed operations from an aircraft.

Among several Mau Mau prisoners was Field Marshal Mbaria Kaniu, who had remained with a girlfriend when she had been wounded in the thigh. An affable individual, he agreed to broadcast surrender appeals from a Psy Ops van sent from Nairobi while it negotiated the few tracks in the swamp, but the results were disappointing. Two days later, a Voice aircraft urged surrender by 3.00 pm or face a heavy mortar 'stonk', but there was no response, and for the next hour the British and three KAR mortar platoons drenched the swamp with high explosive, though with little effect except two Mau Mau killed. Press criticism of the cost of the 'stonk' was rejected on the grounds that the mortar crews needed the practice because such opportunities were rare. Kaniu said of the mortar bombs, 'They would disappear into the soft ground and we would be a little dirtier from before.' By 10 January, the Rifle Brigade had under command:

1 Rifle Brigade, less 'B' Echelon and elements of 'S' Company.
Three companies 1 Glosters.
Three companies 1 KSLI.
East African Armoured Car Squadron.

Nine Police General Service Units. A GSU was the equivalent of a rifle platoon.
Four Police Tracker Teams.
One Tribal Police Unit.
The launch patrolling the lake.
300 prisoners used as labour.
2,000 African civilians.

The 37 Supply Depot Air Despatch Platoon used Valetta aircraft to supply troops. The delegation of command to a battalion HQ of an operation suitable for a brigade proved unrealistic, and on 13 January Brigadier Taylor deployed a Command Post. Shortly before midnight, five Mau Mau from a group of forty who clashed with the Glosters managed to breach the cordon, but dropped six bags of maize. Nine days later, Operation Bullrush was concluded, and its results were limited. At the cost of eight miles of channels cut through the papyrus, nine Mau Mau were killed, among them Major General Mekanika shot dead, nine were captured and six surrendered. Interrogations revealed that when the operation began over seventy Mau Mau were camped in the area, more than half of whom had been undisturbed since September 1955 and had survived by stealing maize from *shambas* north of the swamp, supplemented with wild honey and game. One hide in a cave had a kitchen garden and beds on papyrus platforms. Of those who escaped, some probably evaded the first sweep while others took advantage of dark nights, heavy rain, large gaps between observation posts and incomplete wiring. Several waded out through the shallows of Lake Naivasha. By May, the Rifle Brigade assessed that 72 'ex-swamp' Mau Mau had been accounted for, mostly in unfamiliar countryside.

Such was the reduction of operations in the New Year that the main concern of the KSLI was the visit of the Colonel of the Regiment, Lieutenant General Sir Ernest Down, scheduled for late February. Several officers who climbed Mt Kilimanjaro encountered 20° of frost. A Company and 7 and 9 Platoons, C Company conducted periodic sweeps until the beginning of February, when they handed over to B Company and moved to Anderson's Farm, which was pleasant, if chilly, and largely devoid of Mau Mau. When the Colonel visited on the 17th, most platoons happened to be on operations. A Company had been the

Gatundu Company for several weeks. Private Humphries was part of 4 Platoon patrol when he saw a thin trail of smoke rising from the forest and, accompanied by a tracker, found a warm fire and heaped ashes, a sure indicator that its user would return, which he did with a bundle of firewood. But he managed to avoid the only shot fired by the patrol.

In mid-December, Catling had formed a small committee consisting of Assistant Commissioner Prendergast, Chief Superintendent Ian Henderson and Superintendent Anthony Lepage and tasked it specifically to neutralize Dedan Kimathi. Lepage had arrived in Kenya before the war to farm but had then turned to studying the forest. They planned first to persuade members of Kimathi's gang to surrender and then to induce them to betray him. Naming their operation Blue Doctor, they were initially based at Naivasha Police Station. A surrendered Mau Mau wrote three letters addressed to the 'People of the Forest' urging surrender, and these were posted in Mau Mau forest dead letter boxes between 19 and 21 December, one of them by Henderson and Lepage at a large boulder at the end of Wanderer's Track in the central Aberdares. A Pembroke Voice aircraft broadcast where the letters could be found, and each box was covered by an ambush. On Boxing Day morning a KAR patrol found a letter in a cleft stick addressed to 'Kinanjui', Henderson's Kikuyu name, seeking a meeting on the Jerusalem Track that connected the North Kinangop timber mills with Nyeri. Having decided to infiltrate a pseudo-gang into Kimathi's group, Henderson and an escort of several constables drove up the slopes made slippery by heavy rain to the rendezvous, where he found a note asking him to return the next day. Determined to prove his commitment, Henderson did so and was met by two extremely suspicious Mau Mau: Quartermaster-General Gati, a former farm handyman from Kipiriri who had raided European farms; and Hungu, who had fallen foul of Kimathi when he had sex with a woman without permission and who had escaped from custody after being sentenced to eighty lashes. Both had been hiding until they heard the Voice aircraft and decided to surrender. Henderson persuaded them to switch sides, but because he needed men who had not lost their forest edge, he decided on a high risk strategy, leaving them at large and arranging for a Voice aircraft to broadcast that both were wanted and had bounties on their heads. Welcomed back into the Mau Mau fold and Kimathi's inner circle, the intelligence that these two provided included that the information that the letters and broadcasts would probably drive Kimathi from the locality.

At the end of January, Henderson and Lepage transferred the two Mau Mau, plus four others recently captured from the forest, to a house named Mayfield in Nairobi, where he began the indoctrination process. This turned out to be easy. Villagisation had made living in the forest a matter of sheer survival, of living off the land and stealing from farms, both high risk activities. The threat of the gallows meant that switching sides became a realistic option. By December, 13,500 people had been convicted of offences connected with the Mau Mau and 45,400 were in detention camps. To test their loyalty, the Mau Mau selected by Henderson and Lepage were not held as prisoners and were kept in the same physical state as when they were captured; for instance, they were not permitted to wash or change their forest clothes. By February, Henderson was confident that he had recruited six reliable former Mau Mau, but he needed a total of twelve. Gati had emerged as a leader. When one of the four mentioned that a meeting was planned for the 8th beside a stream on Mt Kipipiri, Henderson instructed the six to attend and thus prove they were still in circulation. Leaving four at the stream, Gati and Hungu, bored with waiting in the rain, found shelter in some fire-damaged timber mills. There they picked up human tracks, intercepted two disillusioned Mau Mau carrying wheat bundles and took them to Henderson. Their interrogation suggested that, following the 1955 surrender negotiations, the remnants of Mau Mau had moved to the isolated northern forest of the Aberdares. Henderson took advantage of the seasonal warm weather to move his base into a small tent beside the River Mathioya below Mt Kinangop, in the hope that Mau Mau foraging for honey would join him. Meanwhile, Gati, checking fruit-bearing trees and patches of edible stinging nettles for evidence of foraging and wisps of smoke, sensed his patrol was being tracked; as they stopped to check out the other side of a small crest, four Mau Mau stepped on to the track. As had become the practice when two gangs met, Gati instructed his patrol to scatter until the four appealed for them to stop. Three turned out to be from Fort Hall and included an expert in making weapons and an insurgent who had once been with the Mt Kenya Mau Mau. Gati persuaded them to join Henderson, who recalled:

> But they were frightened of meeting a European. They had, after all, only caught fleeting glimpses of them during the forest operations of the past three years. My first impression of them was their nauseating smell. It was so strong that I found I could not stand near them. The feeling was evidently mutual, for one of them instantly vomited on smelling a bar of soap taken from Gathieya's pocket. In the days to come I saw many terrorists sickened by the smell of soap on our bodies. Nothing seemed to revolt them more than cleanliness.

It had taken Henderson seven weeks to select his final twelve. His first target was to track down Kahiu Itina and Chege Karobia, both known to be close to Kimathi. Kahiu Itina had been influential in the Nyeri area, and Chege had placed his hideout near a large timber mill at the foot of Mt Kipipiri in the belief that no one would search for Mau Mau near population centres. Henderson split his force into two patrols, one led by Gati, the other by Hungu. Climbing Mt Kipiriri, they had just reached an empty cave close to the summit which they planned to use as a base when they were hailed across the valley by several Mau Mau who obviously recognised Gati. The gang turned out to number twelve, four of whom carried automatic weapons, and they were led by Gaichuhie, whom Gati had last seen in August 1954 when Kimathi selected him to preside over a jungle trial at which a Mau Mau was accused of attempting to assassinate Kimathi by throwing several bullets into the campfire during one of his periodic inspections. When some of those present demanded proof of the accused's responsibility, Kimathi was forced to defuse the argument by selecting four elders. One of Kimathi's fiercest critics was Gaichuhie, who consequently won widespread respect by standing up to him. Although Gati knew the accused had not been responsible and he presented a strong defence, the man was convicted but spared execution by strangulation. Gaichuhie mentioned to Gati that about nine gangs were gathered around the summit and more were expected in response to a meeting called by a Mau Mau witch-doctor named Muraya.

Next day, Gati and Gaichuhie trekked with their men to the meeting place, where Gati found that his own reputation was still strong enough to take command and record in a dairy farmer's milk ledger the names of the 88 Mau Mau present. Muraya had failed to turn up by the late afternoon, and as the insurgents were dispersing Hungu fired a shot. Overpowered and threatened with having hot coals placed on his stomach to extract the truth, he claimed that his revolver had gone off accidentally and proved it by showing a bullet hole in his trousers. The insurgents quickly left, except for two stragglers from a gang that had been destroyed several months earlier who joined the pseudos. The incident taught Henderson an important lesson:

> If we had gone with our teams on the operation we would have compromised every single man. No retreat would have been possible over the open grassland, and no disguise, however good, would have enabled us, as Europeans, to mingle with the mob at the meeting place. From that moment we resolved never to lead our teams in person unless the operation was one based on such good information that we could go straight to a target and attack it . . . we would leave things to our teams and restrict our own activities to ambushing key points, providing support, checking Mau Mau letter boxes, and contacting our teams at prearranged rendezvous in the forest. Having gone to all this trouble to establish a friendly Mau Mau gang in the Aberdares, no risk which might betray them was justified.

Henderson was co-ordinating his operations with 1 Glosters and supplied them with the names of forty-four active Mau Mau. The absence of Kahiu Itina at the meeting convinced him to transfer the hunt to 'Wuthering Heights' in the northern Aberdares, which had been his quarry's stamping ground; although four insurgents were captured and two killed, of Itina there was no sign. Tony Lepage was then recalled to routine duties and was replaced by Inspector Richard MacLachlan, from Glasgow. After a toe-to-toe fight on a forest track in mid-March in which one of his four teams killed two more Mau Mau, Henderson withdrew all teams for the next fortnight to allow normal military operations and lull the Mau Mau into a false sense of security. On April Fool's Day, a patrol learnt that Itina's gang were setting game traps and that he and eleven others were 15 miles to the east; however, the foragers scattered when they were ambushed by an SFT. A captured Mau Mau then agreed to lead Henderson to Itina's hideout on the Ngobit River, but as they neared it after a back-breaking journey up the Elephant Entry Track, the prisoner became reluctant to co-operate. Henderson, in the knowledge that he would be executed on rejoining his gang, assured him that he would be free to go.

Next morning, Henderson's team captured Kingori, the most influential of the Aberdare Mau Mau witch-doctors, and, at last, Kahiu Itina. The ease of the capture worried Henderson, until it emerged that Kingori had predicted the previous day that 'Ngai would send messengers of peace and that when they arrived Ngai would be angry if anyone fled.' The gang had therefore waited in the hideout for the 'messengers'. Kahiu and Kingori resisted supplying information about Kimathi until they were separated from the gang, but then information also flowed from the lesser members, in particular the fact that Kimathi, paranoid about pseudo-gang operations and terrified of betrayal, was eliminating those who were not part of his gang. Two of his couriers who had deserted him told Henderson that he rarely stayed in the same place for more than a few hours and had a sixth sense about danger. It then emerged that Kimathi was based in the Tree Tops Salient, about ten miles west of Nyeri, an area that contained about seven times as many wild animals per square mile as most parts of the Aberdares or Mt Kenya, many aggressive after months of bombing. It also contained the wreckage of Treetops, burnt by the Mau Mau on 27 May 1954, as they had the Nyeri Polo Club.

Henderson launched his next operation in mid-April. He now had twenty-two pseudos, mostly former members of Kimathi's gang and familiar with the Salient. He displayed his trust in them by dividing them into two patrols and equipping them with four Patchetts, revolvers, knives and one or two homemade rifles. Knowing that the search would continue into the long rains, the patrols gradually narrowed the likely location of Kimathi's hideout to an area of 50 square miles containing eight patches of forest, three around a river. Henderson planned to drive Kimathi from the five remaining patches by simulating a major operation. Soaked by heavy rain and accompanied by screeching monkeys, he and his men slithered along paths through the bamboo, opening fire about every five minutes and always ready to climb trees to get away from terrified rhinos and trumpeting elephants. At midday he simulated a 30-minute engagement, but the volleys rolling through the gorges failed to induce any response.

On the 18th, when Henderson planned to search the Salient, his pseudos packed food in animal-skin bags, rubbed strong tobacco on their bodies to remove non-forest smells and smeared their knife blades with goat's blood. Henderson told them that their prime task was to snatch a member of Kimathi's gang. After 36 hours passed quietly, four areas had been searched without result. Gati then returned to an area that he had avoided because of noisy Sykes monkeys, in the belief that Kimathi might use their calls as alarm signals; but as the patrol crossed the third of three rivers at midday on the 21st, fresh tracks were found, including one made by sandals, which Wambararia, Kimathi's brother, regularly wore. They followed the spoor along a buffalo track until they reached a hidden trail where the quarry had split into two groups. Faced with every patrol commander's dilemma of whether or not to split his forces, Gati decided to do so. The smaller group led by Kingarua was challenged by several Mau Mau led by Jeriko, one of Kimathi's toughest lieutenants, and a decidedly anxious Kingarua was spinning a yarn that he was on his way to find food in the Kikuyu Reserve when a KPRAW Piper Pacer flew overhead. Wary of aircraft because they normally indicated Security Forces and pseudos nearby, Jeriko's men grabbed Kingarua and hustled him up the hill to their camp – straight into a hail of Patchett fire from Gati's patrol. As the Mau Mau frantically scattered, they abandoned Brigadier Thurura, who had been wounded in the back. A running battle ensued until the patrol broke contact short of ammunition. Meanwhile, Gati arrived at the camp and, seeing Thurura stuffing paper into his mouth, used a knife to retrieve half-chewed documents, then carried him to a bivouac, where Thurara admitted that Kimathi was about five miles east of the skirmish. By the time that Thurura was delivered to Henderson next day, it was clear that he had been shot in the lungs. Inspector MacLachlan dressed the wounds, and under interrogation Thurura told Henderson that Kimathi would go to the Mwathe region; the chewed documents, however, suggested that he was loath to leave the Tree Tops Salient and the River Mwathe.

During the debrief after the clash the pseudos emphasized that Jeriko's flight was a sign that the Mau Mau's resolution was fading. Henderson suggested that scouts should lead patrols to reduce the risk of the whole team being compromised. On 5 May, the long rains now over, two teams of eleven pseudos, mainly from Fort Hall District, searching the Kahare-ini sector, found an elaborate hideout used by Kimathi consisting of seven bamboo huts, with water supply from a spring and a stone food store that kept chilled meat safe from rodents. Interrogation of two Mau Mau captured while checking a trap revealed that Kimathi was in the Salient and had split his forty-nine followers into six groups; the two then guided the pseudos to a dying insurgent abandoned by Kimathi as a meal for rats and hyenas. For several frustrating weeks pseudos combed the hills, valleys and ravines of the Kiraatfai area, losing two killed by a buffalo dragging barbed wire and another badly injured by a rhino. A patrol on the moorlands was taunted by insurgents singing from crests, until it turned out that they were led by a general who hated Kimathi and who thought that the patrol were part of his gang. Henderson's frustrations deepened when hyenas raided ration drops and a Mau Mau removed a cache after watching Henderson bury it.

During the month, the Rifle Brigade sailed for Malaya. Acting Corporal Daniels and Rifleman Atkins were killed in a 'blue on blue' Headquarter Company ambush in early 1955 when they became separated from the rest of their party. After the femoral artery of Corporal Madden of 'B' Company was pierced by a bamboo, his leg had to be amputated. In June, Rifleman Keen, who was attached to Brigade Headquarters, drowned whilst bathing. Acting Corporal Baker of I Company was killed in an accident involving a Bren gun on 23 October, and Corporal Conley was seriously wounded in a similar accident on the same day. Acting Corporal Jackson of C Company died of acute leukaemia in BMH Nairobi in September. The Glosters left for Aden, where Egyptian subversion was disrupting South Arabia. General Hinde also left, retiring in 1957.

In early June, Mau Mau who had raided a potato field near the Nyeri Polo Ground were tracked to a labour camp and then to the forest, where they were captured. Among the prisoners was Wambararia, and a satchel of documents that he threw into the fire was recovered. On the way back to the rendezvous, the party was charged by a rhino. Wambararia agreed to lead Henderson to Kimathi's hideout but deliberately took a circuitous route, thereby giving his brother and gang time to escape. This was the first time that Kimathi had been forced on to the run, abandoning precious cooking pots and food. Thereafter, he became increasingly paranoid about his security and frequently moved at very short notice.

When Henderson was asked to resolve an epidemic of cattle-rustling that was costing farmers thousands of pounds, the trail led to Ndungu Gicheru, a well-known Mau Mau. Throughout July, Henderson's pseudos patrolled the forest, and then, on the 22nd, Juma Abdalla, one of Kimathi's commanders, was captured. Intelligence emerged that Kimathi's paranoia was running wild, with talk of conferences attended by ghosts, and captures and desertions reducing his gang to fewer than twenty men and Wanjiru, his mistress. Henderson concluded that the gang 'was losing its punch'. When a vital piece of intelligence emerged during the interrogation of Jeriko that Kimathi prayed to Ngai every morning at one of forty sacred *mugumo* (wild fig) trees, Henderson launched Operation Wild Fig to plot likely trees. The species was not common, and by the 8th just eighteen had been located, of which ten were unlikely candidates. Henderson immediately sent patrols to ambush the eight likely ones. These marches tested the pseudos' bushcraft skill in avoiding open spaces, but within the day all were blending into the gloom, lying motionless on the forest floor, typically with chins resting on knuckles, and communicating by tapping on a small stick or crunching a leaf and slowly raising the head and turning in the direction of movement. The biggest problems were screeching Sykes monkeys and a small bird that became agitated when it detected movement. When on the third day the wind blew two large, mating puff adders on to a pseudo, the ambushers believed that Ngai was angry and abandoned the position. Next day, their patience was rewarded when a Mau Mau was spotted checking tree number four. This resulted in a 13-mile pursuit that ended above the River Zaina when the pseudos were challenged by the distinctive, high-pitched voice of Kimathi. A brisk battle broke out in the mixture of undergrowth and bamboo during which Kimathi's gang was reduced to thirteen, but its leader escaped.

In early August, a prisoner said that Kimathi intended to meet Chege Karobia on the 26th and absorb Chege's gang into his own, but he did not know the venue. Two days later, an SFT patrol captured Chege in his hideout and reported that he was due to meet Kimathi somewhere on Rurimeria Hill in the central moorlands. Chege was passed to Henderson and agreed to show him and his fourteen team leaders the rendezvous, but when Henderson reconnoitred the hill it proved impossible to infiltrate the area without being seen. Gati then suggested that Chege should write to Kimathi confirming his attendance, and by dawn on 25 August sixteen five-strong patrols were strung in a cordon around the hill. At 10.00 am Chege and four of his men climbed the hill and waited for four days. It later emerged that Kimathi had intended to meet Chege, but his sharp sixth sense had persuaded him to abandon the plan the night before.

By mid-1956 the pseudo-gangs managed by the Police and Army had such a firm grip on Central Province that any Mau Mau who left the forest risked arrest. The few reserve-based Mau Mau gangs generally lived in underground bunkers beneath houses, only emerging to steal and raid, and were thus less easy to root out. Henderson's SFT had grown to ninety pseudos, with those joining asked only 'to change their regiments, not their souls'; three Kenya Regiment soldiers, three police inspectors and two African constables acted as patrol leaders, in addition to MacLachlan. In mid-September, Henderson decided to flush Kimathi from the eastern uplands of the Aberdares down to the Tree Tops Salient. After the eleven Land Rovers carrying twelve teams had been hidden in thick bush, Henderson divided his force into five detachments and, holding one in reserve, gave the remainder separate tasks:

1. Ambush two wild fig trees near the Kinaini stream.
2. Check a hideout where the tracks of Kimathi had last been seen.
3. Search the Mathakwa-ini forest for game traps.
4. Descend 26 miles to the edge of the forest bordering the Nyeri Native Reserve and search for evidence of foraging parties. It was thought that shortage of food would force Kimathi to raid the Reserve.

No contacts were made during the first two days and the hideout was empty, but in the Mathakwa-ini area there was evidence of trapping. On the 17th a patrol watched a Mau Mau challenge a baboon troop for a drink at a small, muddy pool and pounced before he sensed danger. On the same day, Gacheru was challenged while following the tracks of three men picked up near Wuthering Heights and making for a dead letter box in the Mwathe sector. As the Mau Mau made for high ground, Gacheru shouted to imaginary colleagues across the valley that Mau Mau were heading for them. The bluff worked, and as one of the trio ran back down into the valley he was captured after a tough scrap. It turned out that, three days earlier, Kimathi had sent him and three others, one being the man who challenged the baboons, to search for trapping wire from a Harvard that had crashed east of the National Park Track. Soon after leaving Kimathi's camp they were charged by a rhino and its calf and fled in different directions. The trio eventually met up and, returning to Kimathi's hideout, found that it was abandoned, then spent the next two days foraging for food and searching for Kimathi. They were returning to Wuthering Heights, a round trip of 70 miles, when they were seen. Mbaka, the leader, said that Kimathi had twice spoken of suicide and, in preparation, had destroyed letters sent to him. At the end of September, Henderson withdrew his force to Mayfield to rest. Kimathi was the only noted senior Mau Mau still at large. Stanley Mathenge had disappeared, escaping from arrest during the surrender negotiations. In assessing the intelligence, Henderson concluded that in addition to nine prayer trees, there were fourteen places Kimathi might visit, including: two letter boxes beneath the roots of a large tree near Tree Tops; an old beehive at the junction of the Muringato and Itha rivers six miles up the mountain; food stores in Juma Abdalla's cave beside the River Muringato and under a fig tree in the Ruhotie Valley; and a trapping area. All of these were within the 50 square miles of the Tree Tops Salient.

With the small rains due, Henderson planned to cover the fourteen locations in Operation Hot Scrum. On 7 October he established Camp Kinaini beside a river and Camp Frost, so named because of the cold nights, at the top of the Kiandangurst track on the edge of the moorlands. With a reserve patrol left at each camp, two days later the pseudo patrols fanned out and found footprints leading to dead letter boxes and food stores. During the afternoon of the 15th a letter from Kimathi was found in the old beehive. He was nearby. A patrol in the Ruhotie Valley following aimlessly wandering tracks clashed with two men in a swamp south of Mihuro stream on the eastern Aberdares and wounded and captured Brigadier Gitahi, Kimathi's most trusted veteran. From the information that he divulged at Camp Kinaini, Henderson deduced that

Kimathi's gang had been reduced to six; he quickly assembled an assault force, including the sick, and instructed three two-man patrols to cover three fords, but wild animals and a pack of wild dogs running down a bushbuck compromised them. Directing that his two camps were to be guarded by one man, he sent Gati and his assault force with Gitahi strapped to a stretcher to find and follow Kimathi's spoor. Gati, who soon dispensed with the stretcher, pointed in the dusk to Kimathi's hideout, a bamboo hut about 50yds ahead, but it proved to have been empty for some time. As the pseudos followed the spoor to a spring, Gitahi was pushed into the lead; he had gone barely 200yds when he dropped to the ground and signalled Gati to join him. About 30yds ahead was a buckskin coat hanging on a branch, and a small hearth. The team quietly surrounded the hideout, then searched it, finding freshly-cut nettle under a bush, an old pot, the leg and ribs of a buck and, near the entrance, two skin bags, a tattered army blanket, a bed of flattened grass and nettles and Kimathi's Kikuyu Bible. In the expectation that Kimathi would return, the patrol spread out, but he failed to appear by first light the next, so Gati then split his patrol to cover the hideout and the approaches.

A heavy shower heralding the rains obliterated the tracks the patrols had made over the previous eight days, but Kimathi could not now move without leaving footprints in the mud. Most of his traps had been found and thus he was forced to scavenge in the Reserve. Henderson therefore sent five patrols from Camp Kinaini to comb the forest, and when a team came under fire as they shook into extended line, its leader, Ruku, cut his foot on a tree stump. While he was applying a dressing it, he saw Kimathi cross a clearing and twice squeezed the trigger of his Patchett, but it misfired. It later turned out that some 9mm ammunition given to paramilitary units was of poor quality. Gati's patrol picked up Kimathi's tracks and were covering his last two traps when Kimathi, Maragua and Wanjiru, his mistress, approached one in the early afternoon. But once again Kimathi sensed danger, and as the trio escaped, pursued by Gati's team, at about 1.00 pm they collided with Gachenu's team climbing from the Zaina Valley. In a short close-quarter battle involving firearms and *pangas*, Maragua was wounded and the exhausted Wanjiru captured. Kimathi got away by climbing a steep cliff towards the moorlands. It later emerged that Kimathi wanted to check the two traps and then return to the hideout at daylight. Henderson had covered all the possibilities but he needed more information and therefore sent several former insurgents, including three women, to commiserate with Wanjiru, who refused to respond. A long conversation with several of Kimathi's old guard paid dividends, however, and she named two places where Kimathi was likely to cross into the Kikuyu Reserve, namely near the Zaina River and at a village. Since Henderson did not have enough men to cover all bases, and in order to minimize the risk of friendly-fire clashes, he asked Colonel Eric Hayes-Newington, formerly Indian Army and now Kenya Police Reserve and Operational Staff Officer at Provincial Police Headquarters in Nyeri, to guard both crossing points. He sent several teams to Frost Camp to collect rations and establish a line of night ambushes above the forest line. The KAR and Kenya Police placed ambushes on the forest edge opposite Kihuro, while the Tribal Police and Tribal Police Reserve formed a stop along the forest edge between Njogu-ini and the Zaina River, thereby blocking access from the forest to the Reserve.

After the clash, Kimathi set off on a non-stop circular run that took him about 80 miles up and down hills and across rough ground. He re-entered the Tree Tops Salient by dashing across open country and pressed on until he reached the steep valley of the River Mwathe. Then, at about 4.00 pm the next day, 28 hours after he had started, he collapsed exhausted half a mile from the forest edge at Njogu-ini, where he spent the night. After dawn on 19 October he crept along the forest fringe until he was overlooking Karums-ini, which he knew from his youth, and before the moon rose he crossed the mile-wide restricted zone and entered the Reserve, 40 months after he had left it. Cutting sleeves of energy-giving sugar cane and a few unripe bananas, he crossed back into the forest. Next morning, one of Henderson's patrols found his resting place. During the day, Henderson left by air for Nairobi, where he and his wife were presented to Her Royal Highness Princess Margaret at a Government House tea party. That night, Kimathi again entered the Reserve to cut sugar cane.

Meanwhile, a Tribal Police Reserve patrol that had been covering the Chania River spent the night in the forest edge. At dawn, they split into two detachments and were crossing the restricted zone when they saw a man carrying a bundle making for the forest and ordered him to stop.

When the man ignored the challenge, Constable Mau Ndirangu fired two shots and then pursued him, firing a third time. At the forest edge he found, lying among undergrowth in a ditch, an unkempt man wearing a leopard skin cloak, armed with a rifle and a *panga* and bleeding from a wound in his right thigh. Ndirangu asked for his name. 'Field Marshal Dedan Kimathi Waciuri' was the answer. On hearing the shots, Henderson's patrols had fanned out to cover escape routes. Kimathi was taken to the Chief's Centre at Ihururu, from where he had escaped when the Emergency was declared, and was then transferred to Nyeri Civil Hospital and placed under guard. About three weeks later he was convicted of possession of arms and ammunition by a tribunal of African assessors in Nairobi and four and half months later was executed – an act that saw him promoted to the status of martyr in the cause of black liberation. Politically he was naïve, nevertheless by 1956 he had become a figurehead that destabilized any political negotiations. He was eventually cornered because he failed to retain the loyalty of his followers.

While Anderson in his *Histories of the Hanged* describes Henderson's hunt as 'obsessive' and his men as 'turncoats', better words would have been 'persistent' and 'loyalist'. Henderson was given an order, which he fulfilled by recruiting a cohort of former Mau Mau, and then he systematically destroyed Kimathi's gang. Interestingly, the British failed to capture other insurgent leaders of the time: the Greek-Cypriot General Grivas in Cyprus and the Comunist Chin Peng in Malaya. The capture of Kimathi meant that East Africa Command could release the last British battalion, the KSLI, for deployment to Aden.

By mid-October about 330 former Mau Mau had been talent-spotted into police pseudo-gangs and a further 100 were working with military intelligence, included three gangs controlled by an MIO in the Rift Valley Province. When Henderson persuaded Prendergast to extend pseudo-gang operations to round up the remnants of the Mau Mau, Assistant Superintendent Lionel Brands GM launched Operation Silver Dollar in Naivasha District on 7 November; however, the patrol leaders encountered morale problems, which led to Henderson temporarily withdrawing them from operations.

Although the Emergency was essentially over, Governor Baring decided that the detention camps should remain in order to rehabilitate captive Mau Mau after their years in the forest. Under normal circumstances, a facet of peace negotiations is the release of prisoners, and by June 1957 Attorney-General Eric Griffith-Jones had become so concerned about conditions in the camps that he wrote to Baring of scenes and a regime that were 'distressingly reminiscent of conditions in Nazi Germany and Communist Russia'. It was a dark period of Kenyan history, which led to the British Government being accused of war crimes. The Nuremberg Principles define a war crime as 'violation of the laws or customs of war, such as massacres, bombing of civil targets, murders and torture of prisoners of war and detainees and terrorism'. Revisionist historians of the Kenyan Emergency claim that most abuse was committed by the Administration and rarely hold the Mau Mau to account for murder, mutilation and mayhem, things currently evident in Kenya and other parts of East Africa. Nevertheless, in 2013 the British Government was compelled to express 'sincere regret' to those who suffered ill-treatment and stated that victims, mainly Mau Mau, would receive compensation. The Government also agreed to finance the Memorial in Uhuru Park, Nairobi to those victims. No such memorial exists to the others who died during the Kenyan Emergency.

In 1958, Special Branch uncovered the Kiamu Kia Muingi, a secret society that was an offshoot of the Mau Mau; it was emasculated with arrests when it was found to be compiling lists of Africans who had helped the Security Forces. General Service Units conducted Operations Tusker One and Two against Mau Mau hardliners in the Aberdares forest and Embu and Meru Districts respectively. In December 1958, as part of the British strategic re-alignment of Middle East Command, HQ 24 Infantry Brigade moved into new barracks at Kawaha, eight miles west of Nairobi, to take command of a brigade group, minus armour; two years later, in Operation Vantage, it was rushed to Kuwait when Iraq threatened invasion, and it was also involved in quelling mutinies in Tanganyika, Uganda and Kenya. The State of Emergency was lifted on 12 December 1960. An unintended consequence of the Emergency was that it delayed the United Nations drive for European colonies in Africa to be given their independence; nevertheless, as the Colonial Office promoted self-government and greater African representation, 'one man, one vote' thrust the Europeans and Asians into the minority. During this embryonic political process, the KAU was reformed as the Kenya

African National Union (KANU) under the leadership of Kenyatta and the labour leader, Tom Mboya. Although essentially non-ethnic or anti-tribal, Mboya was attacked as an instrument of Western capitalism and a split in KANU produced the Kenya African Democratic Union (KADU). On 12 December 1963 Kenya was given its independence, with Kenyatta as its first president. In 1960, Frank Corfield, a former Colonial Office official, published his *Historical Survey of the Origins and Growth of Mau Mau* from the selected official records, and when he concluded that Kenyatta and the KAU had led the Mau Mau rebellion, the colonists were delighted and his view was accepted by the new Governor. But Kenyatta, however, declared the book was a pack of lies ('If I had my way I'd put it in the fire'.) Keen to maintain good relations with Kenya, after independence the British Government tabled the Report in the House of Commons and then shelved it.

A substantial number of colonists left Kenya and some were unable to sell their farms and businesses, most of which were given to Kikuyu, Embu and Meru farmers. Those who stayed could apply for Kenyan citizenship. Of the Indian minority, most retained their British passports and later left for the United Kingdom. By 1978, the minority Kikuyu, with Kenyatta's support, had expanded beyond their traditional homelands and taken over land they claimed to have been 'stolen by the whites', a move that outraged the majority and induced long-term ethnic tension. Squabbles over land ownership remain an issue. In 1964, HQ East Africa Command was replaced by British Land Forces Kenya. The way that the Kenyatta clan and its allies held on to power through questionable elections and corruption has led to political instability, poverty in the townships and communal violence. The plains that once teemed with the Big Five – buffalo, elephant, leopard, lion and rhino – now teem with vehicles filled with tourists, as well as armed patrols intercepting poachers who have slaughtered thousands of elephants and rhino to sell their ivory and horn in Far Eastern markets. Since about 2012, Kenya has been troubled by the *Harakat al-Shabaab al-Mujahideen* (Mujahideen Youth Movement), a terrorist group based in East Africa that has kidnapped and murdered tourists in Kenya and conducted bombings and shootings. The British military presence remains, with a Cooperation Agreement that allows the British Army to conduct exercises in the rugged terrain of the Great Rift Valley.

Conclusions

The rebellion known as the Kenya Emergency took place in a relatively small part of Kenya and was confined almost exclusively to the Kikuyu, Embu and Meru tribes, whose culture had been undermined by European colonists striving to establish a white state. It was not a widely popular uprising; indeed, the majority of Kenyans were content to abide by the Emergency measures and many threw in their lot with the Administration by joining the KAR, Home Guard and Reserve Police. Initially, the Kikuyu simply wanted their seized ancestral land to be returned to them. After 50 years of colonialism, a period which included two world wars, they were no longer prepared to be subservient employees exiled to congested, disease-ridden, poverty-stricken reserves or to live as squatters on low wages, paying progressively higher taxes, wearing the degrading *kipendi* and subject to policies that discriminated against African competition. Returning veterans from the world wars, in particular the Second World War, had seen another life and agitated for a fairer society, but the powerful colonist lobby proved a major stumbling block, even though international opinion was moving toward granting indigenous government.

During the first nine months of the Emergency, the Mau Mau made ground against Kenyan local Security Forces which had forgotten that there are laws of armed conflict. The violence never adopted a national character. There were no major attacks on infrastructure, in particular the railways, and there was little disruption to public services. However, the Mau Mau's attacks on whites drew international outrage which far outweighed any condemnation of their violence against loyalist Africans and continues to resonate today. While not a sophisticated enemy, the Mau Mau were masters of the forest, bamboo belt and moorland and had extensive support networks; but their cause was doomed by the arrival of two British brigades, by air power, by the application of counter-insurgency tactics in low intensity operations first learned in Ireland after the First World War, then in Palestine after 1945 and being developed at the time in Malaya. The use of uniformed and non-uniformed special units raised from Security Forces in Kenya proved crucial, and would become a feature of British operations. Mau Mau's failure to identify a charismatic leader who was not jailed did not help their cause. While it is easy to criticize the actions of many National Servicemen, all had lived through the Second World War and used atlases in geography and history lessons showing the British Empire in red; they were understandably paternalistic towards its members, and they were fighting a war in which friends and colleagues were killed and wounded.

Appendix A

Order of Battle

39 BRIGADE				
	ARRIVED	**DEPARTED**	**UNIT**	**DEPARTED**
Lancashire Fusiliers	Dec 1952	Aug 1953	Black Watch	
Buffs	Apr 1953	Dec 1954	KOYLI	Oct 1955
Devons	Apr 1953	Jan 1955	Rifle Brigade	April 1956
49 BRIGADE				
Royal Northumberland Fusiliers	Aug 1953	Jan 1955	1 Royal Irish Fusiliers	Nov 1955
Black Watch	Aug 1953	Apr 1955	Glosters	Mar 1956
Royal Inniskilling Fusiliers	Sep 1953	Jun 1955	KSLI 1955	Nov 1956

70 (East African) Brigade
2/3 (Kenya) KAR
4 (Uganda) KAR
5 (Kenya) KAR
1/6 (Tanganyika) KAR
2/6 (Tanganyika) KAR
7 (Kenya) KAR

Kenya Regiment
East African Armoured Car Squadron
156 East African Heavy AA Battery

39 Corps Engineer Regiment (72 and 73 Field Squadrons, 75 Field Park Squadron)

39 Independent Infantry Brigade Signal Squadron
49 Independent Infantry Brigade Signal Squadron
40 Infantry Brigade Signal Squadron

East African Signal Squadron
Army Wireless Chain Signal Squadron
77 Company (Motor Transport) RASC
16 Army Fire Brigade RASC

37 Supply Depot, East African Army Service Corps:
67 Animal Transport Company, East African Army Service Corps
70 Supply Depot, East African Army Service Corps
90 Company (Motor Transport), East African Army Service Corps

REME
47 Command Workshop REME

ROYAL AIR FORCE

East Africa Communications Flight			1xProctor, 1xValetta, 2xAnson. Psy Ops	Eastleigh
No. 82	Jul 52	Dec 52	Lancaster 1 PR	Eastleigh
1340 Flt	Mar 53	Jan 56	Harvard 2B close support	
No.49 Sqn	Nov 53	Jan 54	Lincoln B2 bombers	Wittering
No.100 Sqn	Jan 54	Mar 54	Lincoln B2	Wittering
No.61 Sqn	Mar 54	Jun 54	Lincoln B2	Upwood
No.214 Sqn	Jun 54	Dec 54	Lincoln B2	Upwood
No.8 Sqn	Apr 54	Jun 54	Vampire FB9 FGA	Aden
No.13 Sqn	Aug 54	Jun 55	Meteor PR 10	Fayid
No.21 Sqn	Sep 54		Canberra-B2	Scampton
Army Air Corps			Auster AOP	
			Sycamore helicopter	

Appendix B

Casualties

SECURITY FORCES CASUALTIES					
European		African		Asian	
Killed	Wounded	Killed	Wounded	Killed	Wounded
63	102	524	465	3	12

The Palace Barracks Memorial Garden in Holywood, Northern Ireland lists 94 deaths, of which eleven are known to have been killed in action. The remainder died from a variety causes, including friendly fire, traffic incidents and disease. They are buried in one of the Commonwealth War Graves Commission cemeteries. So far as can be determined, none were repatriated. The highest ranking casualty was Brigadier Ernest Western DSO (Queen's Own Royal West Kents), then serving with HQ East Africa Command, who died of a heart attack on 19 December 1952. A breakdown of British casualties is as follows:

ARMY	**Officers**	**Other Ranks**	**Total**
3rd King's Own Hussars	1		1
Royal Engineers	1	2	3
Royal Signals		1	1
Royal Scots		1	1
Queen's (Royal West Surrey) Royal Regiment		1	1
Buffs (Royal East Kent) Regiment		4	4
Royal Northumberland Fusiliers		3	3
Royal Warwickshire Regiment	1		1
Devonshire Regiment	1	10	11
Lancashire Fusiliers		1	1
Royal Welsh Fusiliers	1		1
1 Royal Inniskilling Fusiliers	1	2	3
1 Gloucestershire Regiment	3	3	6
1 Black Watch	1	3	4

1 Sherwood Foresters		1	1
1 Royal Irish Fusiliers		2	2
1 Berkshires		1	1
Queens Own Royal West Kent Regiment	1		1
1 King's Own Yorkshire Light Infantry		1	1
1 King's Shropshire Light Infantry	1	2	3
1 Middlesex Regiment		1	1
Rifle Brigade		4	4
Royal Army Service Corps (RASC)		2	2
Royal Army Medical Corps (RAMC)		1	1
Royal Army Ordnance Corps (RAOC)		1	1
Royal Electrical and Mechanical Engineers (REME)		4	4
Royal Military Police (RMP)		1	1
Royal Army Pay Corps (RAPC)		1	1
Royal Army Education Corps (RAEC)		1	1
Army Catering Corps (ACC)		2	2
Royal Army Veterinary Corps (RAVC)		1	1
Total	**12**	**55**	**69**
ROYAL AIR FORCE			
Eastleigh, Kenya	2	5	7
Luqa, Malta	2	5	7
Upwood, UK	3	3	6
Wittering UK	3	2	5
Total	**10**	**15**	**25**
GRAND TOTAL	**12**	**68**	**94**

	1952	**1953**	**1954**	**1955**	**1956**
Army	2	21	25	14	7
RAF			18	7	

Statistics of other casualties vary. The figures provided by Anthony Clayton provide a decent benchmark:

CIVILIAN CASUALTIES					
European		**African**		**Asian**	
Killed	**Wounded**	**Killed**	**Wounded**	**Killed**	**Wounded**
32	26	819	916	26	36

Mau Mau casualty figures vary to a far greater extent and largely depend on the standpoint from which the assessor is making the calculation.Thanks to pressure from public interest lawyers in Great Britain, in 2013 the British Government funded a memorial to those Kenyans killed and tortured by British forces during the Kenya Emergency, agreed to pay £20m in compensation to Mau Mau veterans and expressed 'sincere regret' for abuses committed under colonial rule. So far as can be determined, no such memorial and no such compensation has been sought for the victims of Mau Mau atrocities.

MAU MAU 1952–6				
Killed	**Captured**	**Surrendered**	**Executed**	**Detained**
11, 503	2,585	2,714	1,015	c50,000

Glossary

Askari	Soldier (Swahili)
BMH	British Military Hospital
CID	Criminal Investigation Department
DSO	Distinguished Service Order
EAASC	East African Army Service Corps
FBS	Forces Broadcasting Service
FIA	Field Intelligence Assistants
GHQ	General Headquarters
GM	George Medal
GOC	General Officer Commanding
GSO	General Staff Officer
HMT	Her Majesty's Troopship
HF	High Frequency
HQ	Headquarters
JAPOIT	Joint Army and Police Operational Intelligence Teams
KAR	King's African Rifles
KASU	Kenya African Study Union
KAU	Kenya African Union
KCA	Kikuyu Central Association
KLFA	Kenya Land and Freedom Army
KOYLI	King's Own Yorkshire Light Infantry
KPA	Kikuyu Provincial Association
KPR	Kenya Police Reserve
KPRAW	Kenya Police Reserve Air Wing
KSLI	King's Shropshire Light Infantry
MBE	Member of the British Empire
MC	Military Cross
MIO	Military Intelligence Officer
Muhima	The Movement
NAAFI	Navy, Army and Air Force Institute

NCO	Non Commissioned Officer
PI	Photographic Interpretation/Interpreter
Psy Ops	Psychological Operations
RAF	Royal Air Force
RAMC	Royal Army Medical Corps
RAOC	Royal Army Ordnance Corps
RAPC	Royal Army Pay Corps
RASC	Royal Army Service Corps
RMP	Royal Military Police
TCT	Tactical Combat Tracker
SFT	Special Forces Team
SIB	Special Investigation Branch
SLR	7.62mm Self Loading Rifle
VE	Victory in Europe
VHF	Very High Frequency
VJ	Victory over Japan
WOPC	Warrant Officer Platoon Commander
YKA	Young Kikuyu Association

Bibliography

Books etc.

Anderson, David, *Histories of the Hanged: Britain's Dirty War in Kenya and the End of Empire*, W.W. Norton & Co, New York and London

Bailey, Bill, *Hearts and Minds, Pseudo Gangs and Counter-Insurgency: Based upon Experiences from Previous Campaigns in Kenya (1952–60), Malaya (1948–60) & Rhodesia (1964–1979)*, Edith Cowan University, Perth, Western Australia

Barnes, Juliet, *The Ghosts of Happy Valley: Searching for the Lost World of Africa's Infamous Aristocrats*, Aurun Press, London, 2013

Beck, Ann, *Some Observations on Jomo Kenyatta in Britain 1929–1930*, Cahiers d'Etudes Africaines, Vol 6, No 22, 1966

Beckett, Ian, *Modern Insurgencies and Counter-Insurgencies: Guerrillas and their Opponents since 1750*, Routledge, 2001

Beckett, Ian and Pimlott, John, *Counterinsurgency: Lessons from History*, Pen & Sword, Barnsley, 2011

Bennett, Huw, *Fighting the Mau Mau: The British Army and Counter-Insurgency in the Kenya Emergency*, Cambridge University Press, Cambridge, 2013

Berman, Bruce, *Control & Crisis in Colonial Kenya: The Dialectic of Domination*, James Currey, Oxford, 1996

Campbell, Guy, *Charging Bull: A History of the Kenya Regiment 1937–1963*, Leo Cooper, 1986

Charters, David A., *Counter-Insurgency Intelligence: The Evolution of British Theory and Practice,* Journal of Conflict Studies, University of New Brunswick

Clayton, Anthony, *Counter-Insurgency in Kenya 1952–1960*, Sunflower University Press, Kansas, 1984

Crawshaw, Colonel (retd) Michael, *The Evolution of British COIN*, Security and Stabilisation, Ministry of Defence Joint Document Publication 40, November 2009

Crow, Lieutenant Colonel James E., *Insurgency: A Case for the Kenya Police*, US Army War College, 1971

Dinges, Lieutenant Colonel Edward A., *The Role of the Military in the Campaign against the Mau Mau in Kenya*, US Army War College, Pennsylvania, 1971

Duder, C.J.D., *Beadoc – the British East Africa Disabled Officers Colony and the White Frontier in Africa*, The Agricultural History Review,1974

— *The Soldier Settlement Scheme of 1919 in Kenya*, University of Aberdeen, 1978

— *'Men of the Officer Class': The Participants in the 1919 Soldier Settlement Scheme in Kenya*, African Affairs, Vol. 92, No. 366, 1993

Du Toit, Brian M., *The Boers in East Africa: Ethnicity and Identity*, Praeger, 1998

Eaton, Captain Hamish, *APIS: Soldiers With Stereo*, The Intelligence Corps Museum, 1978

Egerton, Robert B., *Mau Mau: African Crucible*, The Free Press, New York, 1989

Farmer, Alexander, *Mau Mau Rifles, the Red Hackle*, Method Publishing, Sutherland, 2011

Flintham, Vic, *High Stakes: Britain's Air Arms in Action 1945–1990*, Pen & Sword, Barnsley, 2008

Franklin, Derek, *A Pied Piper in a Cloak: Memoirs of a Colonial Police Officer (Special Branch)*, Janus Publishing, London, 1997

Fremont-Barnes, Gregory, *History of Counterinsurgency*, Praeger, 2015

Friedman, SGM Herbert (retd), *PSYOP of the Mau-Mau Uprising*, PsyWar.org, 2006

Furedi, Frank, *The Mau Mau War in Perspective*, James Currey Publishers, London, 1989

Gathogo, Julius, *Kenya: Remembering General Chui Wa Mararo – Was Mau Mau a Revolution Betrayed?*, *The Star* (Nairobi), 2015

Heather, Randall W., *Intelligence and Counter-Intelligence in Kenya 1952–1956*, Intelligence and Security, 5:3, 57–83, 1983

— *Of Men and Plans, The Kenya Campaign as Part of the British Counterinsurgency Experience*, Conflict Quarterly

Henderson, Ian and Goodhart, Philip, *Man Hunt in Kenya*, Doubleday & Co, New York, 1958

Hickman, Tom, *The Call Up: A History of National Service*, Headline, Chatham, 2004

Hodges, G.W.T., *African Manpower Statistics for the British Forces in East Africa 1914–1918, Journal of African History*, XIX 1 (1978) pp 101–6, Cambridge University Press

Huttenbach, Virginia, *The Boy Is Gone: Conversations with a Mau Mau General*, Ohio University Press, Athens, Ohio, 2015

Johnson, Malcolm, *Yield to None: The History of the King's Own Yorkshire Light Infantry,* Propagator, 2005

Kassimeris, Dr George, *Warrior's Dishonour: Barbarity, Morality and Torture in Modern Warfare*, Ashgate, 2007

Kitson, Frank *Bunch of Five,* Faber & Faber, London, 1977

— *Low Intensity Operations, Subversion, Insurgency & Peacekeeping*, Faber & Faber, 1971

Lonsdale, John, *Mau Mau & Nationhood: Arms, Authority & Narration*, Ohio State University Press, 2003

Maxon, Robert M., *Struggle for Kenya: The Loss and Reassertion of Imperial Initiative 1912–1923,* Fairleigh Dickinson University Press, 2001

Morelli, Virginia, *Ancestral Passions: The Leakey Family and the Quest for Humankind's Beginnings*, Touchstone, 1956

Newark, Tim, *Empire of Crime: Organised Crime in the British Empire*, Mainstream Publishing, 2011

Nicholls, Christine, *Red Strangers: The White Tribe of Kenya*, Bloomsbury, 2015

Ochieng, William Robert, *Economic History of Kenya*

Osborne, Myles & Kent, Susannah Kingsley, *Africans and Britons in the Age of Empires 1660–1980*, Routledge, 2015

Page, Malcolm, *King's African Rifles, A History*, Pen & Sword (Military), Barnsley, 1998

Percox, David, *Britain, Kenya and the Cold War: Imperial Defence, Colonial Security and Decolonisation*, IB Tauris, 2004

Royle, Trevor, *The Best Years of their Lives: The National Service Experience*, Michael Joseph, London, 1986

Shapiro, Jacob, *The Terrorist's Dilemma: Managing Violent Covert Organizations*, Princeton University Press, 2013

Stapleton, Timothy,

— *Warfare and Tracking in Africa, 1952*–1990 (Warfare, Society and Culture No.11), Routledge, 2015

— *Bush Tracking and Warfare in Late Twentieth-Century East and Southern Africa,* Historia Vol 59, n.2: Durban, November 2104

Steer, Brigadier Frank, *To the Warrior his Arms: The Story of the Royal Army Ordnance Corps 1918–1993*, Pen & Sword (Military), Barnsley, 2005

Sutton, Brigadier D.J., *The Story of the Royal Army Service Corps and Royal Corps of Transport 1945–1982*, Leo Cooper, London, 1983

Van Brugen, Second Lieutenant M.J., *Establishing Collective Security in Kenya,* British Army Review

Van der Bijl, Nick, *Sharing the Secret: A History of the Intelligence Corps*, Pen & Sword, Barnsley, 2013

Vinen, Richard, *National Service: A Generation in Uniform 1945–1963*, Penguin, 2015

Warner, Philip, *The Vital Link, The History of the Royal Signals 1945–1985*, Leo Cooper, Barnsley, 1989

West, Nigel, *Historical Dictionary of International Intelligence*, Scarecrow Press, 2006

Windeatt, Lieutenant Colonel, *The Devonshire Regiment August 1945–May 1958*, Forces Press (NAAFI), Aldershot, 1980

Regimental Journals

The Dragon (The Buffs)

The King's Shropshire Light Infantry

Gallipoli Gazette (The Lancashire Fusiliers)

Other

The High Court of Justice, Queen's Bench Division

Ndiku Mutua & Others v Foreign and Commonwealth Office

Witness Statements: Huw Charles Bennett, John Cato Nottingham

Index